Face-to-Face Communication over the Internet

Social platforms such as MySpace, Facebook and Twitter have rekindled the initial excitement of cyberspace. Text-based, computer-mediated communication has been enriched with face-to-face communication such as Skype, as users move from desktops to laptops with integrated cameras and related hardware. Age, gender and culture barriers seem to have crumbled and disappeared as the user base widens dramatically. Other than simple statistics relating to email usage, chat rooms, and blog subscriptions, we know surprisingly little about the rapid changes taking place. This book assembles leading researchers on nonverbal communication, emotion, cognition and computer science to summarize what we know about the processes relevant to face-to-face communication as it pertains to telecommunication, including video conferencing. The authors take stock of what has been learned regarding how people communicate, in person or over distance, and lay the foundations for solid research helping to understand the issues, implications, and possibilities that lie ahead.

Arvid Kappas is Professor of Psychology in the School of Humanities and Social Sciences at Jacobs University Bremen.

Nicole C. Krämer is Professor of Social Psychology, Media and Communication at the University of Duisburg-Essen.

STUDIES IN EMOTION AND SOCIAL INTERACTION
Second Series

Series Editors

Keith Oatley
University of Toronto

Antony S. R. Manstead
Cardiff University

Titles published in the Second Series:

The Psychology of Facial Expression, edited by
James A. Russell and José Miguel Fernández-Dols

Emotions, the Social Bond, and Human Reality: Part/Whole Analysis, by
Thomas J. Scheff

Intersubjective Communication and Emotion in Early Ontogeny, edited by
Stein Bråten

The Social Context of Nonverbal Behavior, edited by Pierre Philippot,
Robert S. Feldman, and Erik J. Coats

Communicating Emotion: Social, Moral, and Cultural Processes, by
Sally Planalp

Emotions across Languages and Cultures: Diversity and Universals, by
Anna Wierzbicka

Feeling and Thinking: The Role of Affect in Social Cognition, edited by
Joseph P. Forgas

Metaphor and Emotion: Language, Culture, and Body in Human Feeling, by
Zoltán Kövecses

Continued on page following Index

Face-to-Face Communication over the Internet

Emotions in a web of culture, language and technology

Arvid Kappas
Nicole C. Krämer

CAMBRIDGE UNIVERSITY PRESS
Cambridge, New York, Melbourne, Madrid, Cape Town,
Singapore, São Paulo, Delhi, Tokyo, Mexico City

Cambridge University Press
The Edinburgh Building, Cambridge CB2 8RU, UK

Published in the United States of America by
Cambridge University Press, New York

www.cambridge.org
Information on this title: www.cambridge.org/9780521619974

First published 2011

Printed in the United Kingdom at the University Press, Cambridge

A catalogue record for this publication is available from the British Library

Library of Congress Cataloging-in-Publication Data

Face-to-face communication over the internet : emotions in a web of culture,
language, and technology / [edited by] Arvid Kappas, Nicole C. Krämer.
    p. cm. – (Studies in emotion and social interaction)
    ISBN 978-0-521-85383-5 (Hardback) – ISBN 978-0-521-61997-4 (pbk.)
    1. Social networks.   2. Internet–Social aspects.
3. Teleconferencing.   I. Kappas, Arvid.   II. Krämer, Nicole C.
III. Title.   IV. Series.
    HM741.F33 2011
    302.30285–dc22
                                                          2010045993
ISBN 978-0-521-85383-5 Hardback
ISBN 978-0-521-61997-4 Paperback

Dedicated to Harald Wallbott – our esteemed colleague – who would have loved to contribute to the book. We miss him.

Contents

Preface

In 2010, almost all laptop computers are sold with built-in cameras and microphones. Together with bundled software, such as Skype, everybody with access to a fast connection can easily engage in face-to-face communication over the internet. FaceTime, in conjunction with Apple's iPhone, provides a convenient and portable face-to-face application. Other solutions have been announced and will be released at a rapid pace. Thus, while text-only, computer-mediated communication (CMC) is likely to have its place for years to come, face-to-face mediated communication is here for real and it is here to stay. Concurrently, threats to global mobility, due to the environmental consequences of air travel, or challenges to air travel, such as the global disruptions caused by threats of terrorism and natural disasters, have led to increased calls to use alternative ways to achieve communication and collaborative work goals that so far had been mainly dealt with in physical, face-to-face interaction. At the same time, social networks meld many-to-many communication with one-to-one communication in different chat systems, with and without video. In other words, mediated face-to-face communication has become a commodity in business and private contexts. Thus, a volume dealing with different facets of internet-based, face-to-face communication is timely and we hope it will be of interest to readers who want to learn more about the topic. One goal of the present volume is also to stimulate further research on this topic.

It is possibly strange to think that, just a few years ago, mediated face-to-face communication seemed an exotic topic. The costs of hardware, software, and fast internet connections were high, and professional video-conferencing systems in business contexts were rather an exception and notorious for their incompatibilities and complexity. About 25 years ago, in the context of my master's thesis, I was interested in presenting face-to-face communication in a believable way on video with somebody looking into the eye of the experimental subject to test the effects of nonverbal behavior on the attribution of emotions and attitudes. The idea of videophones was then already old, so participants in the study could probably well imagine such a system, despite the fact that they had never seen one for real. Attempts to introduce videophones had failed for many reasons – cost was always one of the most cited. However, indications of their socially problematic nature were obvious to everybody who thought about the implications of having a moving image accompany a telephone-like conversation.

I have very clear memories of watching the German science fiction TV series *Raumpatrouille* as a child in the 1960s. The series predated *Star Trek* slightly and, while looking a bit quaint by today's standards, has gained cult status in Germany and still sells on DVD. The episodes contained many futuristic elements, ranging from humanity living under water due to the effects of global warming (!) to various techno-logical advances, including a videophone communication system called *visiophone*. The following scene comes from the fifth episode of the series called "Kampf um die Sonne," first televised in November 1966 (script by Honold and Larsen). From his apartment, Commander Cliff McLane calls his security officer Tamara Jagellovsk on the visio-phone. She answers "Hello?" but the screen of the visiophone remains dark. Surprised and a bit irritated, McLane starts, "Is that you, Tama——Lieutenant Jagellosvk?" and after she identifies herself, he asks Tamara why she does not switch on the screen. She replies that he might guess, and he, apparently a bit embarrassed, says, "Oh, you are probably not alone." She laughingly says that it is nothing like that but that she has just run a bath, to which he replies that this is a silly concern because he could, in any case, see only her head and neck. She answers, embarrassed, that she would feel that her neck looked too exposed for a work-related conversation when she was not dressed. After he persuades her to put on a bathrobe, Tamara finally switches on her screen. At the end of the conversation, McLane compliments her on her bathrobe. She answers, "Why, thank you!" to which he replies, "Particularly if you forget to close it completely." Flustered, Tamara terminates the connection. Apart from the fact that this little scene underlines McLane's reputation as a flirt and tease, there is much interesting here regarding communication via video-phone: (1) having a visual connection has an influence on identifying the interaction partner, avoiding the type of misidentification that happens occasionally on the telephone; (2) if the video channel is available but not used, the interaction partner is likely to have suspi-cions as to the motivation; (3) at times, one might not feel comfortable in using the video channel (particularly with superiors when one is undressed, apparently); and (4) mixing different contexts involving dress, makeup, and the like that are not an issue when taking a voice-only call becomes relevant if the visual channel is added.

Figure 0.1 Participants of the ESF Workshop, Face-to-Face Communication Over the Internet: Emotions in a Web of Culture, Language, and Technology, April 6–7, 2002, Hull, UK. First row from left to right: Malathy Rengamani, Eva Krumhuber, Pierre Philippot, Arvid Kappas, Pio Enrico Ricci Bitti, Monique De Bonis. Second row from left to right: Gary Bente, Karl Grammer, Nicole C. Krämer, Brian Parkinson, Antony S. B. Manstead. Third row from left to right: Veikko Surakka, Arto Mustajoki (SCH representative), Harald Wallbott, José-Miguel Fernández-Dols.

Inspired by these childhood memories from the 1960s, my own research in the 1980s (see Hess *et al.*, 1988) and the discussions with Harald Wallbott, then working in Klaus Scherer's group at the University of Giessen, I felt at the outset of the new millennium that the time had come for a concerted effort to focus research on such a medium. In 2002, I convened an exploratory workshop "Communication over the Internet: Emotions in a Web of Culture, Language and Technology," funded by the Standing Committee for the Humanities of the European Science Foundation, inviting eleven researchers from nine European countries to identify the issues involved in face-to-face communication over the internet. The workshop was held on April 6–7 and concluded with the intention to produce a book that would address several of the issues identified. Most of the authors in this volume participated in this workshop (see Figure 0.1).

Some time after the workshop, the idea of an edited volume came into being, and I was truly happy to recruit Nicole C. Krämer, who had attended the workshop as a junior member, as a co-editor for this task. Many people have helped this project along the way, ranging from the local support during the workshop by Eva Krumhuber, Dimitrios Xenias, and Malathy Rengamani, to several student assistants who helped with the editing. I am particularly indebted to the reviewers who have graciously given their time and of course to the European Science Foundation for their support early on, specifically Philippa Rowe. Our partners at Cambridge University Press have always been very helpful and patient, and we hope they like the finished product. I would like to thank particularly Sarah Caro for help in the early stages and, more recently, Hetty Reid.

One of the participants in the workshop, Harald Wallbott, a pioneer in nonverbal communication research with a particular interest also in social psychological processes in mediated communication, died unexpectedly in 2003. It was Harald who was supposed to write the first chapter, highlighting some of his early research, such as the relevance of image size to the perception of emotions (e.g., Wallbott, 1992). All authors agreed that this volume should be dedicated to his memory. Those who knew him appreciated his sense of humor and creative spirit. His death is a loss to our science.

Arvid Kappas
Bremen, June 2010

References

Hess, U., Kappas, A., and Scherer, K. R. (1988). Multichannel communication of emotion: synthetic signal production. In K. R. Scherer (ed.), *Facets of Emotion: Recent Research* (pp. 161–182). Hillsdale, NJ: Erlbaum.

Wallbott, H. G. (1992). Effects of distortion of spatial and temporal resolution of stimuli on emotion attributions. *Journal of Nonverbal Behavior*, *16*, 5–20.

Contributors

Gary Bente,
University of Cologne, Germany

Pilar Carrera,
Universidad Autonoma de Madrid, Spain

Céline Douilliez,
University of Lille 3, France

José-Miguel Fernández-Dols,
Universidad Autonoma de Madrid, Spain

Agneta Fischer,
University of Amsterdam, The Netherlands

Pier Luigi Garotti,
University of Bologna, Italy

Jeannine Goh,
University of Manchester, UK

Karl Grammer,
University of Vienna, Austria

Martin Lea,
University of Manchester, UK

Antony S. R. Manstead,
Cardiff University, UK

Elisabeth Oberzaucher,
University of Vienna, Austria

Brian Parkinson,
University of Oxford, UK

Pierre Philippot,
Université de Louvain, Belgium

Pio Enrico Ricci Bitti,
University of Bologna, Italy

Susanne Schmehl,
University of Vienna, Austria

Veikko Surakka,
University of Tampere, Finland

Toni Vanhala,
University of Tampere, Finland

Joseph B. Walther,
Michigan State University, USA

Abbreviations

2D	two-dimensional
3D	three-dimensional
AI	artificial intelligence
AU	action unit (see FACS)
CASA	computers are social actors paradigm
CAVE	cave automatic virtual environment
CMC	computer-mediated communication
DSM-IV	*Diagnostic and Statistical Manual of Mental Disorders,* 4th edition
ECG	electrocardiography
EDP	extended desktop platform
EEA	environment of evolutionary adaptedness
EMG	electromyography
FACS	facial action coding system
FNE	Fear of Negative Evaluation Scale
FTF/FtF	face-to-face
FTFC	face-to-face communication
GAQ	Geneva Appraisal Questionnaire
HCI	human–computer interaction
HMD	head-mounted display
HNF	Heinz-Nixdorf-MuseumForum
H.320	technical specification for videoconferencing services
IADS	international affective digitized sounds
IAW	integrated avatar workbench
ICQ	"I seek you" (instant messaging software)
IP	Internet Protocol
LifeFX	commercial software aimed at providing facial expressions to internet messages
MAX	Multimodal Assembly Expert (embodied conversational agent developed at the University of Bielefeld)
MNs	mirror neurons
MUD	multiuser dungeon
NVB	nonverbal behavior

PA   pleasure and arousal
PAD   pleasure, arousal, and dominance
PANAS   Positive and Negative Affect Schedule
PD   panic attack disorder
RB2   Reality Built for Two
REA   Real Estate Agent (embodied conversational agent
          developed at MIT)
SIDE   social identity model of deindividuation effects
SMS   short message service
TCP-IP   Transmission Control Protocol-Internet Protocol
TIC   time-independent collaboration (asynchronous videocon-
          ferencing system)
VCE   virtual communication environment
VCR   videocassette recorder
VMC   video-mediated communication
VR   virtual reality
VVC   virtual videoconference

Introduction

Electronically mediated face-to-face communication: issues, questions, and challenges

Arvid Kappas and Nicole C. Krämer

In our globalized world, communication and interaction increasingly happen online and are mediated through computers and the internet. This is true not only for organizational settings and teams working together, but also for private contacts with family, friends, and even strangers (e.g., Bargh and McKenna, 2004). Theories on computer-mediated communication (CMC) that have described internet-based communication as deficit-laden compared to face-to-face communication (e.g., Kiesler, 1997; Kiesler et al., 1984; Kiesler and Sproull, 1992; Short et al., 1976; Siegel et al., 1986; Sproull and Kiesler, 1986; Strauss and McGrath, 1994) might have difficulty to explain these current developments. On the other hand, these approaches have argued that the cues we rely on in everyday face-to-face interaction are filtered out in computer-mediated communication. While this was certainly true for mere text-based interactions, more recent forms of communication via the internet have adopted numerous additional features and incorporate several of these cues (Antonijevic, 2008; Fullwood and Orsolina, 2007). This is, on the one hand, due to technological advancements, but has, on the other hand, been fostered by creative efforts of the users, as had been predicted by Walther (1992, 1996) in his social information processing and hyperpersonal communication theory. In fact, recent developments in the field of the so-called Web 2.0 show that users themselves often developed several strategies and technologies to support at least partial surrogates for face-to-face interaction, which have led to a steady increase of immediate and increasingly multimodal communication (Ramirez et al., 2002; Walther and Burgoon, 1992; Walther and Parks, 2002). Nowadays, when people either are forced to interact via a computer, or they wish to do so, they increasingly use new technologies that at least partly incorporate aspects of everyday face-to-face communication.

1

Table 0.1 Forms of text-based communication

Form	Synchronicity	Specific addressee	Enhancements
Blogs/microblogs (Twitter)	Partly	No	Photos
Social networking sites (Facebook, MySpace)	No	No (except when using mail function)	Photos, status messages
Email	No	Yes (mostly)	Emoticons
ICQ/chat	Yes	Yes (mostly)	Emoticons/ smileys

In the following, an overview of current internet-based communication opportunities is presented, outlining the diversity of interaction forms and also demonstrating that, even within the realm of text-based communication, more and more enhancements are integrated to compensate for the lack of nonverbal cues (see Table 0.1). In this respect, the recent advent of so-called Web 2.0 platforms, revolutionizing text-based communication within cyberspace, deserves special attention. Although several elements of Web 2.0 (e.g., wikis) are not explicitly targeted at fostering direct communication between individuals, other platforms, such as blogs, microblogs, and social networking sites (Boyd and Ellison, 2007), render possible, if not encourage, detailed self-presentation and also enable interaction between friends and strangers. Although these platforms started out by permitting merely asynchronous messages, they continue to adapt toward more synchronous forms (e.g., microblogs such as Twitter) or include ability to display the current status and activity (e.g., via status messages in Facebook). The conventional forms of text-based internet communication, such as email and ICQ/chat, have long been enhanced by the opportunity to include emoticons and smileys (e.g., Antonijevic, 2008; Derks, 2007; Fullwood and Orsolina, 2006; Walther, 2006; Walther and D'Addario, 2001).

The ability to conduct voice interactions via the internet has also improved. People use numerous voice-over-IP (Internet Protocol) technologies and software such as Skype (see below) to talk to friends and family all over the world with low or no cost. While these options do not provide significant additional features compared to conventional telephone (apart from lower cost), other technologies considerably enhance the usual audio- and even face-to-face communication. Avatar technologies have developed such that elaborate human-like figures can be used to represent oneself in various cyberworlds and in the internet. Recently, people can, by means of so-called virtual presence software, convey that they are visiting a specific internet site. With the help of a small avatar, one can chat there with other users represented by a so-called weblin (http://weblin.en.softonic.com; www.clubcooee.com). Moreover, 3D online worlds populated by avatars that allow basic nonverbal communication, as well as either chat or voice over IP conversations, have gained popularity (see *Second Life* or *World of Warcraft*). In particular, nonverbal interaction is still very indirect and limited and does not yet reach the elaborateness of avatar research platforms (Bente *et al.*, 2008; Blascovich *et al.*, 2002).

However, the option of video transmission via the internet has also improved dramatically in the past 10 years. Not only can we convey personal messages and engage in impression management via various video platforms (e.g., YouTube), but actual video-mediated interactions (in the sense of private or job-related videoconferences) have become easier since the launch of Skype. By means of this software and a small webcam, as integrated in conventional PCs or laptops, one can conduct video-mediated conversations with people all over the world who use the same technology.

Thus, recent developments demonstrate that if technology renders possible the convenient usage of face-to-face communication elements, and the cost of the required bandwidth is sufficiently low, a significant number of people will use it. This was not self-evident in the past and was discussed controversially within the last decade. However, although the massive use of technologies such as Skype suggests that, at least under some circumstances, people prefer the most direct and face-to-face-like communication form, still the heavy usage of *Second Life*, *World of Warcraft* or the status messages within the social networking sites has to be explained. The massive popularity of these apparently more indirect communication possibilities suggests that there might also be specific gratifications and perceived advantages related to the fact that not all information is conveyed, and, more importantly, that these forms provide additional aspects that are not available in usual face-to-face communication. For instance, within *Second Life* or *World of Warcraft*, additional options for creative self-presentation are given that might enhance the interaction experience and increase control over self-presentation. Against this background, the pros and cons, the chances and risks of face-to-face communication over the internet, on the one hand, and innovative forms of communication which might provide additional opportunities that are not present in face-to-face interaction, on the other hand, have to be considered carefully.

Besides the fact that face-to-face communication in CMC is becoming increasingly popular, the same seems to be true for human–computer interaction (HCI). Unlike 20 years ago, when merely text-based interaction with computers was possible (which, moreover, was basically derived from human language and had to be learned), nowadays human-like embodied agents are available that autonomously interact with the human user. In the future, these artificial agents should dramatically facilitate – by means of natural speech and multimodal nonverbal interaction – the handling of computers or the internet (Cassell *et al.*, 2000; Krämer, 2008a).

Common applications are the so-called chatbots, which are especially used in e-commerce (e.g., "Anna" by IKEA). While most of these industrial applications still rely on text-based interaction, simple dialogue structures, and merely basic nonverbal behavior, some research platforms demonstrate that speech input and output and more elaborate forms of nonverbal behavior are possible (Cassell *et al.*, 2000; Gratch *et al.*, 2007; Kopp *et al.*, 2005). Most interestingly, research using even the most basic human-like interface agents demonstrates that human reactions to virtual agents are remarkably similar to those to human interlocutors (Krämer, 2008a; Nass and Moon, 2000; Sproull *et al.*, 1996). It has been found that virtual, anthropomorphic agents interacting with users trigger impression management on the part of the human user (Krämer *et al.*, 2003; Sproull *et al.*, 1996), foster cooperation (Parise *et al.*, 1999), lead to social inhibition (Rickenberg and Reeves, 2000), or evoke communication behavior that is equivalent to that which would be expected in a human face-to-face conversation (Kopp *et al.*, 2005; Krämer, 2005). Additionally, several studies demonstrate the importance of carefully designing the nonverbal behavior of the agent: it has repeatedly been shown that the nonverbal behavior of the artificial agent matters and that human users' reactions depend on the agents' nonverbal signals – just as in human–human interaction (Bente *et al.*, 2001; Krämer *et al.*, 2007; von der Pütten *et al.*, 2008, 2009; Rickenberg and Reeves, 2000). It thus becomes increasingly important not only to focus on computer-mediated, face-to-face interactions but also to address issues of humans interacting in a face-to-face mode with virtual agents. Two chapters of the book will therefore comment on these aspects.

Understanding the usage of computer-mediated, face-to-face communication, as well as nonverbally rich HCI, is clearly not simply a matter of solving engineering problems. Similarly, the behavior of users and the acceptance of such technologies cannot be understood simply from questionnaires targeted on wishes and preferences. Instead, a variety of processes are involved, linked to communication processes, empathy, social self-presentation, group processes, and the like that require a dialogue between the social sciences and engineering. This book is intended to address such issues.

Structure and contents of this book

This book tries to address the issues mentioned above by contributions that address several psychological aspects of face-to-face interaction via the internet. The chapters are predominantly based on social psychological assumptions and considerations, but also personality psychology, clinical psychology, media psychology, and the psychology of emotions play a major role. The chapters partly discuss rather general aspects such as the promises and pitfalls of face-to-face communication over the internet while some chapters raise more specific research questions. For instance, the role of gender differences is discussed, the question of whether shy people benefit from more anonymous communication is tackled, and cultural aspects are taken into account.

The book is divided into three parts. In the first part, three chapters focus on general aspects of CMC and the effects of visual cues. In the second part, five chapters present specific forms of video- or avatar-based technologies and corresponding findings. The third part consists of two contributions that address some of the questions mentioned above with respect to HCI instead of computer-mediated communication forms.

General aspects of visual cues in CMC

More specifically, the book starts with a review by Joseph B. Walther, who discusses the promise and the pitfalls of visual cues in CMC. The first section reviews theories advocating the utility of visual cues in telecommunication. He states, however, that observational results indicate that visual cues often fail to enhance virtual groups' work. The second section targets the conditions of these effects and presents research that shows when and how visual cues detract from CMC social impressions and evaluations. In parallel, the author discusses why there is still a subjective preference for multimedia and visual cues.

In the second chapter, José-Miguel Fernández-Dols and Pilar Carrera combine general approaches from psychology and philosophy to discuss new, technology-enhanced ways of managing one's facial expression. Starting with an account of the usage of pictures, the authors discuss how telecommunications can give rise to new forms of "artificial" facial information and speculate on the effects of this potential development.

The third chapter, written by Agneta Fischer, is also concerned with general aspects of visual cues in CMC but, in addition, relates the effects to gender issues. She discusses three hypotheses with regard to the importance of gender in social interactions in face-to-face interaction and CMC: (1) due to the fact that gender is less salient in chat-based CMC, equalization and less sex-stereotypic behavior is observed; (2) in line with SIDE theory, it is assumed that social categories are emphasized, leading to larger gender differences; (3) gender differences will emerge depending on context. Empirical evidence largely seems to support the third hypothesis.

Video- and avatar-based communication

Chapter 4 by Pio Enrico Ricci Bitti and Pier Luigi Garotti focuses on videoconferences and their implications for intercultural aspects. Based on an account of communication forms on the internet, the authors summarize the functions of nonverbal behavior in face-to-face communication. They discuss the pros and cons of videoconferences via the internet and, referring to these considerations, present an account of the intercultural implications of the usage of videoconferences via the internet.

In Chapter 5, Brian Parkinson and Martin Lea investigate the factors that impact the transmission of emotions in videoconferencing (e.g., restriction of movement and orientation, sensory information, temporal parameters). In their own study, they especially focused on the delay of the transmission. They demonstrated that in high-delay situations, more difficulties arose. However, if friends were conversing, they were not negatively affected by delays.

In Chapter 6, Pierre Philippot and Céline Douilliez examine the relationship between social anxiety and internet communication. They discuss different hypotheses with regard to the relationship between internet use and social adjustment (social anxiety and loneliness). They present evidence that socially anxious and lonely individuals show specific patterns of communication on the internet that differ from those people who do not suffer from social anxiety. The authors conclude that the introduction of a video channel might constitute a difficulty for socially anxious people.

In Chapter 7 by Antony S. R. Manstead, Martin Lea, and Jeannine Goh, the issue of co-presence is considered as the most profound difference between normal face-to-face interaction and video-mediated face-to-face interaction. The authors discuss the implications of co-presence, or its absence, in the communication of emotion, self-disclosure, and relationship rapport. In order to achieve this, they refer to some recent studies that have examined the effect of presence on the facial communication of emotion. In an attempt to decompose presence further into its different social psychological aspects, they describe a study that investigated how these various aspects impact upon self-disclosure and rapport independently. The authors conclude that the absence of co-presence in video-mediated interaction can liberate the communicators from some of the social constraints normally associated with face-to-face interaction while maintaining others and introducing new constraints specific to the medium.

In Chapter 8 by Gary Bente and Nicole C. Krämer, various avatar-based interaction approaches are discussed. Based on a functional model of nonverbal behavior they comment on the psychological factors determining the effects of different systems. By this, they aim to achieve a deeper understanding of the function of nonverbal cues in CMC. Additionally, an avatar-based communication platform is introduced that allows real-time transmission of gaze, head movements, and gestures in net communication. By means of this platform, various studies in various research paradigms can be conducted.

Emotions and visual cues in HCI

Chapter 9 by Veikko Surakka and Toni Vanhala starts with the observation that people show strong emotional reactions when interacting with computers. In consequence, they investigate how synthesized emotional information might affect human behavior in the context of information technology. They assume a (supposedly positive) effect of utilizing any kind of emotional cues or messages in human–technology interaction. After presenting several possibilities to have a computer analyze human emotion-related processes (physiological measures, technologies to measure the computer users' behavior), they present studies that show the potential of emotionally expressive intelligence and demonstrate how perceptual and expressive intelligence can be merged to create functional loops. The overarching goal of their research and their chapter is to provide a basis for a new generation of emotionally intelligent systems and to provide a theoretical and empirical basis for integrating emotions into the study of HCI.

Against the background of evolutionary approaches, Elisabeth Oberzaucher, Karl Grammer, and Susanne Schmehl, in Chapter 10, suggest that even in communication with and by machines, humans tend to react socially and use communication mechanisms, which are primarily social and embodied. Therefore, it is seen as important that human-like agents are able to use human-like communication on their part. The authors thus present an approach to producing communicative feedback which is based on a pleasure-arousal-dominance space. Using a "reverse engineering" approach, the authors implement FACS on a 3D computer face. By producing a large number of random faces and subsequent evaluations, they were able to identify relevant emotional feedback that can be implemented in future systems. Similarly, they analyzed body postures.

Where do we go from here?

The future will see increasing integration of different levels and types of reality. Already there are various applications in the context of mixed and augmented reality that blend computer-generated imagery with video-based textures. While most efforts in this area have probably been put into the development of user interfaces (e.g., in military aircraft or in cars), there are now attempts to use such paradigms in the context of face-to-face interaction, such as videoconferencing (e.g., Regenbrecht *et al.*, 2003). For example, it is possible to have virtual boardrooms or other meeting places that mix agents tracking actual nonverbal behavior of interactants that are transmitted from various remote locations, avatars that represent artificial systems, and integrated video streams.

As the quality of computer-generated imagery increases, a point will come at which *authenticity* will become more of a concern to users – this applies not only to avatar representations of interactants but also to advanced videoconferencing software that allows augmentation in the sense of modification and addition of synthetic material. In this context, authenticity refers to the authenticity of the *identity* of people (am I talking to the person I think I am talking to?), the authenticity of the *attributes* of the person I am interacting with (age, gender, looks . . .), and the *dynamic authenticity of behavior* (did the interaction partner really smile – did the interaction partner smile in a particular way?). The latter is likely, as it is plausible that the intensity of particular expressions could be modified on the fly. For example, desired expressions could be amplified, and undesired expressions could be inhibited. In addition, expressions could be augmented – for example, wrinkles around the eyes could be added to increase an impression of genuine smiles on the fly. This would correspond to an implementation of emotion-expression rules such as Ekman and Friesen's display rules (1969) in *socially intelligent mixed-reality environments*.

However, whether such automatic corrections are likely to be implemented in the near future is only partially an engineering problem. At present, it appears that the theoretical knowledge regarding what expression would be appropriate and in which context is not available and will not be available in the near future (see Kappas, 2003). However, despite all the criticisms that have been raised in this respect, it is possible that in highly domain-specific applications proper rules can be defined – for example, in a service environment, such as remote e-commerce. In this case, there are certain levels of politeness required that could be defined today given present theories – even taking cultural variations into account. Thus, it is not implausible that mediated interactions with members of other cultures could be improved by slight modifications of the intensity of smiles and related movements, such as nodding or variations of gaze. Similarly, the feedback of a therapist could be filtered according to clearly defined rules. These are examples where technology is not used to recover the information "lost in translation" from offline to online communication, but instead to augment and improve interaction. There is much potential here for the reduction of conflict by reducing misunderstanding. Of course, there is always the possibility of abuse and notions such as a "charisma amplifier" that might transform a lacklustre politician into the next voter magnet linger potentially at the horizon.

The impact of such developments is difficult to predict. On the one hand, one could imagine that knowledge of "tampering" with reality would change the perception of the interaction partner. However, this need not be the case. The perception of nonverbal indices is not primarily driven by conscious evaluation, but by a parallel series of largely automatic processes (Burgoon *et al.*, 2000; Choi *et al.*, 2005; Krämer, 2008b), some of which might be biologically prepared, and others learned at an early age and automatized beyond conscious access (see also Kappas and Descôteaux, 2003). In particular, researchers focusing on an evolutionary framework of communication pointed out long ago (e.g., Leyhausen, 1967) that expression and impression have most likely not co-evolved. Instead, according to them, impression processes are based on phylogenetically later developments. In consequence, we should consider the contemporary developments in augmented face-to-face interaction as a hyperrapid evolution of expression processes that is not matched by biological processes in our impression apparatus – in our social brains. Just as we are likely to "adopt" simple artificial entities, such as dolls or robots (Kappas, 2005), and react socially to all kinds of artificial objects (Reeves and Nass, 1996), so are we likely to be "fooled" by augmented face-to-face interaction displays. Once such systems have gained sufficient acceptance, this is a likely consequence.

Is it possible that technology would be used for countermoves to increase authenticity in interaction? Yes, to a certain degree. However, then it is likely to be integrated also into nonmediated interaction as well. For example, there have been numerous attempts to identify deception in the voice – in some cases, displays next to a telephone that are supposed to indicate speaker stress as symptoms of lying. Although there is, at present, not a single, well-controlled, scientifically sound study that would show such systems to be valid and reliable, there seems to be, unfortunately, a ready market for such gadgets. It is thus conceivable that in real face-to-face interactions augmented displays might come into play; for example, separating glass panels in banks or at customs, or even eyeglasses that overlay the actual face with markers that might highlight "suspicious" twitches, tics, or other signs. At this point the boundary between making mediated face-to-face communication more real and making real interaction benefit from augmentation becomes moot.

Lastly, one wonders how offline communication and interaction is affected in the long run by the changes in behaviors, patterns, and networks. This is an interesting question and the brief experience with present-day mediated communication technology is not sufficient to make any predictions. Apparently, when confronted with the first attempts of the brothers Lumière, the audience in the cinema jumped out of their seats in panic when a (shaky black-and-white!) film of a train heading toward the camera was presented. These effects seem unbelievable in hindsight. Surely, some of the early reactions to the affordances and possibilities of cyberspace will look equally silly after one generation. We should not assume that the perception of these media, and their use and acceptance, will remain constant as they permeate the fabric of everyday life of users for whom a world that is not constantly blending online and offline work would be just as hard to imagine as a world without cars, airplanes, telephones, or readily available electricity would be to the readers of this book.

None of the contributions in this chapter touch the frontiers evoked in the last few paragraphs. However, some of the developments suggested in this last, speculative, section are near. It is specifically the interaction of social and behavioral sciences with engineering and computer science that is needed to develop human and human–machine interactions, to study the effects on humans, and perhaps, to a certain degree, to point to a responsible use of such technologies. There are issues that have ethical ramifications, just as there are issues that might cause harm to humans. A naive embrace of all technological progress is obviously highly misplaced. However, a Luddite rejection is neither appropriate nor realistic. New forms of interaction in the guise of Web 2.0 are already permeating every sphere of life. Often media come and go in ways that were not predicted. The success of SMS (Short Message Service) was not anticipated, just as the success of the related microblog platform Twitter could not have been fore-seen. With affordable real-time, high-definition, 3D, immersive environments around the corner – who knows how consumers/users will react? Is it possible that lovers will decide to ban all technology and focus on decidedly "retro" dates, or instead don augmented reality "pink" glasses that allow them to have a perfect, idealized version of their beloved with them at all times?

To borrow the title of a recent conference organized by the European Union's Future and Emerging Technologies initiative, "Science Beyond Fiction" is here today in research laboratories. In everyday life the level of acceptance of face-to-face interaction over the internet has already dramatically increased in the time between the workshop funded by the European Science Foundation at the University of Hull in 2001 on "Face-to-Face Communication over the Internet" and the writing of this chapter. We consider the research presented in this book relevant not only to developments in the next decade but also to an understanding of an important facet of human interaction in a rapidly developed mixed-reality world: face-to-face interaction over the internet.

References

Antonijevic, S. (2008). Expressing emotions online: an analysis of visual aspects of emoticon. Paper presented at the Annual Meeting of the International Communication Association, Sheraton New York, New York City.

Bargh, J. A. and McKenna, K. Y. (2004). The internet and social life. *Annual Review of Psychology*, *55*, 573–590.

Bente, G., Krämer, N. C., Petersen, A., and de Ruiter, J. P. (2001). Computer animated movement and person perception: methodological advances in nonverbal behavior research. *Journal of Nonverbal Behavior*, *25* (3), 151–166.

Bente, G., Rüggenberg, S., Krämer, N. C., and Eschenburg, F. (2008). Avatar-assisted net-working. Increasing social presence and interpersonal trust in net-based collaborations. *Human Communication Research*, *34* (2), 287–318.

Blascovich, J., Loomis, J., Beall, A. C., Swinth, K. R., Hoyt, C. L., and Bailenson, J. N. (2002). Immersive virtual environment technology as a methodological tool for social psychology. *Psychological Inquiry*, *13*, 146–149.

Boyd, D. M. and Ellison, N. B. (2007). Social network sites: definition, history, and scholarship. *Journal of Computer-Mediated Communication*, *13* (1), article 11. http://jcmc.indiana.edu/vol13/issue1/boyd.ellison.html.

Burgoon, J. K., Berger, C. R., and Waldron, V. R. (2000). Mindfulness and interpersonal communication. *Journal of Social Issues*, *56* (1), 105–127.

Cassell, J., Sullivan, J., Prevost, S., and Churchill, E. (eds) (2000). *Embodied Conversational Agents*. Cambridge, MA: MIT Press.

Choi, V. S., Gray, H. M., and Ambady, N. (2005). The glimpsed world: unintended communication and unintended perception. In R. R. Hassin, J. S. Uleman, and J. A. Bargh (eds), *The New Unconscious* (pp. 309–333). New York: Oxford University Press.

Derks, D. (2007). *Exploring the Missing Wink: Emoticons in Cyberspace.* Heerlen: Open Universiteit Nederland, Academisch proefschrift. www.ou.nl/ Docs/Onderzoek/Definitieve%20versie%20Exploring%20the%20Missing %20Wink.pdf.

Ekman, P. and Friesen, W. V. (1969). The repertoire of nonverbal behavior: categories, origins, usage, and coding. *Semiotica, 1,* 49–98.

Fullwood, C. and Orsolina, I. M. (2007). Emoticons and impression formation. *Applied Semiotics, 19,* 4–14.

Gratch, J., Wang, N., Okhmatovskaia, A., Lamothe, F., Morales, M., and Morency, L. P. (2007). Can virtual humans be more engaging than real ones? In Julie Jacko (ed.), *12th International Conference on Human-Computer Interaction, Beijing, China 2007* (pp. 286–297). Berlin: Springer.

Kappas, A. (2003). What facial expressions can and cannot tell us about emotions. In M. Katsikitis (ed.), *The Human Face: Measurement and Meaning* (pp. 215–234). Dordrecht: Kluwer Academic Publishers.

(2005). My happy vacuum cleaner. Presented in the context of a symposium on artificial emotions at the 14th Conference of the International Society for Research on Emotion in Bari, Italy, July 11–15, 2005.

Kappas, A. and Descôteaux, J. (2003). Of butterflies and roaring thunder: nonverbal communication in interaction and regulation of emotion. In P. Philippot, E. J. Coats, and R. S. Feldman (eds), *Nonverbal Behavior in Clinical Settings* (pp. 45–74). New York: Oxford University Press.

Kiesler, S. (1997). *Culture of the Internet.* Mahwah, NJ: Lawrence Erlbaum.

Kiesler, S. and Sproull, L. (1992). Group decision making and communication technology. *Organizational Behaviour and Human Decision Processes, 52,* 96–123.

Kiesler, S., Siegel, J., and McGuire, T. W. (1984). Social psychological aspects of computer-mediated communication. *American Psychologist, 39,* 1123–1134.

Kopp, S., Gesellensetter, L., Krämer, N. C., and Wachsmuth, I. (2005). A conversational agent as museum guide – design and evaluation of a real-world application. In T. Panayiotopoulos *et al.* (eds), *Intelligent Virtual Agents, LNAI 3661* (pp. 329–343). Berlin: Springer-Verlag.

Krämer, N. C. (2005). Social communicative effects of a virtual program guide. In T. Panayiotopoulos *et al.* (eds), *Intelligent Virtual Agents 2005* (pp. 442–543). Hamburg: Springer.

(2008a). *Soziale Wirkungen virtueller Helfer.* Stuttgart: Kohlhammer.

(2008b). Nonverbal communication. In J. Blascovich and C. Hartel (eds), *Human Behavior in Military Contexts* (pp. 150–188). Washington, DC: National Academies Press.

Krämer, N. C., Bente, G., and Piesk, J. (2003). The ghost in the machine. The influence of embodied conversational agents on user expectations and user behaviour in a TV/VCR application. In G. Bieber and T. Kirste (eds), *IMC Workshop 2003, Assistance, Mobility, Applications* (pp. 121–128). Stuttgart: Fraunhofer 1RB.

Krämer, N. C., Simons, N., and Kopp, S. (2007). The effects of an embodied agent's nonverbal behavior on user's evaluation and behavioural mimicry. In C. Pelachaud *et al.* (eds), *Intelligent Virtual Agents 2007* (pp. 238–251). Berlin: Springer.

Leyhausen, P. (1967). Biologie von Ausdruck und Eindruck. Teil I. *Psychologische Forschung, 31,* 113–176.

Nass, C. and Moon, Y. (2000). Machines and mindlessness: social responses to computers. *Journal of Social Issues, 56* (1), 81–103.

Parise, S., Kiesler, S., Sproull, L., and Waters, K. (1999). Cooperating with life-like interface agents. *Computers in Human Behavior*, *15*, 123–142.

Pütten, A., von der, Reipen, C., Wiedemann, A., Kopp, S., and Krämer, N.C. (2008). Comparing emotional vs. envelope feedback for ECAs. In H. Prendinger, J. Lester, and M. Ishizuka (eds), *IVA 2008, LNAI 5208* (pp. 550–551). Berlin: Springer.

(2009). The impact of different embodied agent-feedback on users' behavior. In S. Ruttkay *et al.* (eds), *Intelligent Virtual Agents 2009*. Berlin: Springer.

Ramirez, A., Walther, J.B., Burgoon, J.K., and Sunnafrank, M. (2002). Information-seeking strategies, uncertainty, and computer-mediated communication toward a conceptual model. *Human Communication Research*, *28* (2), 213–228.

Reeves, B. and Nass, C. (1996). *The Media Equation: How People Treat Computers, Television, and New Media Like Real People and Places*. Cambridge University Press.

Regenbrecht, H., Ott, C., Wagner, M., Lum, T., Kohler, P., Wilke, W., and Mueller, E. (2003). An augmented virtuality approach to 3D videoconferencing. *Proceedings of the Second IEEE and ACM International Symposium on Mixed and Augmented Reality* (ISMAR '03) (pp. 290–291). Tokyo: IEEE Computer Society.

Rickenberg, R. and Reeves, B. (2000). The effects of animated characters on anxiety, task performance, and evaluations of user interfaces. In T. Turner, G. Szwillus, M. Czerwinski, F. Peterno, and S. Pemberton (eds), *Proceedings of the ACM CHI 2000 Human Factors in Computing Systems Conference, April 1–6* (pp. 49–56). The Hague, Netherlands: ACM.

Siegel, J., Dubrovsky, V., Kiesler, S., and McGuire, T.W. (1986). Group processes in computer-mediated communication. *Organizational Behavior and Human Decision Processes*, *37*(2), 157–187.

Sproull, L. and Kiesler, S. (1986) Reducing social context cues: electronic mail in organizational communication. *Management Science*, *32*, 1492–1512.

Sproull, L., Subramani, M., Kiesler, S., Walker, J.H., and Waters, K. (1996). When the interface is a face. *Human–Computer Interaction*, *11*(2), 97–124.

Walther, J.B. (1992). Interpersonal effects in computer-mediated interaction: a relational perspective. *Communication Research*, *19*, 52–90.

(1996). Computer-mediated communication: impersonal, interpersonal, and hyperpersonal interaction. *Communication Research*, *23*, 3–43.

(2006). Nonverbal dynamics in computer-mediated communication, or :(and the net :('s with you, :) and you :) alone. In V. Manusov and M.L. Patterson (eds), *Handbook of Nonverbal Communication* (pp. 461–479). Thousand Oaks, CA: Sage.

Walther, J.B. and Burgoon, J.K. (1992). Relational communication in computer-mediated interaction. *Human Communication Research*, *19*, 50–88.

Walther, J.B. and D'Addario, K.P. (2001). The impacts of emoticons on message interpretation in computer-mediated communication. *Social Science Computer Review*, *19*, 323–345.

Walther, J.B. and Parks, M.R. (2002). Cues filtered out, cues filtered in: computer-mediated communication and relationships. In M.L. Knapp and J.A. Daly (eds), *Handbook of Interpersonal Communication* (3rd edn., pp. 529–563). Thousand Oaks, CA: Sage.

PART 1

General aspects of visual cues in computer-mediated communication

CHAPTER 1

Visual cues in computer-mediated communication: sometimes less is more

Joseph B. Walther

Overview: This research reviews the promise and the pitfalls of visual cues in computer-mediated communication (CMC). The first section reviews theories advocating the utility of visual cues in telecommunication. Empirical research consistent with such theories has shown that communicators express preference for multichannel communication, whereas observational results, in contrast, indicate that visual cues often fail to enhance virtual groups' work. The second section extends this paradox by reviewing research that shows when and how visual cues detract from CMC social impressions and evaluations. Alternative uses of visual information, focusing on objects rather than people, show dramatically different effects. Taking into account the persistent preference for multimedia despite its disappointing results, the final section attempts to redirect theories of media selection to include a component about the principle of least effort in media preferences and how visual cues are at the same time easier and inferior to text-based CMC in many settings.

> Talking with another individual is still the easiest way to share information, because other people have the ability to see our gestures and facial expressions, listen to our tone of voice and understand what we are trying to communicate.
> Microsoft (1999), "Knowledge Workers Without Limits"

The epigraph reflects a common presumption that an abundance of nonverbal cues is the easiest way to facilitate shared understanding. In contrast, some of my students' course evaluations reflect our regular face-to-face encounters in class:

Portions of this chapter were presented at the International Communication Association, and the Annenberg Public Policy Center Conference on Digital Media and Communication.

"Prof. Walther means well but he is not the best instructor."

"He was not concerned with our retention of information and his presentation of it was poor."

"The way the lecture was presented was not beneficial to learning."

Others in the same course wrote:

"This class was extremely interesting and enjoyable. Walther's enthusiasm of the material made it easier to learn."

"Very attentive and understanding..."

"I felt like he taught us a lot."

Perhaps the presence of nonverbal cues, even in a face-to-face setting, is not a sufficient predictor of shared understanding. How valuable are they in a mediated context?

As several chapters in this volume illustrate, among the advances upon us and awaiting us in digital media, many researchers, prominent computer developers, and media analysts are enthusiastic in their welcome of high-quality, inexpensive videoconferencing in the mix of tools currently comprising computer-mediated communication (CMC). The delivery of natural-appearing video addresses users' intuitive desires and many theorists' claims that more communication cues are better – that the ability to convey nonverbal communication cues allows communicators to appreciate each other interpersonally and facilitates understanding their messages, or both. As a counterpoint to many of these illustrations and advocacies, however, this essay will argue that unqualified optimism about the inherent value of visual cues in online communication may be as scientifically unfounded as it is intuitive. Research exploring the utility of visual images of participants in CMC has tended to reflect two trends. First, great consistency in users' ratings of the desirability of video communication, and, second, no consistent support for the material benefits of the channel, despite its appeal. This discrepancy suggests that, in the truest sense of the word, visual cues in CMC are "overrated."

This chapter will review the theoretical arguments for the use of visual cues in CMC, and then look at the evidence for their perceived appeal and their actual utility. Research is discussed that shows how visual information in object-oriented interaction shows more promising effects of visual information, while some social processes are enhanced due in large part to its absence. A perspective on the use of easy versus onerous communication systems in general is discussed, considering the costs and benefits of various cue systems.

In the final analysis, it is argued, people pursuing task-related functions gravitate to media following principles of least effort; however, research shows that you get what you pay for. Greater effort, undesirable though it may be, yields greater effects. Visual cues have a limited place in optimizing CMC.

Theoretical attraction to nonverbal cues and CMC

A good deal of theory pertaining to CMC can be taken to advocate the use of video cues, in all or in some cases. Social presence theory (Short *et al.*, 1976) is one of the first grand theories applied to CMC, and it was originally intended to explain the advantages and disadvantages of videoconferencing systems. Among the entire literature pertaining to CMC, this work singularly takes an exhaustive account of the cues, combinations, and functions known to pertain to nonverbal communication and interpersonal phenomena. The theory centers on the social relations and reactions of remote collaborators during task-related work, but it does not focus on outcomes related to task effectiveness or efficiency. The theory argues that the greater the number of (nonverbal) cue systems users have in communication, the more social presence – a sense of the other – they experience, leading to interpersonal warmth, friendliness, and satisfaction with the interaction.

   Media richness theory (Daft and Lengel, 1986; see also Daft *et al.*, 1987) also predates the widespread use of CMC, and also focuses on multiple cue systems. This theory focuses not on interpersonal evaluations, but on the efficiency and effectiveness of task resolution (specifically, the reduction of uncertainty and equivocality in instrumentally oriented communication). It also differs from social presence theory in that it does not predict linear benefits from greater cue system use. Rather, it suggests that the greater the number of cue systems (along with natural language potential, immediate feedback, and personalization potential, resulting in "richer" media) the better when the topic is equivocal, whereas "leaner" media are adequate – even more efficient – for simple exchanges.

Inconsistent support and challenges

A generous amount of empirical scrutiny has been devoted to these theories. Much empirical research has included not digital media or video, but other text-based CMC programs, often telephones, and frequently face-to-face (FTF) interaction. Theorists and researchers assume that FTF interaction exceeds the effects of video or photos, so we may conclude that if FTF communication differs from text-based CMC, video and photos also might, whereas if FTF does not differ, other visual media will not. Among these studies, two kinds may be identified: projective and observational research. Projective research refers to studies in which users – often managers – are asked to indicate (often, select from a list) what medium they would be likely to select to communicate with another person, for various respective purposes. In Daft *et al.*'s (1987) research, for example, managers completed questionnaires assessing their media sensitivity, or the degree to which their projective choices of communication media, including email, matched the theoretical richness requirements of a variety of situations. Daft *et al.* found a positive relationship between these managers' media sensitivity and their existing professional personnel evaluations within their company. In a summary analysis of many studies assessing social presence, Rice (1993) similarly found consistent support across numerous organizational sites, levels, and time periods in users' projective assessments of the desirability of wider "bandwidth" communication channels – i.e., those with more cue systems, with FTF communication having the most – for communication tasks requiring greater interpersonal uncertainty or delicacy. While most of these studies did not examine videoconferencing, or the use of visual images in CMC, per se, they followed the logic of the theories holding that more bandwidth and FTF cues are superior for some types of communication for which CMC without such cues might be suboptimal.

Observational studies, ironically, yield systematically contrary results. This is to say that several types of studies reliably support, while others reliably challenge, these theoretical relationships. Markus' (1994) naturalistic observations, for instance, showed that while managers' *self-reported responses* reflected media richness dictates, they did not *follow* them in their spontaneous, behavioral media selections. Nor were they ineffective in their managerial communication, as projective media richness research elsewhere suggested they would be. In experimental research using groups, a number of time-limited, one-shot studies supported the basic social presence approach; however, longer-term or time-unlimited groups tend not to suffer the social problems previously expected of limited bandwidth media in experiments using CMC and FTF comparisons. This is not just a matter of failing to find significant differences. Rather, longer time frames and other facilitating circumstances have been predicted and found to yield superior results in social assessments for CMC (see, for review, Walther, 2002; for a meta-analysis, see Walther *et al.*, 1994).

Indeed, recent theories have suggested that minimal, text-based CMC interaction is quite capable, and in some cases likely, to foster exceedingly intimate and affectionate communication to levels greater than those common in parallel off-line FTF interaction. The hyperpersonal communication perspective on CMC (Walther, 1996) argues that users exploit the characteristics of CMC and shape their interactions in positive ways. Using text-based communication, users present themselves in selective ways, concentrating on purposeful message construction, and eliminating the role of involuntary nonverbal appearance and behavior features from interaction. Reciprocally, they magnify their sense of the similarity and desirability of others, becoming more friendly and attractive. Naturally, this depends to some extent on the desires of the users and the contexts in which they operate. Nevertheless, research has supported aspects of this model, as seen among student teams composed of virtual and co-located partners (Walther, 1997): Over two projects' duration, virtual partners with a common group identity and an expectation of long-term interaction rated each other more socially attractive, more affectionate, and even more physically attractive than those who expected a short-term acquaintance. Those who were prompted to look for interindividual differences, unlike those with the group identity, seemed to be immune to these hyperpersonal effects and their partner ratings were similar to those of FTF partners: average rather than extreme.

These results are similar to those of some SIDE theory investigations (Lea and Spears, 1992; see, for review, Postmes *et al.*, 1998). This theory, the name of which is an acronym for social identification/deindividuation, argues that when a common social identity is salient among communicators who cannot observe individuating nonverbal cues, norms are reinforced and reflected, overattribution of similarity occurs, and social attraction increases. When visual characteristics conveyed by video (or FTF) communication are present, they depress the overattribution and magnification processes that take place when CMC fosters "visual anonymity" (Lea *et al.*, 2001). This research strongly suggests that text-based CMC, because of several properties not the least of which is its lack of visual cues, facilitates rather than inhibits users' cognitive and behavioral efforts, providing extraordinary effects unparalleled by FTF interaction.

While these contrasts regarding social dimensions are noteworthy, they do not tell the whole story of virtual group work. Groups have to do things such as solve problems and produce products as well. Yet, in this domain also, the data do not support a rich medium advantage. Hollingshead *et al.* (1993), for example, also report the benefits of time and experience in virtual groups with regard to their decision-making effectiveness. In their research, over several decision-making tasks over time, CMC groups overcame an initial disadvantage to become as effective as FTF groups. One may wonder why, if FTF dynamics are not superior to text-based CMC, at least under some circumstances, we would expect their electronic simulacra, video, or pictorial images, to be so.

Still pictures

Returning to social presence theory's notion that visual cues help us to assess the personalities of others, and considering that full-motion video or FTF may be overrated, we may consider whether still photographs might convey enough about electronic partners' apparent self to facilitate social presence without overburdening the human and machine system with superfluous data. To develop a sense of the social characteristics of one's partners, it may be adequate to offer static physical appearance cues, as people make judgments about others to a great extent based on the way they appear. Indeed, Bill Gates (1999, n.p.) advocates a system in which, "depending on the bandwidth, it would either just put up a still image of the person you are talking to or, if it is preferred, you can have actually a video link." Yet, once again, this notion raises concerns from the perspective of hyperpersonal and other perspectives.

Several studies have tested the social presence hypothesis that a picture of one's CMC partners would promote attraction and affection among virtual partners, providing some support (Tanis and Postmes, 2003, Study 1; Walther *et al.*, 2001). In one of these studies, however, the social presence hypothesis was boundaried within the relatively narrow domain in which social presence principles are still held to pertain (see Walther, 1996): zero-history, virtual groups with no anticipated future interaction. For long-term groups, the opposite dynamic was predicted. Based on the hyperpersonal perspective, people should develop extraordinarily affectionate and attractive relations through CMC, through mutual and reciprocal construction via text. A picture was hypothesized to dampen attraction and affinity for long-term groups. The hypotheses were tested, using student groups from international locations addressing a decision-making problem using a MOO space, in groups of three and four. Using a 2 × 2 experimental design, half of the groups were familiar – they had worked with each other on prior projects via CMC over the course of a semester – and half were new; half of each were exposed to pictures of their partners, on web pages, before beginning discussions, while the other half were not. The results confirmed the hypotheses: new groups were more affiliative with pictures than without, while established CMC groups favored their partners *without* pictures more than the long-term groups *with* photos did. In all conditions, the hyperpersonal, long-term/no-photo groups rated their partners best. Moreover, when photos were absent, there were significant correlations between participants' self-reported efforts at impression management and the physical attractiveness ratings partners made of the subjects; that is, the more they worked at making a positive self-presentation, the better looking partners who had never seen each other "appeared," psychologically speaking. However, among those whose photos were present, the more efforts they made at self-presentation, the worse their physical attractiveness ratings were. It seems that once a photo is shared, an individual's attractiveness becomes fixed, and efforts to make oneself seem more attractive actually backfire. While much research on visual cues in CMC focuses on the clarification of meaning, the attractiveness of users is an issue that may underlie other important interpersonal dynamics when visual information is offered.

Videoconferencing

Direct evidence about the utility of videoconferencing is similarly paradoxical, with several studies providing negative results from added video cues, others demonstrating complex interaction effects, and yet others showing ironic uses of the video information. While Mühlfelder *et al.* (1999) found no differences in interpersonal trust between videoconferencing and FTF communication, Storck and Sproull (1995) found that users of a videoconferencing system in an educational setting *disparaged* their partners more in this system than in FTF communication, suggesting that video may not only fail to approximate the feel of non-electronic communication, but also degrade communication even more. In an extension of SIDE theory, video plus text-chat was compared to text-chat alone in mixed, international groups. Video both mitigated perceptions of ingroup similarity and reduced out-group antagonism compared to text-only CMC, where visually anonymous in-group and out-group members otherwise garnered respectively more extreme reactions (Lea *et al.*, 2001).

In several studies there was a direct and striking contrast between perception and behavior regarding the value of video. Galagher and Kraut (1994) found that text-based CMC groups were less satisfied with their communication than video-mediated groups, but that there were no significant differences in the quality of the outputs that these conditions produced. Likewise, Dennis and Kinney (1998) found that media richness did not account for decision quality or interpersonal perception effects in a detailed study using text-based CMC and videoconferencing, once again despite its users rating video as more satisfying. These studies are noteworthy, in that participants seemed to think the videoconferencing medium was superior, when in an objective, output-related sense, it was not. Nowak *et al.* (2009) tested an *asynchronous* group videoconferencing system – the time-independent collaboration (TIC) system. Small groups of three or four members developed presentations either using TIC or working FTF over several weeks. Self-administered questionnaire results showed higher scores on social presence and conversational involvement for FTF communication, but self-reported meeting effectiveness scores did not differ between conditions, and external coders' ratings of meeting effectiveness also did not distinguish the formats from one another.

Three independent studies suggest that video information distracts users from their tasks, leading to inferior performance and/or social outcomes. One study concluded that having to attend to visual cues of the person as well as visual properties of a common task object can be problematic: Hinds (1999) found that the management of competing visual cues in such a manner is so cognitively taxing that it leads to stress, decrements in information-processing performance, and biased impressions of co-participants. Matarazzo and Sellen (2000) ironically found that a low-grade, synchronous video system provided better support than a high-grade videoconferencing parallel; subjects rated the poor-quality video system more favorably than the comparable high-quality system, and they completed their tasks more quickly with the inferior system, effects which the researchers attribute to the distraction factor that full-quality video provided in directing attention away from the task in hand.

Another study provides important insights into the effects of video by examining concurrently the perceptions its users held as well as the minutiae of its use. Research by Gale (1991) put project designers in one of three electronic communication conditions: a shared electronic white plus text-based, real-time CMC; whiteboard plus audio; or whiteboard plus audio and video. As might be expected, users rated communication significantly higher in social presence in the CMC/audio/video condition than in CMC-plus-audio or the CMC-alone conditions. However, the video-augmented system did not help them produce a better design product. In fact, no differences between conditions were found in the quality of the groups' outputs. Time spent working, however, was affected: whiteboard plus audio only was the most efficient condition, with text- or video-augmentation both significantly slower than audio. Furthermore, detailed analyses of the actual use of the systems revealed that users did not depend much on the interactive aspects of the video channel. Users' attention to the specific behaviors of their video-relayed partners was minimal. Rather than using the video as a channel to help promote message understanding, they tended to rely on it to see if their partners were still attending to the discussion, in the remote room. It does not appear from these results that the subtleties of affect expression, personality/appearance, or attitude – which we often believe we need, and use nonverbal cues to detect – played much of a role here. It signaled a binary – an on or an off – whether people were still there or not. A remote pressure sensor on the partners' chairs could have done as well!

Seeing who is paying attention, and who is saying what, may be a very satisfying aspect of videoconferencing that has little to do with what people think the benefits may really be. Anyone who has been in a distributed group conference call – with audio only – among strangers or relatively unfamiliar people, knows how difficult it can be to sort out who is saying what. Knowing who is who more or less comes down to being able to associate ideas and utterances with their respective contributors over the course of a conversation. When many participants share similar fundamental vocal pitches – several men, for instance – with no distinguishing accents or notably persistent disfluencies, it is difficult to imagine and sort out who said what and who is who. Thus, video may provide the "scaffolding" on which cognitively to hang the utterances and arguments of the individuals within the group with which one is working. This is no mean feat, but it is unmentioned in the literature on the benefits of videoconferencing over voice and text. In cognition research (Brewer and Nakamura, 1984; Housel, 1985; Housel and Acker, 1981), it is well established that cognitive schemata that provide scaffolding for encoding and evaluating incoming information are useful and enhance information processing and recall. Whether this aspect of videoconferencing is one of its implicit bases for appeal is an empirical question requiring clever research designs.

These findings deserve further analysis and comment. According to Bill Gates (1999), even with the modest quality of internet videoconferencing, "You do get enough video fidelity to get a sense of is somebody engaged, are they agreeing with you, are they bored with the meeting, the kind of clues that you would like to get that help a lot in face-to-face meetings." Yet the example he gives in the same presentation of a dramatic use of videoconferencing involves sharing digital photos of a remote problem to distributed engineers, who were able to direct problem solving via voice. Maybe, if scaffolding is a meager benefit, videoconferencing ought not to be pointing at visual facial cues at all.

Alternative conferencing systems involving video have been developed where, indeed, the shared visual image does not present the nonverbal features of the communicators involved: the camera is not on the people or at least their faces. According to Brittan (1992), several conferencing systems share images of some design object, or the hands-on-the-mouse systems of the users (in order to facilitate switching of system control between users). The point is that when people are working together on some thing that can be represented visually – a model or a document, for instance – one's ocular attention is trained on what Geisler (1999) refers to as the "common virtual object," and that common focus shapes the discourse of collaborators. This approach is similar to the position articulated in Clark and Brennan's (1991) theory of communication grounding. When a common visual referent is available for communicators, it allows discourse to be more referential, efficient, and cogent. Thus, nonverbal visual cues *about the people involved* are not important enough to take precedence over that which is actually the focus of the meeting: the object. An empirical study by Gergle *et al.* (2004) offered a remote helper, who was in a separate physical location from a worker, the view of the worker's electronic workspace, so that the helper could see what the worker was doing when the helper gave instructions on the assembly of puzzle pieces. When dyads had a high-resolution, rapidly refreshing electronic display, puzzles were assembled correctly more often, more quickly, and language became more efficient through the use of more deictic references. These results mirror other studies that also address the superiority of sharing visual information about the objects workers discuss rather than the characteristics of the workers themselves. For instance, Kraut *et al.* (2003) connected a worker by means of a head-mounted camera – pointed away from the worker at a bicycle being repaired – and audio microphone to an expert at a separate location. By speaking about the object, and showing the object via the camera, the expert was better able to guide the worker than in other combinations, or directions, of audio and video.

These experiments offer a sharp contrast not only to desktop videoconferencing techniques but also to common larger-scale videoconferencing arrangements. When considering how videoconferencing is often deployed in conference rooms, where conversations focus on reports or documents and the video depicts the speakers and listeners, it is ironic to review how we handle such discussions FTF when there are no cameras guiding our attention. In an FTF conversation that involves a physical object about which people are talking, and the affectively oriented concerns of the people themselves, listeners may freely switch their visual attention between speaker and object, opportunistically, even surreptitiously. Unfortunately, most videoconferencing systems preclude such opportunism. In some systems, such as

H.320 compatible videoconferencing, the sender may switch the view being transmitted to partners, from self to object and back. In other systems, such as PictureTel, where a remote user is video-connected to an otherwise FTF group, the remote user may pan or switch a camera from one member of the group to another, but must choose one target, or choose a broad and undifferentiated view. In some of these cases, the proximal audience also sees a monitor that reflects that at which the distant viewer is looking – so much for surreptitious glances, which are no longer casual or secretive, and therefore avoided! Obviously, to provide an analogue to FTF interaction, the receiver rather than the sender must be allowed to choose where he or she focuses attention, from a panoply of options that are persistently displayed by multiple monitors, windows, or other viewing devices. Such technology arrangements are expensive and seldom seen in practice. Porting such suboptimal routines from the boardroom to the desktop is prone to disappoint also.

Ease, effort, and optimal multiplicity

Simply put, talking to, listening to, and looking at someone provides a simple and efficient interface for the transmission and reception of information, and for the management of turn taking. It is simple because the face, voice, and words convey highly familiar code systems. It is efficient because they are radically multiple. Even if the face only sent one system (let's say affect and, for the moment, ignore physical/personality impression cues), and the voice transmitted only cues conveyed by vocal variety (and not, say, tempo, vocal quality, etc.) and words (which we will allow to carry content and style as they do across any verbal medium including text-based CMC), even under these conditions we are exchanging a great quantity of information. Cues are exchanged across all levels simultaneously through specialized receptor channels that do not compete for exclusive attention (i.e., eyes track appearance and kinesic cues, ears track verbal and vocalic cues, and neither receptor has to split attention). The simplicity and the simultaneity of non-object-oriented FTF speech transacts information rapidly and is gratifying. This would not be advantageous if the information conveyed by appearance, kinesics, verbiage, and vocalics was always redundant (as it often is), but often these cues are divergent enough to be complementary or even enough to be contradictory (see Ekman and Friesen, 1969). In any event, we track these cues rather well FTF.

In this sense, communication is "easy" FTF (*ceteris paribus*), whereas accomplishing the same communication effects by using restricted-code media is not impossible, but it is "hard." That is, at least within the social information-processing perspective (Walther, 1992; see, for review, Walther and Parks, 2002), users of text-based CMC can adapt their multiple meanings, and social- as well as task-oriented intentions, into the single channel of language online. For instance, Walther *et al.* (2005) tested the expression of liking in CMC and FTF dyads, finding no difference in the level of affinity expressed in the two conditions, but a preponderance of variance in FTF interaction accounted for by clusters of vocalic and then kinesic cues, while CMC affect was managed by the form of disagreements expressed, overt verbal expressions of liking, and other discernible verbal behaviors. Despite the translatability of functions from one cue system to another, however, social information-processing theory holds that it takes more time and/or deliberate effort to accomplish these functions in CMC than to use simultaneous verbal and nonverbal behaviors FTF. If we may assume that those things which are easier and quicker are more gratifying than those which are more effortful and slower, despite the prospects for equivalent outcomes (just as, in learning, "television is easy and print is tough"; Salomon, 1984), it should not be surprising that CMC (and other effort-requiring communication media) is disparaged in relation to FTF or video-mediated communication.

When videoconferencing requires additional effort, it, too, might be perceived less favorably than FTF. In applications where videoconferencing adds rather than reduces cognitive demands, by making attention to disparate aspects of the conversation even more difficult, it should be no surprise that videoconferencing is rated poorly. When the visual focus of videoconferencing is on a person, when it may be better to see an object (such as a model or document), communication must be more effortful. This may explain why videoconferencing research detects cognitive overload (Hinds, 1999) and suboptimal usage (Gale, 1991) in studies with videoconferencing accompanying object-oriented work. The efficiency advantage, however, is also lost if it offers no particular net gain: as Kraut (in Brittan, 1992, p. 65) observes, "There's a huge amount of redundancy between the information you can pick up from voice and what you get over the video channel."

On this basis, the inclusion of nonverbal cues with verbal signals might or might not make communication easier and more efficient than communication through text alone. However, it is precisely ease and efficiency that are not always to be prized, even in instrumental efforts. This is to say that increased effort at the cognitive level (to think through and keep track of messages and other users) and at the behavioral level (in the construction, editing, and management of text-based messaging) invites certain benefits that are lost when communication is grounded in nonwritten, visual information.

Communication that requires more mindful work may yield more effective communication (see Salomon, 1984; Salomon and Globerson, 1987) at both the relational and instrumental level. A simple illustration may help. A virtual group may wish to work FTF or via videoconferencing on their collaborative report. This is an intuitive impulse. Doing so may yield the participants some quicker decisions, within a short time interval, about their approach to the work, than they would get using text-based CMC (especially if it is asynchronous CMC). It will not, however, produce the paper. For that, the participants must write. Writing through their organizing decisions would be more effortful and time intensive. However, it may more likely be deliberative and mindful, and it is certainly more readily store- and retrievable. And, as research has shown, with physical cues they may get to know each other more quickly than, but not necessarily better or as positively as, if they engaged in the more onerous yet beneficial hyperpersonal processes to which text-based communication may lead (Walther *et al.*, 2001).

How do we resolve the consistent attraction to, and high projective ratings for, video or FTF communication, despite its failure to yield superior communication outcomes? Multimodal communication provides the path of least resistance; it is the technique that satisfies the principle of least effort, despite, at times, offering less effective communication as well. When users do not have a choice – they are separated by distance, time, or the arbitrary demands of some experiment – and must rely on bare-bones CMC, they are often wonderfully adaptive and effective, and seem not to mind the effort as much.

Korzenny (1978) foreshadowed this position in another theory that considered videoconferencing and that predated CMC. Korzenny's theory of electronic propinquity argues that the fewer one's choices of media, the more closeness one may experience even through the lowest of bandwidths. Korzenny predicts that users will adopt the widest bandwidth communication medium available to them. As one becomes unavailable, however, the next richest channel is perceived as being able to sustain greater "perceived propinquity" among participants than it would have otherwise. Essentially this position runs counter to Daft and Lengel's (1986) notions that lean media are incapable or generally unavailable for personalized focus and language variety, assumptions which were the weakest parts of Daft and Lengel's theory in the first place and which have received no support; if the counter-evidentiary tests of media richness have shown us anything, it is that these assumptions were misplaced. In a series of formal propositions, Korzenny's theory argues that there is what we may call an accommodation of effort. That is to say, if forced to rely on the structurally least expressive of media choices, the user expands the otherwise limited range of the medium through greater application of communication skills and the reduction of formality, thus expanding the expressive potential of that medium.

A recent small-group communication study supported several of propinquity theory's contentions (Walther and Bazarova, 2008). Groups using videoconferencing, audioconferencing, or text-based conferencing were no less satisfied than groups using FTF communication when all members of a small group used the same medium. When a group used a combination of high-bandwidth and low-bandwidth media (FTF and video, video and audio, or audio and text), the lower-bandwidth medium was less satisfying than the higher-bandwidth alternative. Moreover, users with greater communication skills overcome cue system limitations better than those with lesser skills. The ability to apply social skills in order to accommodate the lack of nonverbal cues, i.e., to make efforts to make text-based or audio-only communication as satisfying as FTF, is an important finding when considering the necessity utility of visual cues in CMC or FTF conferencing.

An (in)efficiency framework of multimedia benefits

We may extend this perspective on complexity, efficiency, and ease to our thinking about the utility of hearing spoken language in CMC or multimedia communication systems, especially auditory cues and their fit with visual object-oriented activity. We assume that there is great efficiency when we can transmit language and vocal information by speech and hearing, while ocular attention is focused on an object. Not only is this efficient in its own right, but also the content of speech becomes more efficient as it becomes referential and contextual (e.g., in watching a shared representation of a collaboratively written paper), referring to "this" and "here" rather than "the section part-way down the third page that starts 'Media Richness Theory.'" I wish to argue one more step, however. From this perspective, the key to the successful speed and efficiency of information exchange relies upon two factors: allocation of cues among noncompeting sensory systems (i.e., eyes for looking at an object, ears for hearing verbiage discussing that object), and the utility of complementary information. If this is so, then it is a theoretical possibility (but by no means necessary) that the vocal channel offers little more than a carrier of language. It remains a theoretical and empirical question whether vocalics are also beneficial because they provide affective or other paraverbal information. It is likely that they do so when needed, but it remains to be seen whether they are indeed needed in task-oriented discussions. Thus, it is possible, and a conservative first stance to assert, that when partners are engaged in a task, vocalic cues take a utilitarian background to (or are at least alternate in salience with) the vocally conveyed verbal content they might simultaneously transmit.

Such an argument is not likely to appeal to those who believe that the voice conveys essential qualities (as it certainly does, when they are attended to), some of which are thought to have evolved over millennia. But ideological views of the essential requirement for vocalic (or visual) cues in order to accomplish rudimentary relational functions are betrayed by reports that we can get to know one another, or have affectionate and even arousing relations online. It becomes necessary to put aside our loyally humanistic but vague devotion to the essentiality of nonverbal cues in communication. We flaunt them when we have them, but as scientists we must not cling to their value unless necessary, and their inherent necessity is precisely the question that CMC raises, the answer to which must guide the deployment of digital media in human communication.

Thus, an (in)efficiency approach to the utility of multiple cue systems in telecommunication suggests that the simplicity of an FTF or electronically simulated FTF meeting system will garner *projective* appeal based on its assumed ease of use, but that it will be relatively inefficient when a task object is involved in communication, and that participants will dispense with it in actual use. For virtual work involving the co-creation of something, common control over that thing plus an audio channel offers optimal matching, regardless of the vocalics themselves. This pairing constitutes a complementary system of information exchange that matches human processing capacity, using voice as a conveyor of real-time language alone. In comparison, text alongside of an object would not work as well, even though text also conveys language, because visually attending to both text and a visual object occludes attention to each source.

When a task-object is *not* involved, however, such as in traditional idea generation, decision making or problem solving, the FTF representation's beneficial help in turn-taking, and in "framing" what comments are associated with which speaker, may reassert its actual beneficial effects. None of these elements so far pertain to any aspect other than information processing and management; there is no spiritual or emotional aspect to this formulation. The traditional appeal of visual cues may be not that they provide visuality but that they provide information multiplicity. But it is another matter altogether for *socially oriented* CMC where, once again, the relationship of nonverbal cues and text is somewhat surprising and paradoxical.

Social interaction as social interaction

As Murray and Bevin stated in 1985 (p. 34), even in computer conversations in which the main goal is "a task involving giving or receiving information . . . any human conversation will also seek to achieve a number of social goals," such as "social acceptance and developing relationships." Yet, a variety of internet communication spaces are not intended to facilitate information goals aside from social acceptance and developing social relationships. As these goals change, the role of virtual objects and the value of multiple, realistic cues diminish as well. In what Armstrong and Hagel (1996) refer to as "communities of fantasy" (e.g., chat spaces), nonverbal visual cues may be undesirable altogether. Spaces where people explore alternative personae or go to escape the hassles of FTF gender stereotyping have no place for visually identifying cues – at least not real ones that replicate actual offline appearance.

Likewise, in some of what Armstrong and Hagel call "communities of interest," users are attracted to features of internet communication that FTF interaction does not provide. One domain in which visual cues seem much less preferable to text-based CMC is in the domain of online social support groups. These ad hoc groups, many of which occur via Usenet but more of which are being intentionally designed (e.g., McTavish *et al.*, 2003), bring together individuals with similar health problems, psychological issues, or social problems in order to share information, provide comfort, and bolster esteem (Braithwaite *et al.*, 1999). Many of these discussions are intensely personal and often deal with potentially stigmatizing issues. They often attract hundreds if not thousands of users. Interestingly, their immense attraction is based in part on anonymity, the ability to type carefully and edit one's comments as they are prepared for dissemination, and the ability to extricate oneself from the conversation without notice to others (Walther and Boyd, 2002).

The previous discussion focused on the efficiency of multiple-cue systems, and is limited to communication focusing on instrumentally oriented tasks. An efficiency goal, in which time is precious, may be the hallmark of many instrumental transactions, where single-channel, text-based media may indeed be a lesser choice. In the realm of relational dynamics and play, however, efficiency and progress are not as important. Moreover, there are aspects of social life in which the important functions of "privacy, secrecy, and deception" are common

(Parks, 1982, p. 89) – processes certainly facilitated by less-revealing CMC. The intriguing and sometimes desirable aspects of getting to know someone online may include some aspect of novelty, collaborative flattery, collusion, and validation. When these processes are more important than, or even coexistent with, getting a task completed, then reduced-cue interaction may offer a superior alternative to the stark reality that FTF can offer, even better than the potential negativity that videoconferencing sometimes provides (Storck and Sproull, 1995). That was qualified with a "when." These goals and conditions are not always the case, but it appears that sometimes they are. Numerous accounts of online chat spaces, where people talk, flirt, play games, and form relationships, may be such spaces where less is more when it comes to the potential benefits of visual information. Is this an unfair assertion? Would people use videoconferencing in such settings if only it were available with good resolution and high interactivity?

The Starbright Project (see McCarthy, 1996) offers another interesting glimpse of the various uses of real videoconferencing and its disuse. The Starbright Project is a high-tech communication system built to allow interaction among seriously ill children in selected hospitals. Its features include high-speed videoconferencing, as well as an avatar-based virtual reality system. In the avatar portion, or Starbright World, users are represented graphically and bodily by cartoon-like abstract characters, which the user can manipulate through space, accompanied by displays of text that the user types in. The interesting usage noted in material about this project is that the children often use the videoconferencing aspect to locate other users who may be logged in simultaneously, and, once located, the children then switch to Starbright World to continue their interaction. In this case, where chat and social interaction are the primary purpose, it seems to be more fun to communicate without the benefits or detriments that the very expensive and highly realist videoconference system allows.

Conclusion

When communicating in CMC with others who are relatively less well known to us, there is high uncertainty about who our partners are and what they think. Visual cues may be easy to decode and are intuitively attractive. Yet, research has not borne out that they are more beneficial in the completion of communication episodes where other CMC media may be used. Where they have been examined directly, the results range from their being superfluous, to taxing, to socially disadvantageous in the long term. Prudence is warranted in the rush to plug in cameras to our CMC systems.

Yet, our study of visual cues in CMC has tended to be an all-or-nothing affair, an approach which future research needs to dispel. While previous research has given lipservice to various functions that facial cues may perform – signaling attention, signaling affect and attitude, and providing conversation management and physical appearance/personality impressions – they have been discussed as though they all need to take place simultaneously. Indeed, in FTF communication and in standard videoconferencing, they do. That approach is, however, no longer necessary since contemporary technology may facilitate the transmission of some cues (e.g., appearance cues) while withholding other visual cues (e.g., kinesic cues).

What the functions of physical appearance are, compared to dynamic kinesic cues, has not been thoroughly conceptualized since the consideration of social presence theory (Short *et al.*, 1976). One attempt at functional distinctions appears in the work of Tanis (2003; Tanis and Postmes, 2003), who argues that media vary in their capacity to transmit cues to *identity* and cues to *meaning*. Tanis' elaboration of this scheme equates static photographic information or biographical text about participants with cues to identity; dynamic *textual* information constitutes cues to meaning. This dichotomy is somewhat at odds with other positions. While CMC users often indeed report that visual cues are critical for identifying others, research shows that the cues users actually use to signal and/or infer identity among online partners are in many cases textual (e.g., Herring and Martinson, 2004; Jacobson, 1999). Moreover, much of the classic work on CMC privileges not language at all but dynamic visual cues such as facial expressions as those best suited to the disambiguation of complex messages (e.g., media richness theory, Daft and Lengel, 1986; Daft *et al.*, 1987). Whether in the long run this particular framework will or will not help sensitize theorists and analysts to look for the functional nature of cues among "leaner" or "richer" communication channels, ultimately a functional approach is what is needed.

Indeed, the future of the field must, as many of the chapters in this volume begin to do, decipher the functional aspects of communication that physical behavior offers, how these functions can be represented through alternative electronic symbol systems, and/or how they are or are not accommodated in communicative action via electronic surrogates for physical cues or in their absence. In many places, FTF is still a "black box," as though its components and dynamics are metaphysical, immune to deconstruction, irreplaceable, and impossible to isolate and reproduce in alternative symbol systems. However, as communication science and human–computer interaction research evolve, it becomes no longer necessary to convey the whole face, or to convey the face's reactions through facial cues alone.

However, in looking for substitutions and segmentations, we do not yet know which of these functions, and what specific subsystems of cues, might be beneficial after all. The expression of some communicative functions may indeed be difficult to translate from nonverbal cues into textual, temporal, or other persistent cues that do appear in CMC. What these specific functions are, however, has yet to be specified and empirically verified beyond the level of intuition and vague allusions. Only through more specific analysis of functions and cues can we design and advance potentially new, alternative interfaces and digital tools to mimic the functions we employ the face or the hands to do offline. Arrows to point like gaze at specific object attributes, interface agents that signal attendance or attention, graphical indicators of turn requests, and subtle or vague affective indicators may yet prove to be useful in CMC, if they can be translated into signals that do not compete for the level of visual attention that a face demands. By demystifying visual cues, analyzing their functions, and recombining and re-representing them an element at a time, we might find that, like the value of well-chosen words in CMC, a little information can go a long way.

References

Armstrong, A. and Hagel, J. (1996, May–June). The real value of on-line communities. *Harvard Business Review*, *74*, 134–141.

Braithwaite, D. O., Waldron, V. R., and Finn, J. (1999). Communication of social support in computer-mediated groups for persons with disabilities. *Health Communication*, *11*, 123–151.

Brewer, W. F. and Nakamura, G. V. (1984). The nature and functions of schemas. In R. S. Wyer and T. K. Srull (eds), *Handbook of Social Cognition* (vol. I, pp. 119–160). Hillsdale, NJ: Erlbaum.

Brittan, D. (1992). Being there: the promise of multimedia communications. *Technology Review*, *95*(4), 42–50.

Clark, H. H. and Brennan, S. E. (1991). Grounding in communication. In L. B. Resnick, R. M. Levine, and S. D. Teasley (eds), *Perspectives on Socially Shared Cognition* (pp. 127–149). Washington, DC: American Psychological Association.

Daft, R. L. and Lengel, R. H. (1986). Organizational information requirements, media richness and structural design. *Management Science*, *32*, 554–571.

Daft, R. L., Lengel, R. H., and Trevino, L. K. (1987). Message equivocality, media selection, and manager performance: implications for information systems. *MIS Quarterly*, *11*, 355–368.

Dennis, A. R. and Kinney, S. T. (1998). Testing media richness theory in the new media: the effects of cues, feedback, and task equivocality. *Information Systems Research*, *9*, 256–274.

Ekman, P. and Friesen, W. V. (1969). The repertoire of nonverbal behavior: categories, origins, usage, and coding. *Semiotica*, *1*, 49–98.

Galagher, J. and Kraut, R. E. (1994). Computer-mediated communication for intellectual teamwork: an experiment in group writing. *Information Systems Research*, **5**, 110–138.

Gale, S. (1991). Adding audio and video to an office environment. In J. M. Bowers and S. D. Benford (eds), *Studies in Computer-Supported Collaborative Work* (pp. 49–62). Amsterdam: Elsevier Science Publishers.

Gates, B. (1999, May 19). 1999 CEO summit keynote. www.microsoft.com/ billgates/speeches/05–19ceosummit.htm.

Geisler, C. (1999). Virtual objects MIA: The problems of mediating multidisciplinary discourse in a software development group. Paper presented at the annual meeting of the American Educational Research Association, Montreal (April).

Gergle, D., Kraut, R. E., and Fussell, S. R. (2004). Language efficiency and visual technology: minimizing collaborative effort with visual information. *Journal of Language and Social Psychology*, **23**, 491–517.

Herring, S. C. and Martinson, A. (2004). Assessing gender authenticity in computer-mediated language use: evidence from an identity game. *Journal of Language and Social Psychology*, **23**, 424–446.

Hinds, P. J. (1999). The cognitive and interpersonal costs of video. *Media Psychology*, **1**, 283–311.

Hollingshead, A. B., McGrath, J. E., and O'Connor, K. M. (1993). Group task performance and communication technology: a longitudinal study of computer-mediated versus face-to-face work groups. *Small Group Research*, **24**, 307–333.

Housel, T. J. (1985). Conversational themes and attention focusing strategies: predicting comprehension and recall. *Communication Quarterly*, **33**, 236–253.

Housel, T. J. and Acker, S. R. (1981). Comparison of three approaches to semantic memory: network, feature comparison, and schema theory. *Communication Quarterly*, **29**, 21–31.

Jacobson, D. (1999). Impression formation in cyberspace: online expectations and offline experiences in text-based virtual communities. *Journal of Computer-Mediated Communication*, **5**(1). http://jcmc.indiana.edu/vol5/ issue1/jacobson.html.

Korzenny, F. (1978). A theory of electronic propinquity: mediated communications in organizations. *Communication Research*, **5**, 3–24.

Korzenny, F. and Bauer, C. (1981). Testing the theory of electronic propinquity. *Communication Research*, **8**, 479–498.

Kraut, R. E., Fussell, S. R., and Siegel, J. (2003). Visual information as a conversational resource in collaborative physical tasks. *Human–Computer Interaction*, **18**, 13–49.

Lea, M. and Spears, R. (1992). Paralanguage and social perception in computer-mediated communication. *Journal of Organizational Computing*, **2**, 321–341.

Lea, M., Spears, R., and de Groot, D. (2001). Knowing me, knowing you: anonymity effects on social identity processes within groups. *Personality and Social Psychology Bulletin*, **27**, 526–537.

Markus, M. L. (1994). Electronic mail as the medium of managerial choice. *Organization Science*, **5**, 502–527.

Matarazzo, G. and Sellen, A. (2000). The value of video in work at a distance: addition or distraction? *Behaviour & Information Technology*, **19**, 339–348.

McCarthy, S. (1996) The good deed. *WIRED, 4.09*. www.wired.com/wired/ archive/4.09/starbright_pr.html.

McTavish, F., Pingree, S., Hawkins, R., and Gustafson, D. H. (2003). Cultural differences in use of an electronic discussion group. *Journal of Health Psychology*, **8**, 105–117.

Microsoft (1999, May 19). Knowledge workers without limits: Gates shares new vision and new technology at Microsoft CEO summit. www.microsoft.com/presspass/features/1999/05–19ceosummit.mspx.

Mühlfelder, M., Klein, U., Simon, S., and Luczak, H. (1999). Teams without trust? Investigations in the influence of video-mediated communication on the origin of trust among cooperating persons. *Behaviour & Information Technology*, **18**, 349–360.

Murray, D. and Bevan, N. (1985). The social psychology of computer conversations. In B. Shackel (ed.), *Human–Computer Interaction—INTERACT '84* (pp. 33–38). Amsterdam: Elsevier-North Holland.

Nowak, K., Watt, J. H., and Walther, J. B. (2009). Computer-mediated teamwork and the efficiency framework: Exploring the influence of synchrony and cues on media satisfaction and outcome success. *Computers in Human Behavior*, **25**, 1108–1119.

Parks, M. R. (1982). Ideology in interpersonal communication: off the couch and into the world. In M. Burgoon (ed.), *Communication Yearbook 5* (pp. 79–107). New Brunswick, NJ: Transaction Books.

Postmes, T., Spears, R., and Lea, M. (1998). Breaching or building social boundaries? SIDE-effects of computer-mediated communication. *Communication Research*, **25**, 689–715.

Rice, R. E. (1993). Media appropriateness: using social presence theory to compare traditional and new organizational media. *Human Communication Research*, **19**, 451–484.

Salomon, G. (1984). Television is "easy" and print is "tough": the differential investment of mental effort in learning as a function of perceptions and attributions. *Journal of Educational Psychology*, **76**, 647–658.

Salomon, G. and Globerson, T. (1987). Skill may not be enough: the role of mindfulness in learning and transfer. *International Journal of Educational Research*, **11**, 623–637.

Short, J. A., Williams, E., and Christie, B. (1976). *The Social Psychology of Telecommunications*. New York: John Wiley & Sons.

Storck, J. and Sproull, L. (1995). Through a glass darkly: what do people learn in videoconferences? *Human Communication Research*, **22**, 197–219.

Tanis, M. (2003). Cues to Identity in CMC: The Impact on Person Perception and Subsequent Interaction Outcomes. Doctoral dissertation, University of Amsterdam, Amsterdam. http://dare.uva.nl/record/220424.

Tanis, M. and Postmes, T. (2003). Social cues and impression formation in CMC. *Journal of Communication*, **53**, 66–693.

Walther, J. B. (1992). Interpersonal effects in computer-mediated interaction: a relational perspective. *Communication Research*, **19**, 52–90.

(1996). Computer-mediated communication: impersonal, interpersonal, and hyperpersonal interaction. *Communication Research*, **23**, 1–43.

(1997). Group and interpersonal effects in international computer-mediated collaboration. *Human Communication Research*, **23**, 342–369.

(2002). Time effects in computer-mediated groups: past, present, and future. In P. Hinds and S. Kiesler (eds), *Distributed Work* (pp. 235–257). Cambridge, MA: MIT Press.

Walther, J. B., Anderson, J. F., and Park, D. (1994). Interpersonal effects in computer-mediated interaction: a meta-analysis of social and anti-social communication. *Communication Research*, *21*, 460–487.

Walther, J. B. and Bazarova, N. (2008). Validation and application of electronic propinquity theory to computer-mediated communication in groups. *Communication Research*, *35*, 622–645.

Walther, J. B. and Boyd, S. (2002). Attraction to computer-mediated social support. In C. A. Lin and D. Atkin (eds), *Communication Technology and Society: Audience Adoption and Uses* (pp. 153–188). Cresskill, NJ: Hampton Press.

Walther, J. B., Loh, T., and Granka, L. (2005). Let me count the ways: the interchange of verbal and nonverbal cues in computer-mediated and face-to-face affinity. *Journal of Language and Social Psychology*, *24*, 36–65.

Walther, J. B. and Parks, M. R. (2002). Cues filtered out, cues filtered in: computer-mediated communication and relationships. In M. L. Knapp and J. A. Daly (eds), *Handbook of Interpersonal Communication* (3rd edn., pp. 529–563). Thousand Oaks, CA: Sage.

Walther, J. B., Slovacek, C., and Tidwell, L. C. (2001). Is a picture worth a thousand words? Photographic images in long term and short term virtual teams. *Communication Research*, *28*, 105–134.

CHAPTER 2

To be seen or not to be seen: the presentation of facial information in everyday telecommunications

José-Miguel Fernández-Dols and Pilar Carrera

Overview: Visual digital devices bring about new ways of managing one's facial expression that consist not of mere amplifications of face-to-face interaction, but rather of sophisticated constructions around different kinds of genre. In our view, these genres are articulated in terms of two main dimensions: the kind of representation of the world included in the message, and senders' social motives with respect to their audience. In terms of the first dimension, *representation*, we distinguish three levels of representation: visual icons of objects or events (we call this first level "copies"), conventional symbols of concepts (we call this second level "allegories and fictional stories"), and idiosyncratic elicitors of basic psychological processes (we call this third level "affect triggers"). In terms of the second dimension (*senders' social motives*), we take into account basic types of social interaction such as aggression, attraction, and helping behavior. The intersection of the two dimensions provides a list of genres in the telecommunication of facial information. We discuss these categories, provide some examples of their use, and make some speculations about their future.

A recognition revolution?

As one might hypothesize from intuition or experience, people derive pleasure from seeing a familiar face. Technology has now allowed us to document this effect; faces we recognize affect us differently from those we do not. Event-related potentials in the electroencephalogram are useful indexes of brain activity. Waves reproduce the synchronized excitation of cortical pyramidal neurons. Human faces produce a special wave around 170 thousandths of a second after the onset of the stimulus. The largest waves correspond to faces of famous people (Debruille *et al.*, 1998). Almost literally, a halo surrounds a famous or infamous person, making his or her face particularly relevant to our mind.

A reasonable hypothesis, considering these data, is that our bodies are not just containers or sustainers of our minds: they are also important landmarks in our everyday representations. Well-known, recognizable bodies – and particularly their "bar code," the face – are among the strongest elicitors of positive or negative affect and, consequently, of emotions.

A corollary of this hypothesis is that "known faces," which can be labeled, represent an extremely powerful psychological phenomenon with fascinating, sometimes scary consequences. Narcissus, in Greek mythology, drowns when he sees his face reflected in the water. For centuries, mirrors were the only way of seeing our own face, and this extraordinary quality made them magical in most cultures. Access to mirrors was the privilege of the fortunate few, and the impressive array of mirrors at Versailles was one of the technological and aesthetic wonders of the eighteenth century.

An alternative to the mirror was the portrait, an artistic genre extremely popular among the powerful and the rich. Portraits also had magic or religious connotations. In fact, the depiction of human faces is forbidden in certain cultures, such as some Islamic cultures, while in others, such as that of ancient Egypt during the time of the Ptolemies, it constituted the passport to life after death.

Daguerreotypes, photographs, films, and videos of faces were not only landmarks of a revolution in mediated communications, but they also heralded a new age for the representation of the face. By the middle of the twentieth century, any citizen of a developed nation had produced far more images of his or her face than the most powerful ruler of 200 years earlier. Our face and body, or their icon, can instantaneously travel thousands of miles, making our physical aspect relevant for people we have never met. Not so long ago, this was only a wild fantasy.

The most obvious evidence of the extraordinary power of this phenomenon is clearly visible: for over a century now, human beings have been playing with their own representation, producing billions of pictures of themselves and spending billions of dollars in the process. People may not agree about the proper food, beverages, ceremonies, or social activities for celebrating important life events, but none, rich or poor, sophisticated or simple, can resist taking pictures of themselves during these events. Representing yourself (and then contemplating the image) in positive events has been the most irresistible and consensual pleasure of the last 100 years.

Additional evidence of the overwhelming psychological power of facial representations comes from elites' success in using them to increase their power or to invent new sources of power. Pictures, and later TV images, became a basic tool in political campaigns. By the 1960s, mass media images were not only instrumental for candidates' popularity, but began to shape their political discourse. Today, many political scientists highlight the extent to which the media has eroded the intellectual quality of political discourse, and produced undesirable side effects, such as massive manipulation.

A further exploitation of the power of broadcast faces is the "star system," a commercial invention of Hollywood. The same actor or actress exposed several times on huge screens becomes "a star," and begins to elicit the pleasure of recognition. A key factor in the enjoyment (and consequent consumption) of a movie is the number of recognizable actors included in its cast. The enjoyment can be generalized to other situations, and the actors and actresses become sources of pleasure in themselves (as unconditioned stimuli in many commercial ads) and unqualified but influential political, social, or cultural leaders.

The concept of stardom transformed the film industry, national elites (stars mixing with the highest ranks of politics, business, and the military; see Mills, 1959), and eventually the notion of success in any professional field, with new waves of star architects, lawyers, doctors, and economists. Whereas exhibition (public shame) was a common punishment for criminals until the nineteenth century, public fame (good or bad) in the twentieth century was not a punishment, but rather an extraordinary reward. Although some law experts argue that public shame is an impractical and inhumane punishment (e.g., Tangney, 2001), some people scramble for fame, even ill fame, as a way of making their faces universally recognized (i.e., becoming more or less transient media stars).

The internet, webcams, and, in general, all the digital representations of human beings, have opened up a new phase in this popular quest for fame. The last relative barrier for the above-mentioned explosion of self-representation was the slow, technically complex processing of photographs or TV broadcasting. Developing pictures and films was a much more time-consuming and complex task than taking or shooting them. People left the processing of their self-image in the hands of experts. Only then could they judge whether these images were satisfactory public representations of themselves.

Because digital representations have overcome the difficulties associated with developing pictures, they have considerably boosted the private production and selection of images. Feedback is instant-aneous, and allows correction at practically no cost. Ordinary people can now do what only the rich and powerful elites could do in the twentieth century: choose, in "backstage" intimacy, a highly con-trolled self-presentation through images. As Goffman (1959) pointed out, people try to present attractive, idealized versions of themselves in front of others. Today, such presentation extends to the audio-visual realm. The impressive success of internet dating and social networking tools, such as Match.com and Facebook.com, opens the way to new forms of social interaction in which self-disclosure is mediated by audiovisual information (conspicuously faces), and users are confronted with the new challenge of balancing accuracy and desirability (see Ellison *et al.*, 2006).

Thus, all visual telecommunication becomes a powerful tool for the everyday self-presentation of common people. How is this power deployed? We can envisage two possible answers to this ques-tion: audiovisual paraphernalia is merely subsidiary to the usual "nat-ural" facial information, or it involves radically new uses of facial information.

In the first option (assumed by most psychology research on the interaction between human behavior and telecommunication devices; e.g., Kraut *et al.*, 1998), telecommunications are explored as new chan-nels that distort, amplify, or transform the usual messages we transmit and the forms of interaction we undertake using our bodies. This approach can inspire a number of fascinating hypotheses, but it depicts telecommunication users as passive recipients of technology, rather than active creators of new ways of communicating.

The second option emphasizes that telecommunications give rise to new forms of "artificial" facial information, with a remote or nonexis-tent link to "natural" self-presentation. In this chapter we will specu-late on this second potential development.

Facial information as genres

About 2,500 years ago, intellectuals regarded poetry the way today's most educated people regard the internet. Plato saw poetry as a sort of pastime, based on appearances, that was ethically dubious and misleading. Plato's attitude, probably typical of educated people in ancient Greece, was contested by Aristotle in his *Poetics*. In the *Poetics*, Aristotle developed a broader framework, in which poetry is a kind of literary text: a genre. Each genre has a different ethical and aes-thetic function, and is aimed at a different kind of audience. Interest-ingly, some of these functions have a strong psychological dimension.

For example, the *catharsis* of tragedy purges the emotions of pity and fear that are aroused in the audience.

Since Aristotle, artistic works supported by a form or medium have been organized in genres. Genres have different structures and subjects, and they are a basic tool for understanding new forms of communication. Aristotle's original typology (epic, lyric, and drama) was based on the way events were represented, from the intimate experience of the lyric to the distant, third-person descriptions of the epic. Subsequently, all the arts have been classified in terms of different genres, including, relatively recently, the movies (comedy, thriller, drama, and so on).

Genres are certainly a theoretical way of classifying complex messages, but they are also conceptual categories: when categories of genres are shared by author and audience, they help to constitute a shared a way of understanding a message and its representational and affective features. For example, today's most conventional genres are cinematographic: everyone has fuzzy but powerful affective and cognitive expectations when renting a video labeled as "comedy" or "drama."

Our prediction is that webcams, video, cellphones with cameras, and other visual digital devices bring about new and revolutionary ways of managing one's facial expression "on the stage" – ways that do not consist of mere amplifications of face-to-face interaction, but rather of sophisticated constructions around different kinds of genre.

In our view, these genres are articulated in terms of the two main dimensions referred to above: the kind of representation of the world included in the message, and senders' social motives with respect to their audience.

In terms of the first dimension, *representation*, we can take inspiration from the typologies used in iconography and iconology, the disciplines dealing with the images conveyed in painting genres. Mainstream typologies of genres from these fields (e.g., Panofsky, 1955) could be roughly translated into three levels of representation: as visual icons of objects or events (we call this first level "copies"), as conventional symbols of concepts (we call this second level "allegories and fictional stories"), and as idiosyncratic elicitors of basic psychological processes (in Panofsky's words: "essential tendencies of the human mind"; we call this third level "affect triggers").

In terms of the second dimension (*senders' social motives*), we can take into account the basic typologies of human interaction provided by social psychologists. Social psychology approaches (e.g., Wallace, 1999) typically include at least three basic interaction processes: aggression, attraction, and helping behavior.

Intended effect in the audience	Representation		
	Copies	Allegories	Triggers
Aggression	Public shame Exposure	Destructive games Dehumanization Insulting caricatures	Disgusting themes Morally repulsive themes
Attraction	Mutual exploration Fads and fashions	Team games Collective identity signs Positive caricatures	"Pure" pleasure (a-representational) themes Virtual beauty
Helping	Defensive spaces Calls for help	Educational games Icons of moral social representations	Compassion triggers

Figure 2.1 Use of potential genres in the telecommunication of facial information.

The intersection of the two dimensions provides a list of potential genres in the telecommunication of facial information (Figure 2.1). In the following paragraphs, we shall discuss each of these categories, provide some examples of their use, and make some speculations about their future. Of course, the list is not exhaustive and the predictions are speculative, but our main goal is to illustrate the potential of the transformation of facial expressions and body information into genres, rather than mere amplifications or reductions of face-to-face interaction.

Copies

The most common and obvious way of using webcams and digital cameras consists of imitating the traditional use of analogical cameras, trying to make a literal copy of reality. Of course, perfect copies of reality do not exist, but the pictures taken by both reporters and tourists are obviously produced within an ontologically realist frame of mind. Reporters and tourists, as well as scientists when they use pictures, try to reflect reality "as it is."

People use digital cameras and send their images in order to share some "real" representations of the world. Sharing these representations is, in itself, a social activity that creates affective ties among those in contact. A conspicuous case, still based on analogical cameras (but with a clear potential for digital audiovisual devices), is lomography (www.lomography.com/). In 1991, a group of Austrian students discovered a forgotten camera, the Lomo, a Soviet replica of Kodak cameras. Within a few years, the camera became an object of cult, and followers of the Lomo movement make millions of instantaneous pictures, have their own congresses, and belong to an international society.

Sharing icons of others' faces and bodies can become, through cellphones with high-resolution digital cameras or videos, a powerful way of building up social ties, as in the Lomo movement. In fact, massive sharing of facial or bodily icons has become a social phenomenon with unexpected consequences: commercial internet sites such as Facebook.com and Twitter.com provide people with tools for massive displays of "bodily signatures" on the internet. For example, Zhao *et al.* (2008) found that a sample of young American Facebook users displayed on average almost 90 pictures in their profiles and 4.5 additional albums of pictures within their accounts.

An example of the potential consequences of these new tools is the spread of innovations related to physical appearance. "Infectious" new faces or manners will have a much faster and more powerful form of triggering the proliferation of fads and fashions. The dynamics of social epidemics, as described by Gladwell (2000), are articulated through connectors, persons with easy access to several social groups; mavens, who like to disseminate knowledge; and salesmen, adept at persuading others. These dynamics could be substantially changed by new telecommunications devices like Facebook. Any individual can become a "social connector" capable of spreading a particular message; the new medium – the digital camera – changes the process of influence. Those with better cameras, and technical skills, will be more influential, and potential "mavens" and "salesmen" will not necessarily be urban, as those from rural or isolated areas gain easier access to social networks.

Sharing "copies" of people can help communities to protect themselves in emergencies. For example, it will be quicker and easier for people to report all kinds of unlawful situations. Pictures of lost children or felons can easily be spread via cellphones, making communities more defensible spaces. At the same time, tiny, high-resolution cellphone cameras are a potential nightmare for citizens' privacy and, therefore, to the management of their own identity. Journalists (e.g., Napolitano, 2003) are reporting cases in which cameras are used to expose people in embarrassing circumstances or, worse, when in showers, toilets, or locker rooms. In fact, the availability of cellphones with tiny, high-resolution cameras has become a serious threat to people's privacy. At any moment, one's photograph can be easily taken and broadcast. Some people may perpetrate such intrusions just for fun, but there may also be more sinister goals, such as discrediting a person's public self-presentation or exposing them to public humiliation. Goffman (1961) coined the term "total institutions" for those places (e.g., psychiatric hospitals or prisons) where complete lack of privacy deprives inmates of any chance of working out a favorable public appearance. Total institutions are powerful and terrible instruments for producing compliance and identity change of inmates. Vicious, systematic use of portable cameras by peers, supervisors, or members of dominant groups can open the way to extremely damaging forms of bullying and harassment, new, informal "total institutions," in which victims can be continuously exposed to the cameras of organized gangs. Unfortunately, cyberbullying has already become a serious problem on the internet (see www.cyberbullying.ca/) and in other contexts. Li (2007) found that 25 percent of a random sample of middle-class Canadian adolescents were victims of cyberbullying, and 15 percent had been perpetrators.

For better or worse, "copies" can become an extremely widespread form of communication. Peirce (1931–8) describes icons as the most primitive written language, in part abandoned because human beings needed more efficient forms of writing (i.e., faster, simpler, and more abstract signs, such as symbols; see Cherry, 1966). New technologies make the use of icons effortless and fast, ushering in a new communicative era in which ideograms will take over or share part of the territory of symbolic language.

Allegories and fictional stories

Allegories, fables, and parables are stories with a moral, in which characters have (at least) a double reading: an immediate, superficial reading, as icons of real people, and a second, deeper, and central reading, as complex symbols of abstract, usually moral concepts. Typical allegories are justice as a blindfolded woman, or love as a blind, winged child. Allegories are usually complex, and some periods of history have been particularly rich in the use of allegories in literature and the visual arts.

Allegories also have a psychological connection with social representations (Moscovici, 1961). Social representations are conventions about objects or persons that make communication about these objects or persons easier. They connect complex concepts to particular images to provide people with the illusion of understanding.

A typical example is Einstein's face icon as an anchor for relativity or atomic physics. Like allegories, social representations make abstract concepts concrete (objectification), and use familiar objects to represent unfamiliar concepts (anchoring).

Massive use of visual telecommunications makes possible new allegories of abstract concepts, and the embedding of personal messages in fictional stories. In fact, the internet is promoting the use of visual paralanguages full of allegories of complex emotions, personality traits, and other psychological processes such as attitudes or identities. For example, rhetoric on the internet is partly based on the use of conventional images, such as emoticons (see Joinson, 2003), which, besides their primitive use as meta-communicative symbols (*smileys* or *smilies*), have become complex allegories. For example, some internet users (e.g., www.muller-godschalk.com/emoticon. html) mention action smileys, celebrity smileys, no-turning smileys, animal smileys, descriptive smileys, people smileys, and so on. Avatars (icons of imaginary bodies in virtual environments) have also become increasingly popular (e.g., Yahoo avatars) for enhancing or idealizing the stable traits of their users, rather than construing other completely imaginary characters (Vasalou and Joinson, 2008).

Doise (1989) distinguished between different levels of resistance to social representations depending on the receivers' beliefs about the message and its consistency. Digital allegories can be faster, more attractive, and more resistant to screening than other social representations, with an easier and more prevalent diffusion.

Digital images are not only accurate but also extremely malleable. Computers and cellphones with cameras are already including a large selection of software capable of receiving and sending pictures and videos (e.g., Pogue, 2004). A potential evolution of this market would involve software capable of editing private images and transforming them into complex, symbolic representations of people's personality, tastes or moods, at the individual level, or of their social identities (e.g., preferences in politics, sports, or sex). In this way, "physical" makeup would be complemented by "electronic" makeup, allowing people to express, in a bolder and more economical language, their own representation of themselves or others.

Physical attraction provided by physical makeup will be reinforced by the ideological attraction provided by electronic makeup of one's own image, helping to establish or reinforce links with groups or individuals. A natural second step would consist in translating the images of one's everyday world into scenes in imaginary worlds, or translating one's own image into the face and appearance of avatars used as allegories of oneself or one's ingroup.

Ingroups can become even closer with these electronic possibilities, keeping users within private worlds, accessible only to them and their peers (see a review of the debate on this effect, called "the internet paradox," in Joinson, 2003). Zhao *et al.* (2008) reported that almost 40 percent of the Facebook users' profile cover pictures were group photos, instead of single-person, reflecting an effort to construct group-oriented identities.

In any case, the transition from "virtual" relationships to "natural," actual relations can be extremely difficult. Impressions through non-visual electronic channels, such as computer-mediated communication, are formed at a slower pace than in natural face-to-face encounters, but they are more affectionate. Walther (1996) calls these relationships "hyperpersonal." On the other hand, Walther and his collaborators (Walther *et al.*, 2001) found that webcams weakened the attraction between people engaged in electronic nonvisual communication, but electronic makeup (see above) could make hyperpersonal relations even stronger.

Furthermore, the allegorical power of editing your own image can also be used for editing others' body and personal appearance, facilitating the process of transforming human beings into animals or disposable objects. This scenario, combined with the electronic harassing mentioned previously, can in the long term make lethal weapons of cellphones or webcams sending denigrating messages. Of course, the same tool could also become an educational resource if people are given the opportunity to play with images and see how changing mere physical appearance can change our attitudes toward ethnic minorities or physically unattractive interlocutors.

Affect triggers

Allegories are complex symbolic messages that have a certain – albeit ambiguous – translation into words. Affect triggers are messages that can elicit affective responses with no direct translation into a verbal message: They are idiosyncratic elicitors of basic affect.

The "affect trigger" is a less obvious category than copies or allegories, but constitutes an important genre for a visual language. Paradoxically, affect triggers are some of the most primitive forms of natural visual communication (e.g., baby facial configurations for most contemporary adults), but also represent one of the most sophisticated steps in the evolution of mediated visual communication. For example, the quest for ideal triggers was prevalent in the Neoplatonic circles of the Renaissance. Botticelli's *The Birth of Venus* was a tangible expression of *humanitas*, a moral virtue that includes all the desirable traits of a

Renaissance gentleman. The contemplation of Venus was a trigger of *humanitas* in the audience (Gombrich, 1972). A long tradition in aesthetics consists in understanding art as a way of transmitting pure, formal beauty.

The evolution of mediated visual messages with affective impact may parallel the evolution of another powerful elicitor of basic affect: music (see Kelly, 2002). Music underwent revolutionary changes with the advent of the analogical technologies of reproduction, leading musicians to change extremely idiosyncratic performances into a standardized practice adapted to the technical requirements of phonographs: shorter, more melodic, and more precise perform-ances. Today, digital reproduction has made universality valueless (copying music is free), and there is a return to idiosyncratic performances, adapted to the tastes and needs of each consumer. As Kelly (2002, p. 30) says, "The only things truly valuable are those which cannot be copied ... for instance: trust, immediacy, personalization."

In the same vein, cellphones and internet screens constitute new territory, for new ways of sending messages with visual affective impact. Like music, visual messages have undergone a process of standardization through the mass media. In the future, effective visual messages will probably have to follow in the footsteps of digital music, seeking more trusting, immediate, and personal ways of eliciting powerful affective reactions.

What are the potential everyday uses of affect triggers? In our view, the use of cellphones and webcams will increase the need for expres-sive messages capable of eliciting the affective reactions that senders want the receivers to experience.

Buffardi and Campbell (2008) have found that narcissism as a trait predicts greater self-promotion in Facebook. In the same vein, aggressive senders will look for ways of eliciting negative affects, such as disgust or fear, in the receiver (e.g., when cyberbullying). Loving senders will look for ways of "cuddling" their receiver. Senders in distress will look for ways of eliciting compassion. Actually, most avatars include facial configurations (e.g., baby face) aimed at eliciting such affective reactions, but if this prediction is correct, "natural" facial expressions are going to play an increasingly important role in tele-comunications (see, for example, LifeFX, a commercial software aimed at providing facial expressions to internet messages). "Baby faces" (Chong *et al.*, 2003), instrumental crying, or disgusting facial behavior (e.g., vomiting) will move into a digital era of new and massive use.

New generations of cellphone users will develop an extremely sophisticated mastery of their facial behavior (like contemporary professional actors), playing with the receiver's affect as contemporary musicians play with the listener's affect through their melodies.

This situation will also push media toward a new and more challenging era, in which audiences will be extremely sophisticated by current standards (as audiences today are extremely sophisticated by silent movie era standards). Celebrities will have to look for new, exclusive ways of sending trusting, personal, and immediate messages to their audiences, and political and commercial marketing will have to redefine some of the basics of visual design.

Conclusion: new sources for the irresistible power of recognition

The genres hypothesis described in this chapter suggests that digital channels of nonverbal information will be more than just channels: they will be new codes that will take the pleasure of recognition to new territories. Stardom and political power will have to open up their visual monopolies to more local forms of visual communication. These local realms of fame could be pleasurable or painful, but will in any case be important references in everyday life. At the same time, elites will have to look for new forms of visual positive discrimination, raising extremely interesting questions that are outside the brief of this chapter.

New genres of face and body communication would be, simultaneously, tools and sources of inspiration for psychologists.

New genres constitute interesting tools: the availability and malleability of devices such as cellphone video cameras will, paradoxically, open the way for currently inconceivable forms of recording the flow of natural nonverbal behavior in interactive and noninteractive situations.

New genres provide sources of inspiration because they present psychologists with new forms of nonverbal communication that are dependent on the context, in an ambiguous territory between "natural" and "artificial" behavior. Is cellphone harassment artificial? Are new forms of cellphone baby-talk natural? As cultural psychology has emphasized, the use of tools extends psychological processes, giving artificial stimuli a natural role in psychological activity (e.g., Vygotsky, 1978). The intrusion of powerful artificial messages in the realm of face-to-face interaction represent a new challenge for defining the borders of natural, universal kinds of nonverbal behavior, and their affective and cognitive messages. In our view, these new challenges could only be confronted through an in-depth review of our current vocabulary and assumptions about emotion (see Fernández-Dols and Russell, 2003) and, from a broader perspective, of the relationships between psychological processes and nonverbal behavior. The current quest for one-to-one correspondence between nonverbal prototypical behaviors and psychological meanings will become a quest for more ecological, situationist approaches in which the meaning of a message is highly dependent on the context. By "context" we mean the interactions held by sender and receiver, but also the codes – shared or not – used by sender and receiver.

The above-mentioned conflict between "natural" interaction and artificial tools will also lead to research taking a more open-minded approach to issues such as emotional expression and the concept of emotion itself. Are the new media opening the way for new "basic" emotions? What is the precise status of the emotions felt through these new tools? Jonathan Dee, a *New York Times* journalist, described his experience with video games as follows:

> There is something there – a curious tension between control and no-control – that seems worth feeling solely on the grounds that … I've never felt it before. The form is miles ahead from the content … But … the form is the whole thrill, and it's more than thrill enough. (Dee, 2003, p. 68)

As for Dee, the new electronic forms of interaction can be an irresistible source of thrills for both layman and expert. Time will tell whether our predictions are wise or laughable.

Acknowledgments

The writing of this chapter was supported by the Spanish government's grant PSI2008–04849/PSIC. We thank Claudia Hernandez for her editorial help.

References

Buffardi, L. E. and Campbell, W. K. (2008). Narcissism and social networking web sites. *Personality and Social Psychology Bulletin*, *34*, 1303–1314.

Cherry, C. (1966). *On Human Communication* (2nd edn.). Cambridge, MA: MIT Press.

Chong, S. C. F., Werker, J. F., Russell, J. A., and Carroll, J. M. (2003). Three facial expressions mothers direct to their infants. *Infant and Child Development*, *12*, 211–232.

Debruille, J. B., Guillem, F., and Renault, B. (1998). ERP's and chronometry of face recognition. *NeuroReport*, *9*, 3349–3353.

Dee, J. (2003). Playing mogul. *New York Times Magazine*, December 21, section 6.

Doise, W. (1989). Attitudes et représentations sociales. In D. Jodelet (ed.), *Les représentations sociales* (pp. 220–237). Paris: Presses Universitaires de France.

Ellison, N., Heino, R., and Gibbs, J. (2006). Managing impressions online: self-presentation processes in the online dating environment. *Journal of Computed-Mediated Communication*, *11*(2). http://jcmc.indiana.edu/vol11/issue 2/ellison.html.

Fernández-Dols, J. M. and Russell, J. A. (2003). Emotion, affect, and mood in social judgments. In T. Millon and M. J. Lerner (eds), *Handbook of Psychology. Volume 5: Personality and Social Psychology* (pp. 283–298). Hoboken, NJ: Wiley.

Gladwell, M. (2000). *The Tipping Point: How Little Things Can Make a Big Difference.* Boston: Little Brown.

Goffman, E. (1959). *The Presentation of Self in Everyday Life.* Garden City, NY: Doubleday.

(1961). *Asylums: Essays on the Social Situation of Mental Patients and Other Inmates.* Chicago: Aldine.

Gombrich, E. H. (1972). *Symbolic Images. Studies in the Art of the Renaissance.* London: Phaidon.

Joinson, A. N. (2003). *Understanding the Psychology of the Internet: Virtual Worlds, Real Lives.* New York: Palgrave-Macmillan.

Kelly, K. (2002). Where music will be coming from. *New York Times Magazine,* March 17, section 6, pp. 29–31.

Kraut, R., Patterson, M., Lundmark, V., Kiesler, S., Tridas, M., and Scherlis, W. (1998). Internet paradox: a social technology that reduces social involvement and psychological well-being? *American Psychologist,* **53**, 1017–1031.

Li, Q. (2007). New bottle but old wine: a research on cyberbullying in schools. *Computers and Human Behavior,* **23**, 1777–1791.

Mills, C. W. (1959). *The Power Elite.* New York: Oxford University Press.

Moscovici, S. (1961). *La Psychanalyse, son image et son public.* Paris: Presses Universitaires de France.

Napolitano, J. (2003) Hold it right there, and drop that camera. *New York Times,* December 11. www.nytimes.com.

Panofsky, E. (1955). *Meaning in the Visual Arts.* Garden City, NY: Doubleday.

Peirce, C. S. (1931–8). *Collected Writings* (8 vols). Ed. C. Hartshorne, P. Weiss, and A. W. Burks. Cambridge, MA: Harvard University Press.

Pogue, D. (2004). Phones, too, get TV time. *The New York Times,* January 4. www.nytimes.com.

Tangney, J. P. (2001). Constructive and destructive aspects of shame and guilt. In A. C. Bohart and D. J. Stipek (eds), *Constructive and Destructive Behavior: Implications for Family, School and Society* (pp. 127–145). Washington, DC: American Psychological Association.

Vasalou, A. and Joinson, A. N. (2009). Me, myself and I: the role of interactional context on self-presentation through avatars. *Computers in Human Behavior,* **25**, 510–520.

Vygotsky, L. S. (1978). *Mind in Society.* Cambridge, MA: Harvard University Press.

Wallace, P. (1999). *The Psychology of the Internet.* Cambridge University Press.

Walther, J. B. (1996). Computer-mediated communication: impersonal, interpersonal, and hyperpersonal interaction. *Communication Research,* **23**, 3–43.

Walther, J. B., Slovacek, C. L., and Tidwell, L. C. (2001). Is a picture worth a thousand words? Photographic images in long-term and short-term computer-mediated communication. *Communication Research,* **28**, 105–134.

Zhao, S., Grasmuck, S., and Martin, J. (2008). Identity construction on Facebook: digital empowerment in anchored relationships. *Computers in Human Behavior,* **24**, 1816–1836.

CHAPTER 3

Gendered social interactions in face-to-face and computer-mediated communication

Agneta Fischer

Overview: This chapter addresses the differences between computer-mediated communication (CMC) and non-computer-mediated, face-to-face communication (FTFC) with respect to gendered interactions by focusing on the consequences of the absence of visual cues. The conclusion based on the present evidence suggests that gender differences do not increase or decrease in CMC compared to FTFC, but in both modes of communication they mainly occur in settings where stereotypes are evoked. This supports the gender-in-context approach, implying that most differences between men and women in social behavior are evoked in a stereotypic context. The absence of visual cues in CMC has little impact on many gender differences in social interaction, but may affect the way in which men and women communicate emotions.

Introduction

Traditionally, computers and everything related to computers were perceived to belong to the masculine domain (Kirk, 1992). However, with the expansion of the internet, and the widespread use of computers in various forms of computer-mediated communication (CMC) (email, chatting, videoconferencing, or social networking sites, such as Hyves, Facebook, and Twitter), we have witnessed an increase of female participation in the virtual world, resulting in more or less equal participating of both sexes. Indeed, there is even evidence that in some contexts women judge CMC more favorably than men do (e.g., Allen, 1995; Hiltz and Johnson, 1990). For example, women consider emailing more effective and easier to use than men, and women seem to be more satisfied with online discussions than men are. The initial rise in female internet users has evoked a debate on whether virtual reality would be able to free interactants from the traditional boundaries of their sex. Some feminist authors, for example (e.g., Haraway, 1990), believed that sexual inequalities would dissolve on the internet. The assumption was that computer-based communication lacks any reference to cues that link persons to the social category to which they belong (later referred to as the cues-filtered-out perspective, Culnan and Marcus, 1987). As a consequence, virtual interactions would not be affected by sex-stereotypical expectancies based on outward appearance or physical cues. Men and women would have equal status and opportunities on the internet, and communication would be free from sex stereotypes. This idea has sometimes been referred to as the equalization hypothesis (Postmes and Spears, 2002).

There is indeed some empirical evidence in favor of this "utopian" view (Bhappu *et al.*, 1997; Dubrovsky *et al.*, 1991; Sproull and Kiesler, 1991). However, there is more evidence that suggests a less "optimistic" view. First of all, the internet does not appear to be such an anonymous place in the sense that interactants can really ignore or hide their sex, as some scholars believed. Yet, on social networking sites and on many discussion forums and email lists, internet users provide their names, and even if no name or face is available, one's sex can be inferred by other cues, such as linguistic style. Second, the internet appears not to be free from sexual harassment and discrimination, given, for example, the greater sexual attention given to female personae in MUD (multiuser dungeon), or the sexual aggressiveness of "female" MUD inhabitants, who often appear to be men, logged on as women (Bruckman, 1993). On the basis of such observations, we may conclude that the World Wide Web is sex-typed: it is characterized by stereotypes and sexism, just like the real world.

Yet, even though the internet does not meet the qualification of a world free from stereotypes and prejudice, computer-mediated and (non-computer-mediated) face-to-face communication (FTFC) differ in some important aspects (see also Baym, 2006), which may have implications for the way in which gender differences manifest themselves. One feature of CMC has especially been considered as having important consequences, namely the absence of visual cues in many forms of CMC. First, this results in relative anonymity and second it implies the absence of nonverbal cues of communication (see also Bargh and McKenna, 2004). These features may not only have consequences for the quality, effects, and more generally, the nature of the social interactions, but are assumed to have an impact on the size of the gender differences in both modes of communication.

This chapter addresses the differences between CMC and non-computer-mediated FTFC with respect to gendered interactions by focusing on these two consequences of the absence of visual cues.

Because I focus on visual cues, I will limit this review to comparisons of text-based CMC with FTFC, and thus exclude other modes of CMC, such as videoconferencing. There are two reasons why I expect visual cues to have a different impact on gender differences in CMC versus FTFC. First of all, in CMC interactions, as in internet discussion groups, there are fewer cues on one's individuality than in other social interactions (e.g., Walther, 1996). For example, when one communicates via email with a person one has never seen before, the only source available about this other person is the text that he or she writes. Although one's sex may be inferred from the text, or the name of the person, we assume that written text makes one's sex less salient than does physical appearance. This may have consequences for the stereotypical nature of the interaction. A second source of difference is that the channel through which emotions can be expressed is clearly more limited in CMC than in FTFC (see also Parkinson and Lea, Chapter 5, this volume; Walther, Chapter 1, this volume). Since gender differences in social interactions are especially apparent in the way emotions are recognized, communicated, and expressed (see Fischer, 2000), the question is whether the communication of emotions by men and women is different in CMC from FTFC (see also Derks *et al.*, 2008).

There are three hypotheses with respect to gender differences in CMC compared to FTFC. The first is the equalization hypothesis, as referred to previously, which states that gender differences in CMC disappear, because the internet's anonymous nature results in a display of uninhibited behavior and less sex-stereotypical behavior (Kiesler *et al.*, 1984). Because one's sex is relatively underexposed, there is no need to conform to sex-stereotypical norms.

A second hypothesis is based on the SIDE model (social identity model of deindividuation effects; Lea and Spears, 1991; Postmes *et al.*, 1998, 2002) and argues the opposite, namely that as, a result of anonymity, social categories rather than individuating information are emphasized, and as a consequence social norms and stereotypes become more rather than less salient, resulting in larger gender differences in CMC. Moreover, anonymity reduces the possibility to differentiate between individuals, but not between social groups, like men and women.

A third hypothesis is based upon the gender-in-context approach (Deaux and Major, 1987; LaFrance and Hecht, 2000) and entails that gender differences are highly variable and depend on the nature of the context. Some contexts elicit highly sex-stereotypical behaviors, whereas other contexts require the same behaviors from men and women.

In the present chapter, I will compare results from studies on gender differences in face-to-face interaction with studies on gender differences in CMC.[1] I will restrict this review to studies of more formal social interactions, and thus I will not include romantic relationships. I will first focus on the role of social, i.e., category-based, versus individual cues in face-to-face and computer-mediated interactions, and then on the way in which emotions are communicated in these two different modes of interaction. More specifically, I will defend the contextual approach, arguing that the extent to which social interaction conforms to stereotypes depends on the context, both in CMC and FTFC. However, in CMC the interaction context may more often be less stereotypical than in FTFC, due to the absence of visual cues.

Gender differences in face-to-face interaction

Sex stereotypes suggest that women are more socially sensitive; more aware of others' needs; more emotionally expressive, warm, and understanding, and more focused on harmony and avoiding conflict; men, on the other hand, would be more dominant, self-confident, independent, and task-oriented, while inhibiting their emotions. One explanation for the existence of these stereotypes is based on Eagly's social role theory, arguing that men and women have different social roles in society (Aries, 1996; Bales, 1950; Eagly, 1987). Instrumental roles, traditionally more often held by men, have more status and are associated with competence, rationality, and autonomy, whereas socio-emotional roles, which are more often occupied by women, are based on their caring role within the family context. Because men more often play instrumental roles and women more often socio-emotional roles, men and women are also assumed to *be* different, women being more warm, emotional, and submissive while men are more rational, dominant, and decisive. These societal roles can be translated into social roles at an interpersonal or group level. For example, instrumental roles would include a focus on task completion, as reflected in giving opinions, asking for information, or criticizing others, whereas socio-emotional roles would imply keeping a harmonious relationship with the other person, thereby focusing on positive emotional expressions, like smiling and agreeing with someone.

The question is whether these stereotypes accurately reflect men's and women's actual behaviors. A study by Hall and Carter (1999) concludes that sex stereotypes with regard to a large number of

---

[1] Throughout this chapter, I use the term "CMC" to refer to text-based CMC only.

behaviors and traits are highly correlated with actual gender differences in these behaviors and traits (as reflected in a score for each behavior or trait, obtained from meta-analyses), although there is high individual variability. Various studies have suggested, though, that the size of these gender differences is not very large. In an early review paper, for example, Anderson and Blanchard (1982) concluded that actual gender differences in social interactions turn out to be not as large as the stereotype would lead us to believe: Women expressed positive emotions only slightly more, and men were only slightly more task oriented. No sex differences were found with respect to negative emotional expressions. Moreover, the majority of interactions in all groups examined in these studies were task oriented, suggesting that only a small part of group interactions gave rise to sex differences. A meta-analysis by Carli (1989) on sex differences in social interactions also showed that gender difference were small to moderate, and also confirmed the stereotypical expectation that women's behavior was more socio-emotionally oriented, whereas men's behavior was more task oriented.

Reviewing the various studies on gender differences in social interactions, Aries (1996) concludes that although gender differences in role differentiation along instrumental and socio-expressive lines are largely confirmed, there are many inconsistencies across studies that may be explained by the situational context of the interaction in each study. Several different contextual determinants may be distinguished, such as the conversation topic, the task at hand, or the sex of the interaction partner(s). Sex differences appear to be larger in interactions between strangers, in meetings for shorter periods of time (see also Wheelan and Verdi, 1992), and in same-sex groups or dyads. Men, for example, express more positive social behavior when paired with a female than with a male interaction partner. Moreover, women and men both show more task-oriented behavior when the task is linked to the participants' own sex rather than to the opposite sex, and if they are allowed to play task-oriented roles. However, women show more stereotypical behavior when they form a minority in the group (Izraeli, 1983; Johnson and Schulman, 1989). In short, gender differences in interactional styles seem to reflect sex stereotypes, which become more salient when interacting with strangers, when being a minority, when interacting with someone of the same sex, or when performing a sex-congruent stereotypical task (Carli, 1989). Similar gender differences in instrumentality and expressivity related to contextual constraints were also found with respect to leadership (e.g., Eagly and Johnson, 1990; Eagly and Karau, 1991).

Distinct gender roles and their associated status have also been studied in language styles (e.g., Tannen, 1990). Lakoff (1975) and Fishman (1983) were the first to argue that women's language is qualitatively different from men's language, as a function of men's greater power and status. As a consequence, female speech forms reflect powerlessness, uncertainty, and hesitance. Examples of these female speech forms are tag questions ("... isn't he?"), politeness ("please"), question forms, or qualifiers and hedges (the use of "I guess," "I wonder," and "perhaps"). On the other hand, men use more statements and opinions, and interrupt more often, as would reflect their greater power position. In a first, often-cited study, Zimmerman and West (1975) indeed showed that in daily mixed-sex conversations men interrupted more frequently than women, whereas in same-sex dyads the amount of interruption was equally divided between the two speakers.

Three decades of empirical research on gender differences in conversational style, however, did not provide convincing empirical support for a distinct female or male language (see Bull, 2002; James and Clarke, 1993). Similar to the conclusions reached in research on social interactions more generally, it seems that the occurrence and size of gender differences depend on the conversational context. Features of speech may have different meanings, depending on the context. Interruption, for example, may be not only an expression of dominance, as suggested by Lakoff, but also an expression of agreement and support. In addition, tag questions may express uncertainty, but also politeness or solidarity. In an analysis of a 43,000-word corpus from radio, television, and daily conversations, Holmes (1985) found that, overall, women used somewhat more tag questions than did men. When considering specific tags, however, she found that women initiated more tags that reflected solidarity, whereas men initiated more tags that expressed uncertainty. Moreover, the use of specific tags depended on the power of the speaker, and the sex composition of the group. With respect to the use of qualifiers and hedges, Holmes (1985) also found that women use "I think" in its deliberative form as frequently as do men, whereas they used the tentative form "I think" – which may express uncertainty – less often than men. Moreover, women used the deliberative "I think" more often in formal contexts than men, whereas the reverse pattern was found in informal contexts. Holmes (1985) explained this in terms of gender-stereotypical expectations, which may force women to add weight and authority to their opinions.

In sum, these studies do not support a general sex difference in language use, and certainly do not provide evidence for the idea that women express more uncertainty in conversations than do men. It seems that "women's language" may indeed reflect a position of social powerlessness, but this is not exclusively reserved for women (Aries, 1996). The general conclusion then that seems to emerge from these different studies in face-to-face interaction and conversational style is that gender differences do not occur in the same form and in the same amount across situations. In contrast, there is more support for the idea that gender interacts with several contextual variables, reinforcing the gender-in-context approach (Deaux and Major, 1987). Sex differences especially occur in settings where stereotypical expectations are activated. This happens especially during interactions with strangers, when one interacts in a same-sex group, when individuals do not have a specific role or task, or when the nature of the task or the content of the conversation conforms to gender stereotypes.

The question is whether a similar interaction between gender and context can also be found in CMC. The absence of the visibility of the other in CMC renders the identification of the other's sex more difficult, yet not impossible, because one may infer a person's sex from text-based cues as well. The question is whether the absence of visual cues would elicit more sex-stereotypical expectations and behaviors (as argued by the SIDE model) or less stereotypical behavior (as argued by the equalization hypothesis). In the next section, we will focus on the role of visual gender-related cues in CMC.

Interaction in CMC: the role of gender cues

The assumption to be explored is whether the fact that we cannot see the other person will increase or decrease gender-stereotypical interactions. In this section, we will first review studies on social context effects in CMC; that is, what effects do the identity of and one's knowledge of one's interaction partner have on the communication process?

It is common knowledge that one of the things we would like to know about our interaction partner is whether it is a man or a woman. In daily conversations we feel uneasy when we are not sure about the sex of the other person. However, would this be different in CMC, given that one's relative anonymity can be seen as one of the advantages of the World Wide Web? A study by Nowak (2003) reported that only about two-thirds of the individuals engaged in a desert survival task across networked computers felt the need to discover the other's sex. Moreover, a third of those who had categorized the other as a man or a woman were wrong. In another study among participants in three internet discussion lists about depression, eating disorders, and football, Wolf (2000) found that the senders of the large majority of the postings could be reliably identified as male or female on the basis of their names, and that only in 11 percent of the cases was the gender of the poster unidentifiable, even after examining the contents. Another study showed that if people play with their identity, their gender is mostly not erased, but rather exaggerated – for example, by emphasizing stereotypical attributes (Donath, 1999). A study on personal weblogs of male and female teenagers (Huffaker and Calvert, 2005) also showed that they use their real names and ages and revealed some quite personal information, as was also the case in social networking sites, where people not only used their real names, but also added photos. The results of these studies suggest that most individuals do not conceal their sex in CMC. Still, in some contexts (e.g., in more or less anonymous discussion lists or in MUD), one may prefer to hide one's sex, or one may not be interested to know the other person's sex.

What is the effect of knowing the other person's sex? Williams and Mendelsohn (2008) directly examined this question by instructing two individuals to have a conversation online, while knowing or not knowing each other's sex. This difference did not have any impact on how they judged each other, nor whether they liked each other. Moreover, guessing the other's sex appeared to be very difficult, and the stereotypical content of the conversation was the best clue for correctly guessing the other's sex.

However, simply knowing that the other is a man or a woman may evoke stereotypic expectations and stereotypical behavior, especially if this person is a stranger, as in face-to-face interactions. For example, women were judged as too talkative, cooperative (Matheson, 1991), or in need of technical assistance (Bruckman, 1993), if they were known only by their names. Postmes and Spears (2002) examined whether the activation of stereotypes is the result of the anonymous nature of CMC or of other features of the context. They compared completely anonymous conditions with conditions where people received information about the other's sex and a unique identifier (in this case a number). Groups (consisting of two men and two women) interacted via a CMC system about the solution of a dilemma, and the contents of the messages were coded. The researchers coded the number of questions asked (stereotypically feminine), the number of explicit autonomous statements (e.g., giving an opinion, stereotypically masculine), and the number of dependent statements (reflection of submissiveness, ignorance, or asking for support; stereotypically feminine). The results showed that there was no sex difference in the length of the messages, but there was a difference in content: In line with the stereotypes, women asked more questions, and made more dependent statements, reflecting a stereotypical feminine style, whereas men made more autonomous statements.

In a second study, the role of stereotype salience and of personal information on gendered interactions was investigated. Stereotypes were made salient by the use of scrambled sentences (a task in which participants were asked to put words in a correct sequence in order to make a coherent sentence; the sentences reflected gender-stereotypical statements and had been demonstrated to elicit stereotypes), and individuated information was manipulated by telling participants that their autobiographical feedback (not about their sex) would be shared among the other group members or not (depersonalized condition). Results showed that only in the anonymous condition, when stereotypes were made salient, and when they talked about a masculine topic, did men make more autonomous statements. When discussing a feminine topic, the pattern of results was reversed, with women making more autonomous statements. These results clearly suggest that it is not merely the anonymous nature of CMC, but also the construction of a stereotypical context in an anonymous setting that creates most gender-stereotypical behavior in CMC.

A direct comparison between interactions in FTFC and CMC was reported by Adrianson (2001), who compared male and female interactions in a group discussion. Groups of students (mixed sex) had to solve two problems in different conditions: FTFC, CMC (in which the other person was anonymous), and CMC (in which the other person was known by his or her real name). They first had to write an individual solution to the problem and then were asked to reach a consensus in the group. The results showed that women wrote more messages than men, but only in the FTFC condition. Women also changed their opinion more often than did men (measured by the difference between their initial individual decision and their group's decision), but this difference was especially significant in the anonymous CMC condition. Further, women expressed a larger number of opinions, but they also agreed more than men, but only in the FTFC condition. The category "opinions," however, included both a stereotypical male style ("this is not the way to do this") and a stereotypical female style ("I think this is not the way to do this"), and therefore it is difficult to draw a conclusion about the more feminine nature of the interactions in the FTFC condition. Given that the task of reaching consensus can be seen as more stereotypically feminine, the more frequent expression of opinions and agreements by women can also be seen as conforming to sex-stereotypical expectations. However, it is unclear why opinion change, which can also seen as typical feminine behavior, is recorded more often in the anonymous CMC condition. The argument provided by the authors that one cannot lose one's face in this condition does not explain the sex difference. All in all, the present study is inconclusive with respect to whether CMC leads to an increase or decrease of stereotypical behavior.

The results of this study show some interesting differences between CMC and FTFC, but it is inconclusive with respect to the size and direction of sex differences in CMC and to what extent this is determined by contextual differences. Savicki and colleagues (e.g., Savicki *et al.*, 1996) examined the role of group gender composition on men's and women's linguistic styles. They analyzed more than 2,000 messages sent by 1,208 individuals from 27 different online groups and coded variables like self-disclosure, opinions, apologies, and use of "we" language. When they merely examined the effect of sex of sender, seven of the 13 coded variables showed a significant difference between men and women, whereas the effect of the sex composition of the group showed a significant difference for only two variables (women made more self-disclosure and men made more assertions of facts). This suggests that the sex composition of the group is an important determinant of sex differences in language style in CMC.

Herring (1996) investigated whether different language styles would prevail in men's and women's discussion groups. She collected data from two internet discussion groups, one linguists' list on issues of interest to academic linguists and one women's studies list discussing the issue of sex differences between male and female brains. All messages were analyzed in terms of their structure and content. The sex of the sender was also coded: women predominated in the women's studies list (26 female and 3 male participants), whereas men predominated in the linguists' list (30 male and 5 female participants). The analyses showed that, overall, the women's studies list less often expressed views, and more often displayed feelings (e.g., "it angers me a great deal that ...") and suggested solutions than the linguists' list. Herring discerned two variants of a basic schema in the messages, namely an aligned and an opposed variant. The aligned variant refers to the idea that the author is aligned with and supportive of the view of the addressee, reflecting a relational orientation. This schema typically starts with a link to a previous message, and an expression of agreement or appreciation. This is followed by a non-critical expression of the writer's views, or by a question, a reference, an answer to a question, or an expression of a feeling about the topic under discussion. The message typically ends with an invitation to the other participant to contribute to the discussion. The opposed variant of the basic schema, on the other hand, contains a critical and opposing stance to the addressee's views. There is typically explicit disagreement and the writer expresses a critical view. At the end, the writer often proposes that the discussion stop rather than inviting others to participate in it.

These two variants on the basic schema of messages on electronic lists reflect a stereotypical male and female style, according to Herring (1996). Not surprisingly, the aligned variant is more in line with the feminine stereotype and more often occurs in the women's studies list, whereas the opposed variant is more in agreement with the masculine stereotype and is more characteristic of the linguists' list. However, neither all men nor all women use a typical male or female style. Especially women who participated in the linguists' list often expressed disagreements and critical views. This is in line with results from other studies both in CMC and FTFC and supports the idea that a masculine topic of conversation or environment evokes a more masculine style of conversation in women.

In another study Savicki and Kelley (2000) investigated the type and nature of CMC interactions in groups by including different tasks (masculine or feminine content) and different gender composition (only female, only male, and mixed). The contents of the messages were coded on the basis of the following categories: extent of first-person use (self-disclosure), number of opinions, number of facts, coalition (agreement with another person), satisfaction with the group process, group development, level of argumentativeness, and the use of coarse and abusive language. The groups were asked to reach consensus on the ranking of a character's moral values in either a lover's scenario (feminine task) or a fallout shelter task (masculine). All messages that were sent during the group discussion were content analyzed. The results showed that the sex composition of the group was more important than the nature of the task, or the mere sex of the participant. In exclusively female groups, more words were sent per message (not more messages) than in the two other groups. These female groups also used the first person (indication of self-disclosure) most frequently, they had the largest percentage of messages containing mild and intense reactions to another person in the group, they sent the largest number of messages reflecting an opinion, and they least often used offensive or angry language (flaming). Moreover, these female groups were also more satisfied, participated more, and reported higher group cohesion than the male-only and mixed groups.

These results indicate that women make more use of an open and positive style that stimulates reciprocity and social support. It should be emphasized, however, that these effects were not determined by the sex of the sender, but by the sex composition of the group. We may therefore refer to this phenomenon as "gendered communication," because "gender has an effect within groups as norms for communication develop" (Savicki and Kelley, 2000, p. 822; see also Herring, 1996).

All in all, these studies do not support the equalization hypothesis, since sex differences were found in CMC, but the size and direction depended on the nature of the interaction context. In line with the gender-in-context approach, there is evidence that some contexts give rise to more stereotypical interactions than other contexts, in both CMC and FTFC. Yet, it may be suggested that CMC may evoke more stereotypical expectations, especially in anonymous conditions, though it should be noted that anonymity in itself is not sufficient to produce stereotypes. Stereotypes in CMC are elicited when interacting with same-sex others, or when they are engaged in stereotypical tasks. This pattern of results is similar to results from studies in FTFC, implying that even when visual information is absent, gender stereotypes are elicited by the nature of the task or the identity of the interaction partners.

The role of emotions and nonverbal displays in FTFC

Studies in face-to-face social interactions have not often explicitly dealt with sex differences in emotions. Although many studies have been conducted on sex differences in nonverbal behavior, emotions have generally not been assessed in these studies (see Hall *et al.*, 2000). We may, however, assume on the basis of gender role norms and gender stereotypes that women would express more overtly emotions that promote harmony, affiliation, and warmth. Reviews of the literature on gender differences in the expression of emotions (Brody and Hall, 2000; Fischer, 1993, 2000) indeed suggest that women signal more warmth and affection through their body language than do men, because, for example, they keep a closer distance to their interaction partner, lean forward, nod and gaze, and smile more than men (Hall, 1984). One of the most studied and robust differences between men and women is that women smile more than men (Hall, 1984; LaFrance and Hecht, 2000), but we may doubt whether this difference indicates that women are actually more happy than men. One explanation for women's more frequent smiling may be a gender role norm: women's role of keeping harmony requires them to smile more than men (e.g., Hochschild, 1983; Stoppard and Gunn Gruchy, 1993). Stoppard and Gunn Gruchy (1993), for example, found that women expected more negative consequences for themselves than did men if they failed to express positive emotions directed toward others. By contrast, men only expected positive consequences when they expressed positive emotions, independently of whether these emotions were self- or other-oriented.

The general gender expressivity normF that women should smile may be overruled by situation-specific norms, however. According to LaFrance and Hecht's (2000) expressivity demand theory, different situations may impose different requirements to smile or not. In some situations, there may be smiling rules that apply to men and women to the same extent, as when one greets someone. In situations where there are no specific smiling rules, the general gender expressivity norm would apply. In a meta-analysis, LaFrance and Hecht (2000) showed that several contextual variables, like camera visibility (increases self-awareness and normative behavior) or presence of others, all resulted in more smiling by women than men. These contexts elicited a gender expressivity norm, as they did not evoke specific smiling rules. As predicted, sex differences in smiling decreased when a situation called for specific expressivity demands, as, for example, when participants were required to lie or to compete with others.

Women's more frequent smiling may also reflect a gender difference in status. The engagement in different social roles has implications for one's status: Task-oriented roles are generally assigned more status and power than socio-emotional roles (Eagly, 1987). Moreover, because high-status members are assumed to be more competent, they are also evaluated more positively, and thus receive more opportunity to engage in task-oriented behavior. In contrast, low-status members are more likely to strive for social acceptance by high-status members. Thus, women's more frequent smiling or display of other positive expressions may also point to their striving for social acceptance by males. Power or status can thus be seen as an important situational demand characteristic, leading to gender differences. Indeed, studies by LaFrance indicate that women's smiling is related to their lower social status, whereas men's smiling is related to positive feelings. LaFrance *et al.* (2003) argued that equal power positions would result in larger gender differences in smiling, because gender norms would be more salient, whereas in unequal power positions expressivity norms would be related to one's powerful or powerless role. Their meta-analysis showed that the highest effect sizes (i.e., largest sex differences) were found for participants with equal power, whereas the lowest effect sizes were found for those who had more power than their partner. In other words, when men and women have equal power, gender-specific norms become more salient, resulting in more stereotypical expressive displays.

Low status may not only lead to more smiling, but may more generally result in the display of emotions that signify powerlessness and vulnerability. This is, for example, reflected in another highly robust sex difference in nonverbal communication, namely crying. Women cry more than men, irrespective of context or culture (Fischer *et al.*, 2004; Vingerhoets and Scheirs, 2000).

Lower status may also lead to the development of a greater sensitivity to nonverbal displays, because low-status individuals are more dependent on the acceptance and positive evaluation by high-status individuals (e.g., Henley, 1977). Snodgrass (1985, 1992), for example, showed that participants who were assigned a low status were more sensitive to others' reactions than participants who were assigned a leadership role, irrespective of their sex. Women's lower status may therefore explain why women have been shown to be better senders and decoders of emotions than men, especially when shown on the face (Hall, 1978, 1984; Rosenthal and DePaulo, 1979; Wagner *et al.*, 1986). Moreover, Coats and Feldman (1996) found that the ability to encode happiness was related to the sociometric status of women, whereas the ability to encode anger was related to the sociometric status of men. Several other studies have also shown that women are better in decoding happiness and less accurate in decoding anger expressions (Coats and Feldman, 1996; Wagner *et al.*, 1986). Thus, women's sensitivity to others' emotional expressions does not seem to apply to emotions that reflect hostility or antagonism.

One explanation for this phenomenon may be that women have been socialized to suppress or avoid any hostility in social interactions, resulting in an overall ignorance of such hostile emotions in others. This does not imply that women never express their anger, however. On the contrary, women seem to express their anger especially to their intimates (e.g., Archer, 2000; Kring, 2000), whereas men seem more aggressive in public settings toward strangers. Moreover, Evers *et al.* (2005) found that women are more likely to express their anger to someone who remains anonymous rather than to a person they will meet, whereas this did not make a difference for men's anger expression. There are also indications that men and women, once angry, express their anger differently. Women often seem to express their anger more indirectly, as, for example, by gossiping about another person, or by crying, rather than by expressing the anger in the other's face (e.g., Timmers *et al.*, 1998). The lower aggression rate of women and their more indirect anger style has been explained by the fact that women are more anxious about retaliation by the target, and by potential negative relationship consequences (Eagly and Steffen, 1986). Indeed, in situations where they are as aggressive or even more so than men – for example, in intimate relations (Archer, 2000) – this seems to be caused by the fact that they believe their anger and aggression to be justified.

In sum, women are generally more accurate in decoding the non-verbal displays of others, with the exception of hostile displays. This may be the result of the fact that they are socialized more to focus on others' displays, because of their own low status or their motive to promote harmony and avoid conflict. In line with this argument, women also tend to smile more, either to gain approval from others or to reassure others, and there is some evidence that women have more difficulty in expressing negative emotions directly. All these differences can be explained by women's more relational orientation and lower status. The question is to what extent these differences would also occur in CMC, where others' reactions are not visible.

Emotion communication in CMC

Expressing emotions may be different in CMC in two ways. First, CMC is slower and less spontaneous, as all information exchange has to be typed and can be read over before being sent (controllability). Second, an important aspect of the emotional information (e.g., face, voice, posture) is not available (cuelessness, see also Philippot, Chapter 6, this volume). In other words, one is aware that the other cannot see one's own emotional reaction, just as the emotional reaction of the other remains invisible. As a consequence, it has been hypothesized (see also Walther, Chapter 1, this volume) that it is easier not only to share one's emotions with others (self-disclosure) but also to express negative emotions, because of the absence of both direct and confronting feedback. In other words, sharing intimate personal information may be less embarrassing, and one may not be inhibited by potential negative or hostile feedback from others.

Starting with the assumption that CMC would facilitate emotional self-disclosure, various studies have confirmed this assumption (e.g., Bargh *et al.*, 2002; Tidwell and Walther, 2002; Valkenburg and Peter, 2007). These studies also suggest that sex differences are not significant. Examining the identity of the interactants in self-disclosure, Valkenburg and Peter have shown that adolescents particularly disclose themselves in cross-sex interactions, although this more often occurred for boys than for girls. This suggests that boys may benefit more from the relatively distant nature of CMC.

Research on the use of emoticons (e.g., smileys ☺ or sad faces ☹) also suggests that individuals at least feel the need to express their emotions not only with words but also with short symbols. Are emoticons indeed more often used in interactions that are emotional? Derks *et al.* (2004) asked respondents to react to a short internet chat, on either a socio-emotional or a task-oriented topic. They could react with texts and/or with emoticons. The results showed that the respondents more often used emoticons in response to the socio-emotional text than to the task-oriented text, and they used more negative emoticons in a negative context and more positive emoticons in a positive context. This study thus suggests that emoticons are more often used when individuals experience emotions.

How frequently are emoticons used? Witmer and Katzman (1997) content-coded a sample of messages from publicly posted newsgroups and special interest groups and found that 13 percent of the messages contained emoticons, or graphic accents. A similar percentage was found in an experiment about online communication versus FTFC by Adrianson (2001). Wolf (2000), however, found that 30 percent of the postings on different internet lists used emoticons, and Huffaker and Calvert (2005) found that even half of the messages posted on weblogs by male and female youngsters contained emoticons. These differences in percentage of emoticon usage may be due to the topic of conversation, as is suggested by the study by Derks *et al.* (2007). In Wolf's research, the topics of the discussion lists were more emotional; for example, depression, football, and eating disorders. This may stimulate more emotion sharing. In addition, emoticons also seem to be used more often in personal and intimate relationships, as in personal weblogs, and this may explain the high percentage of emoticon use in the study by Huffaker and Calvert (2005).

The use of emoticons does not necessarily reflect the intensity of emotional experiences, but it does convey the intentions and motives of the person using an emoticon. Sasaki and Ohbuchi (1999) reported a direct comparison of emotional interactions in CMC and FTFC. They had students participate in a role-playing conflict in interaction with a confederate. They then asked participants to report on their emotions, appraisals, and responses. There were no differences in reported anger, appraisals of intent, and aggressive behaviors between conditions, but there was a difference in the extent to which the person's reaction had elicited aggressive responses in the other person. In the vocal communication condition, angry feelings and perceived negative intentions of the aggressor resulted in aggressive responses of the other party, whereas this effect was not found in CMC. The authors suggest that this difference may be due to the fact that CMC involves typing (rather than just talking), which would distract attention from the other's emotions, decreasing one's own hostility towards the other person. An alternative explanation may focus on the presence of nonverbal signals in the vocal communication condition, which may have increased the inference of anger or aggression in the other person.

The lower salience of others' emotions may thus imply that it is easier to express negative emotions in CMC, because one need not worry about hurting the other person, nor is there any need to be afraid of the other person. The assumption that individuals will be less reluctant to provide negative feedback in a CMC context was investigated by Hebert and Vorauer (2003). In their study they compared the delivery of negative feedback in CMC versus FTFC. They assigned pairs of participants the role of either target or judge. The judges had to evaluate the target's written essay in either CMC or FTFC. After the judge had delivered feedback on the essays, the targets were asked to estimate the judge's appraisals of their skills and how much the judge liked them. In addition, independent coders rated the feedback and estimated the judge's liking of the target as well. An analysis of the coders' scores showed that evaluation of skills by the judge was more positive and also clearer in FTFC than in CMC. Moreover, the discrepancy between targets' meta-perceptions (comparison between perceptions of how they were viewed by the judges with the judge's actual impressions) and their self-perception was smaller in FTFC than in CM interactions. This suggests that it may be more difficult to estimate how the other evaluates one in a CMC context.

These results show that CMC may enhance negative feedback or emotion expressions, possibly because these expressions are not inhibited by another's negative reaction. It is not clear whether these results are due to differences in encoding or decoding of the messages. In other words, judges in the FTFC condition may have tried harder to convey a clear message than judges in CMC, but there may also have been better mutual emotional understanding.

Gender differences in emotional CMC

This brings us to an important theme in this chapter; namely, are emotions in CMC differently decoded and expressed by men and women? Consistent with sex stereotypes, we would expect women to use more positive emoticons, like smileys, to convey appeasement, or to downsize their negative intents. With regard to negative emotions, such as flaming or use of aggressive language, however, we would expect women to use these more in FTFC than in CMC, given the relatively anonymous nature of CMC, and the absence of direct feedback from another person (see also Evers *et al.*, 2005). Witmer and Katzman (1997) studied the use of emoticons by analyzing messages that were sent as part of an international computer-supported collaboration project: 30 percent of the posters of messages containing emoticons were female and 70 percent were male. When considering the number of emoticons in the messages, it indeed appeared that women more often used challenging language and flamed more often than men.

Not all studies provide support for women's more frequent flaming, however. In Adrianson's (2001) study, for example, hardly any flaming or use of emoticons occurred, and no gender differences were found. This may, however, also be due to the fact that these were experimentally induced rather than spontaneous interactions. Participants may have restrained themselves from the use of emoticons. Wolf (2000) also found support for a move away from the emotional sex stereotype. She investigated emoticon use on the internet, and coded messages from four different newsgroups: a predominantly female newsgroup (e.g., an eating disorder support group), a predominantly male newsgroup (football), and two mixed gender newsgroups (a depression support group and a divorce support group). She coded the number of different emoticons (smileys, frowneys) and the meanings of the use of the emoticon (to express teasing/sarcasm, humor, sadness, and despair; to offer an apology, positive feelings, or solidarity). In the predominantly female group, the smiley was the most frequently used emoticon, and the categories of humor and solidarity were the most frequently coded meanings. The use of emoticons in order to tease others was absent. In the predominantly male group, on the other hand, the only emotional use of the emoticon (smiley and frowney) was to express sarcasm or humor. These two groups thus show stereotypical male and female emotion expressions. It should be noted, however, that these sex differences in the use of emoticons may also have been evoked by the topic of conversation. Thus, in an eating disorder support group, one may be more inclined to use smileys as means of showing support or sympathy than in a football newsgroup, irrespective of one's sex (see also Herring, 1996).

This hypothesis is supported by the results of the mixed gender group, where women and men used the same number of emoticons in their messages, although there still appeared to be differences in the way they used emoticons. In these mixed-gender groups, women teased and made sarcastic comments in 17 percent of their postings (following humor in 35 percent of the cases), but men still used sarcasm emoticons more than did women (31 percent of the postings). Men also used emoticons to apologize (7 percent), something they did not do in the predominantly male groups. Thus, men and women both seemed to use emoticons more in a non-stereotypical way than in the sex-segregated groups. It is not clear, however, whether the difference in the way these emoticons were used was due to the sex composition of the group, or to the topic of conversation, as these factors were confounded.

In conclusion, there is no support for the idea that the internet is a cold and impersonal medium (see also Derks *et al.*, 2008). Not only are there many groups and discussion lists on personal topics, like diseases or divorces, but the internet also has become a place to start and maintain romantic relationships. Thus, emotions are part of any CMC. The question is to what extent the absence of visual, nonverbal cues makes the communication of emotions different in CMC, compared to FTFC. One consequence is the absence of direct and thus sometimes confrontational feedback. This may make it easier to share emotions that one may find embarrassing, and it may also make it easier to express emotions to which one expects negative reactions from others, such as anger and feeling hurt. In other words, emotion regulation that aims to avoid direct negative feedback from others may be different in CMC versus FTFC. This may explain why male adolescents are more likely to self-disclose emotionally on the internet than in real life, and it may also explain why women in some contexts may be less inhibited to express their anger directly.

Conclusion

The central question of this chapter was whether and to what extent the absence of visual information in text-based CMC interactions would affect the gender-stereotypical nature of social interactions. I focused my review on the effects of the absence of visual cues, rendering CMC more anonymous and less multichanneled than FTFC. Although the empirical evidence that examines this question is still limited, the conclusion based on the present evidence suggests that gender differences do not increase or decrease in CMC compared to FTFC; in both modes of communication, they only occur in settings where stereotypes are evoked. This supports the gender-in-context approach (e.g., Deaux and Major, 1987), implying that most differences between men and women in social behavior only appear in response to a stereotypical context.

One important aspect of the context is the *identity* of the other person: Is it a man or a woman, and what else do we know about this person? In face-to-face interactions, stereotypes are elicited when one interacts with strangers, or with members of the same sex (in a group). In other words, individuals tend to rely on stereotypes if the other's sex is salient. The same happens in CMC: When the other person is anonymous, that is, when there is no personal information available, stereotypes are more likely to be activated. A second aspect of the context is the composition of the group. For example, women tend to use a more stereotypical female style showing agreement with, and support of the other person, and men tend to use a more stereotypical masculine style by expressing more critical views, but these stereotypical styles disappear in mixed groups or when the task is gender-neutral.

We could argue, however, in line with the SIDE model that CMC may evoke stereotypical contexts more easily, as the result of the absence of visual cues. It is difficult to draw firm conclusions with regard to this question because of the lack of studies in which FTFC and CMC have been directly compared. Postmes and Spears (2002) have shown that an anonymous context only leads to more stereotyping if the stereotypes are already accessible. On the other hand, stereotypes may be less strongly activated because the other's sex is less salient in CMC. Indeed, in some studies fewer gender differences were found in CMC compared with FTFC (e.g., Adrianson, 2001; Sasaki and Ohbuchi, 1999). Other studies, however, did not explicitly report gender differences, and thus it remains unclear whether gender differences were absent or simply not examined.

Most differences between CMC and FTFC should perhaps be found with regard to exchanges that involve emotions (see also Derks *et al.*, 2008). On the basis of studies that have implicitly or explicitly examined emotions in CMC, the conclusion seems justified that interactions on the internet can and do have an emotional content. First of all, individuals use emoticons, especially in personal exchanges, apparently because they need some sort of short and strong displays of emotions. Women do not seem to use more emoticons, however, though they sometimes use them in other ways than men do. As in real life, women tend to use smileys more frequently to communicate humor or solidarity, whereas men use them to display a reserved attitude, or even sarcasm. This sex difference in the use of emoticons, however, also seems to depend on the context: the more stereotypes are activated, the more stereotypical the use of emoticons.

Studies on the communication of negative affect, especially anger, or negative feedback, have shown inconsistent results. Playing a role conflict elicits equal amounts of anger in CMC and FTFC, but CMC elicits less aggression in another person and thus has less harmful effects. This may be due to the fact that one's angry expression is invisible. However, a study on negative feedback (Hebert and Vorauer, 2003) showed that respondents give more negative feedback in CMC than in FTFC. Given that women may be more reluctant than are men to express their anger directly, CMC may motivate a counter-stereotypical anger reaction in women, because the other's response to their anger is less salient. In the case of men, this should not make a difference. Whether men's and women's anger expression would have different effects remains to be seen.

This relates to another important issue, namely women's superior skills in decoding others' faces. This sex difference seems to disappear in CMC, as emoticons are much more explicit and easier to interpret than actual faces. We can only speculate about the consequence of this sex difference for CMC. One implication may be that women will be more inclined to use a masculine, assertive style, because CMC focuses them less on others' reactions. Women may therefore feel less inhibited by others' presumed feelings of hurt or pain, and display more hostility, either in words or by using flames. To date, however, there is no consistent evidence to support this assumption.

Finally, it should be clear from this review of research that we lack a strong empirical basis to draw firm conclusions about the way in which gendered interactions proceed in CMC and how different it is from FTFC. Therefore, the answers I have provided should be considered tentative. So far, the evidence suggests that most gender-stereotypical interactions depend more on the social context than on the mode of communication. The absence of visual cues and direct feedback may especially affect how men and women regulate their emotions.

References

Adrianson, L. (2001). Gender and computer-mediated communication: group processes in problem solving. *Computers in Human Behavior*, **17**, 71–94.

Allen, B. J. (1995). Gender and computer-mediated communication. *Sex Roles*, **32**, 557–563.

Anderson, L. R. and Blanchard, P. N. (1982). Sex differences in task and social-emotional behavior. *Basic and Applied Social Psychology*, **3**, 109–139.

Archer, J. (2000). Sex differences in aggression between heterosexual partners: a meta-analytic review. *Psychological Bulletin*, **126**, 651–680.

Aries, E. (1996). *Men and Women in Interaction*. Oxford University Press.

Bales, R. F. (1950). *Interaction Process Analysis: A Method for the Study of Small Groups*. Reading, MA: Addison-Wesley.

Bargh, J. and McKenna, K. Y. A. (2004). The internet and social life. *Annual Review of Psychology*, **55**, 573–590.

Bargh, J. A., McKenna, K., and Fitzsimons, G. M. (2002). Can you see the real me? Activation and expression of the "true self" on the internet. *Journal of Social Issues*, **58**, 33–48.

Baym, N. (2006). Interpersonal life online. In L. A. Lievrouw and S. Livingstone (eds), *The Handbook of New Media* (pp. 35–55). London: Sage.

Bhappu, A. D., Griffith, T. L., and Northcraft, G. B. (1997). Media effects and communication bias in diverse groups. *Organizational Behavior and Human Decision Processes*, **70**, 199–205.

Brody, L. R. and Hall, J. A. (1993). Gender and emotion. In M. Lewis and J. M. Haviland (eds), *Handbook of Emotions* (pp. 447–461). New York: Guilford.

Brody, L. and Hall, J. (2000). Gender, emotion, and expression. In M. Lewis and J. Haviland (eds), *Handbook of Emotions* (pp. 338–349). New York: Guilford Press.

Bruckman, A. S. (1993). Gender swapping on the internet. *Proceedings of INET'93*, San Francisco, CA.

Bull, P. E. (2002). *Communication Under the Microscope: The Theory and Practice of Microanalysis*. London: Psychology Press.

Carli, L. L. (1989). Gender differences in interaction style and influence. *Journal of Personality and Social Psychology*, **56**, 565–576.

Coats, E. J. and Feldman, R. S. (1996). Gender differences in nonverbal correlates of social status. *Personality and Social Psychology Bulletin*, **22**, 1014–1022.

Culnan, M. J. and Markus, M. L. (1987). Information technologies. In F. M. Fabin, J. L. Putnam, K. H. Roberts, and L. W. Porter (eds), *Handbook of Organizational Computing: An Interdisciplinary Perspective* (pp. 420–443). Newbury Park, CA: Sage.

Deaux, K. and Major, B. (1987). Putting gender into context: an interactive model of gender-related behavior. *Psychological Review*, **94**, 369–389.

Derks, D., Bos, A. E. R., and von Grumbkow, J. (2004). Emoticons en sociale interactie via Internet [Emoticons and social interaction on the internet]. In D. Wigboldus, M. Dechesne, E. Gordijn, and E. Kluwer (eds), *Jaarboek Sociale Psychologie 2003* (pp. 59–67). Groningen: ASPO Pers.

Derks, D., Bos, A. E. R., and von Grumbkow, J. (2007). Emoticons and social interaction on the internet. *Computers in Human Behavior*, **23**(1), 842–849.

Derks, D., Fischer, A. H., and Bos, A. E. R. (2008). The role of emotion in computer-mediated communication: a review. *Computers in Human Behavior*, **24**, 766–785.

Donath, J. (1999). Identity and deception in the virtual community. In M. Smith and P. Kollock (eds), *Communities in Cyberspace* (pp. 29–59). New York: Routledge.

Dubrovsky, V. J., Kiesler, S., and Sethna, B. N. (1991). The equalization phenomenon: status effects in computer-mediated and face-to-face decision-making groups. *Human–Computer Interaction*, **6**, 119–146.

Eagly, A. H. (1987). *Sex Differences in Social Behavior: A Social Role Interpretation*. Hillsdale, NJ: Lawrence Erlbaum.

Eagly, A. H. and Johnson, B. T. (1990). Gender and leadership style: a meta-analysis. *Psychological Bulletin*, **108**, 233–256.

Eagly, A. H. and Karau, S. J. (1991). Gender and the emergence of leaders: a meta-analysis. *Journal of Personality and Social Psychology*, **60**, 685–710.

Eagly, A. H. and Steffen, V. J. (1986). Gender and aggressive behaviour: a meta-analytic review of the social psychological literature. *Psychological Bulletin*, **100**, 309–330.

Evers, C. A. M., Fischer, A. H., Rodriguez Mosquera, P. M., and Manstead, A. S. R. (2005). Anger and social appraisal: a "spicy" sex difference. *Emotion*, **5**, 258–266.

Fischer, A. H. (1993). Sex differences in emotionality: fact or stereotype? *Feminism and Psychology*, **3**, 303–318.

   (2000). *Gender and Emotion: Social Psychological Perspectives*. Cambridge University Press.

Fischer, A. H., Rodriguez, P. M., van Vianen, E. A. M., and Manstead, A. S. R. (2004). Gender and culture differences in emotion. *Emotion*, **4**, 87–94.

Fishman, P. (1983). Interaction: the work women do. In B. Thorne, C. Kramarae, and N. Henley (eds), *Language, Gender and Society* (pp. 89–101). Rowley, MA: Newbury House.

Hall, J. A. (1978). Gender effects in decoding nonverbal cues. *Psychological Bulletin*, **85**, 845–857.

   (1984). *Nonverbal Sex Differences: Communication Accuracy and Expressive Style*. Baltimore, MD: Johns Hopkins University Press.

Hall, J. A. and Carter, J. D. (1999). Gender-stereotype accuracy as an individual difference. *Journal of Personality and Social Psychology*, **77**, 350–359.

Hall, J. A., Carter, J. D., and Horgan, T. G. (2000). Gender differences in nonverbal communication of emotion. In A. H. Fischer (ed.), *Gender and Emotion: Social Psychological Perspectives* (pp. 97–118). Cambridge University Press.

Haraway, D. (1990). A cyborg manifesto: science, technology, and socialist-feminism in the late twentieth century. In A. C. Herrmann and A. J. Stewart (eds), *Theorizing Feminism: Parallel Trends in the Humanities and Social Sciences* (pp. 424–457). Boulder, CO: Westview Press.

Hebert, B. G. and Vorauer, J. D. (2003). Seeing through the screen: is evaluative feedback communicated more effectively in face-to-face or computer-mediated exchanges? *Computers in Human Behavior*, **19**, 25–38.

Henley, N. (1977). *Power, Sex, and Nonverbal Communication*. Englewood Cliffs, NJ: Prentice-Hall.

Herring, S. C. (1996). Two variants of an electronic message schema. In S. C. Herring (ed.), *Computer-Mediated Communication. Linguistic, Social and Cross-Cultural Perspectives* (pp. 81–108). Amsterdam: John Benjamins.

Hiltz, R. S. and Johnson, K. (1990). User satisfaction with computer-mediated communication systems. *Management Science*, **36**, 739–751.

Hochschild, A. (1983). *The Managed Heart*. Berkeley, CA: University of California Press.

Holmes, J. (1985). Sex differences and mis-communication: some data from New Zealand. In J. B. Pride (ed.), *Cross-Cultural Encounters: Communication and Miscommunication* (pp. 24–43). Melbourne: River Seine Publications.

Huffaker, D. A. and Calvert, S. L. (2005). Gender, identity and language use in teenage blogs. *Journal of Computer-Mediated Communication*, **10**. http:// jcmc.indiana.edu/vol10/issue2/huffaker.html.

Izraeli, D. N. (1983). Sex effects or structural effects? An empirical test of Kanter's theory of proportions. *Social Forces*, **62**, 153–165.

James, D. and Clarke, S. (1993). Women, men and interruptions: a critical review. In D. Tannen (ed.), *Gender and Conversational Interaction* (pp. 231–280). New York: Oxford University Press.

Johnson, R. A. and Schulman, G. I. (1989). Gender-role composition and role entrapment in decision-making groups. *Gender and Society*, **4**, 355–372.

Kiesler, S., Siegel, J., and McGuire, T. W. (1984). Social psychological aspects of computer-mediated communication. *American Psychologist*, **39**, 1123–1134.

Kirk, D. (1992). Gender issues in information technology as found in schools: authentic/synthetic/fantastic? *Educational Technology*, *32*, 28–31.

Kring, A. (2000). Gender and anger. In A. H. Fischer (ed.), *Gender and Emotion: Social Psychological Perspectives* (pp. 211–231). Cambridge University Press.

LaFrance, M. and Hecht, M. (2000). Gender and smiling: a meta-analysis. In A. H. Fischer (ed.), *Gender and Emotion: Social Psychological Perspectives* (pp. 97–118). Cambridge University Press.

LaFrance, M., Hecht, M. A., and Paluck, E. L. (2003). The contingent smile: a meta-analysis of sex differences in smiling. *Psychological Bulletin*, *129*, 305–334.

Lakoff, R. (1975). *Language and Women's Place*. New York: Harper and Row.

Lea, M. and Spears, R. (1991). Computer-mediated communication, de-individuation and group-decision making. *International Journal of Man–Machine Studies*, *34*, 283–301.

Matheson, K. (1991). Social cues in computer-mediated communication negotiations: gender makes a difference. *Computers in Human Behavior*, *7*, 137–145.

Nowak, K. L. (2003). Sex categorization in computer-mediated communication (CMC): exploring the utopian promise. *Media Psychology*, *5*, 83–103.

Postmes, T. and Spears, R. (2002). Behavior online: does anonymous computer communication reduce gender inequality? *Personality and Social Psychology Bulletin*, *28*, 1073–1083.

Postmes, T., Spears, R., and Lea, M. (1998). Breaching or building social boundaries? SIDE-effects of computer-mediated communication. *Communication Research*, *25*, 689–715.

(2002). Intergroup differentiation in computer-mediated communication: effects of depersonalization. *Group Dynamics: Theory, Research, and Practice*, *6*, 3–16.

Rosenthal, R. and DePaulo, B. M. (1979). Sex differences in eavesdropping on nonverbal cues. *Journal of Personality and Social Psychology*, *37*, 273–285.

Sasaki, M. U. and Ohbuchi, K. (1999). Conflict processes on computer-mediated communication. *Tohoku Psychologica Folia*, *58*, 50–55.

Savicki, V. and Kelley, M. (2000). Computer mediated communication: gender and group composition. *Cyberpsychology and Behavior*, *3*, 817–826.

Savicki, V., Kelley, M., and Lingenfelter, D. (1996). Gender, group composition, and task type in small task groups using computer-mediated communication. *Computers in Human Behavior*, *12*, 549–565.

Savicki, V., Kelley, M., and Oesterreich, E. (1998). Effects of instructions on computer-mediated communication in single- or mixed-gender small task groups. *Computers in Human Behavior*, *14*, 163–180.

Schouten, A. P., Valkenburg, P. M., and Peter, J. (2007). Precursors and underlying processes of adolescents' online self-disclosure: developing and testing an "internet-attribute-perception" model. *Media Psychology*, *10*, 292–315.

Siegl, J., Dubrovsky, S., Kiesler, S., and McQuire, T. (1986). Group processes in computer-mediated communication. *Organizational Behavior and Human Decision Processes*, *37*, 157–187.

Snodgrass, S. E. (1985). Women's intuition: the effect of subordinate role on interpersonal sensitivity. *Journal of Personality and Social Psychology*, *49*, 146–155.

(1992). Further effects of role versus gender on interpersonal sensitivity. *Journal of Personality and Social Psychology*, **62**, 154–158.

Sproull, L. and Kiesler, S. B. (1991). *Connections: New Ways of Working in the Networked Organization*. Cambridge, MA: MIT Press.

Stoppard, J. M. and Gunn Gruchy, C. D. (1993). Gender, context and expression of positive emotion. *Personality and Social Psychology Bulletin*, **19**, 143–150.

Tannen, D. (1990). *You Just Don't Understand*. New York: Ballantine.

Tidwell, L. C. and Walther, J. B. (2002). Computer-mediated communication effects on disclosure, impressions, and interpersonal evaluations: getting to know one another a bit at a time. *Human Communication Research*, **28**, 317–348.

Timmers, M., Fischer, A. H., and Manstead, A. S. R. (1998). Gender differences in motives for regulating emotions. *Personality and Social Psychology Bulletin*, **24**, 974–985.

Valkenburg, P. M. and Peter, J. (2007). Preadolescents' and adolescents' online communication and their closeness to friends. *Developmental Psychology*, **43**, 267–277.

Vingerhoets, A. and Scheirs, J. (2000). Sex differences in crying: empirical findings and possible explanations. In A. H. Fischer (ed.), *Gender and Emotion: Social Psychological Perspectives* (pp. 143–166). Cambridge University Press.

Wagner, H. L., MacDonald, C. J., and Manstead, A. S. R. (1986). Communication of individual emotions by spontaneous facial expressions. *Journal of Personality and Social Psychology*, **50**, 737–743.

Walther, J. B. (1996). Computer-mediated communication: impersonal, interpersonal and hyperpersonal interaction. *Communication Research*, **23**, 3–43.

Walther, J. B. and D'Addario, K. P. (2001). The impacts of emoticons on message interpretation in computer-mediated communication. *Social Science Computer Review*, **19**, 323–345.

Wheelan, S. A. and Verdi, A. F. (1992). Differences in male and female patterns of communication in groups: a methodological artifact? *Sex Roles*, **29**, 1–15.

Williams, M. J. and Mendelsohn, G. A. (2008). Gender clues and cues: online interactions as windows into lay theories about men and women. *Basic and Applied Social Psychology*, **30**, 278–294.

Witmer, D. F. and Katzman, S. L. (1997). On-line smiles: does gender make a difference in the use of graphic accents? *Journal of Computer-Mediated Communication*, **2**. http://jcmc.indiana.edu/vol2/issue4/witmer1.html.

Wolf, A. (2000). Emotional expression online: gender differences in emoticon use. *Cyberpsychology and Behavior*, **3**, 827–833.

Zimmerman, D. H. and West, C. (1975). Sex roles, interruptions and silences in conversation. In B. Thorne and N. Henley (eds), *Language and Sex: Differences and Dominance* (pp. 105–129). Rowley, MA: Newbury House.

PART 2

Video- and avatar-based communication

Nonverbal communication and cultural differences: issues for face-to-face communication over the internet

Pio Enrico Ricci Bitti and Pier Luigi Garotti

Overview: The various forms of interpersonal communication that take place on the internet are considered and several questions concerning the efficacy of interpersonal communication over the internet are raised (i.e., whether this form of communication can be compared to actual face-to-face communication).

The technologies for communication over the internet do not always allow access to "kinesic" behaviors through the visual channel or to vocal-intonational modulations of speech through the auditory channel; they therefore cannot count on a wide range of nonverbal signals that are of extreme importance for certain communicative processes. Graphic and linguistic strategies permit internet users to compensate for this lack of communicative signals and render communication via the internet more immediate, natural, spontaneous, and expressive. Videoconference might be an effective means for conveying the sense of presence to interlocutors; it can be used in many different areas: in work (long-distance collaboration and meetings between people in different locations), long-distance education (teleteaching, e-learning), and health care (telemedicine, telehealth, psychotherapy), as well as in legal contexts.

This contribution, finally, analyzes the video-based interactions between individuals belonging to different cultures and evaluates the differences in nonverbal communication in this perspective.

Introduction

The internet is now a means of communication widely used in the interaction between individuals: It is used for work, to chat with friends, to meet new people, to discuss matters of social importance, for educational purposes, etc. The videoconference has now been

81

added to the most frequently used systems (email, discussion forums, mailing lists, etc.), and this has made interaction between people more complete and natural.

But can the efficacy of interpersonal communication over the internet be compared to actual face-to-face communication? What are the benefits and limitations of online interaction?

To answer these queries, it is necessary to distinguish between the various forms of interpersonal communication that take place on the internet: The fundamental distinction concerns the fact that most of the means of interaction used up to now have implied an essentially "textual" (written) type of communication, which excludes the possibility of interlocutors seeing or hearing each other and therefore interacting face to face as occurs in everyday life.

These means of communication do not allow access to "kinesic" behaviors through the visual channel or through the auditory channel to vocal-intonational modulations of speech. They cannot therefore count on a wide range of nonverbal signals that are of extreme importance for certain communicative processes, such as turn-taking, the formation of mutual impressions, feedback, and the expression of emotions and interpersonal attitudes, which are typical of face-to-face communication. The impossibility of making full use of the potential of auditory and visual channels in "textual conversations" on the internet has led its users to develop strategies to make the communication more functional and effective. It is well known that linguists have proven human language to be strongly influenced by usages, social conventions, and, above all, by the means of communication used. The fact that written communication on the internet has produced variations in the "linguistic register" that aim to make exchanges more effective is therefore understandable. When exchanging messages in real time without being able to see or hear each other, users seek out new forms of textual (written) communication to make up for this lack of nonverbal behavior. The most typical example of online interpersonal communication through written text is the chat line, a means of communication widely used, especially among younger internet users, to interact in real time with other people. Internet users that communicate through written text have tried to compensate for this lack of communicative signals associated with gestures, facial expressions, prossemics, vocal intonation, etc., by inventing graphic and linguistic strategies for transmitting information relating to emotions, interpersonal attitudes, and regulation of mutual exchanges (attention, turn-taking, feedback, etc.). These strategies have given rise to an "abbreviated" language full of acronyms and alterations, uppercase letters, and punctuation marks often repeated excessively. The function of these strategies is to make communication via the internet, which, given its textual (written) nature, is structurally incapable of transmitting meta-communicative signals (which go beyond the literal meaning of the words), faster, more immediate, natural, spontaneous, and expressive. Emoticons (or smileys) are the most widely used linguistic and graphic strategy used in chat lines to make up for the lack of nonverbal communication. Their task is essentially to clarify the emotional tone of the communication, and they are now a universal iconography exclusive to online communication.

It is no surprise that emoticons, more than other types of strategies such as small capitals, repeated vowels, or repeated punctuation marks, have had so much success. Facial expressions represent the main way of communicating emotional states and constitute one of the main "conversational signals."

Emoticons are now so popular with internet communication users that most sites that feature a chat line have an inventory of smileys that specifies the meaning of each one.

Emoticons are usually placed at the end of a sentence to clarify its emotional tone, but they are often used alone (without words) to replace an entire sentence. Emoticons can therefore be used to abbreviate the length of messages and make the communication more fluent and similar to face-to-face communication.

However effective they may be in casual communications between friends, emoticons are not as useful in interactions with a specific collaborative purpose (e.g., for work or education), in which the regulation of conversational turns, the interpretation of the interlocutor's real intentions, mutual attitudes, etc., are very important.

This is the reason for the development of another type of technology that facilitates direct interaction and conversation between interlocutors that are not physically in the same place: the videoconference via the internet. With the help of the computer keyboard, a video camera, and a microphone, it is possible for two interlocutors in two different places to see and listen to each other in real time via the internet.

A further development of the videoconference is desktop videoconferencing; this means that users located in different places can collaborate. Not only can each user be connected to others via audio and video, but each user can also take part in joint activities on a shared blackboard or document. Audio and video channels are thus combined, and graphics and text files can also be sent and received.

Therefore, the help these technologies provides allows for types of communication very different from those interactions based solely on written text and more similar to "face-to-face" communication.

The term "video-mediated communication" (VMC) is used in these cases; by means of VMC interlocutors can make use, at least in part, both when "sending" and when "receiving" messages, of the repertoire of nonverbal signals that use the vocal-auditory channel (vocal-intonational and paralinguistic aspects of speech) and the visual-kinesic channel (facial expression, gaze direction, gestures, posture, etc.).

Nonverbal communication in face-to-face interaction and its functions

Nonverbal communication has various important functions in people's social behavior. Research carried out in the last few decades has shown a considerable range of nonverbal elements that operate in a particularly complex way: We are now able to evaluate the type of influence that our nonverbal behaviour has on others and to judge people's ability to send nonverbal signals and interpret them; we know that the information provided by words is in some cases contradicted and belied by the nonverbal signals that accompany it and that when verbal communication is not possible, information is transmitted via nonverbal signals.

Many nonverbal aspects of communicative behavior are so connaturalized in everyday interactions that it is difficult to be fully aware of their functions and meaning: When we get to know a person, for example, we essentially use information from their nonverbal behavior, and to recognize the emotional state or interpersonal attitudes of our interlocutor, we pay attention not only to what they are saying, but also to their tone of voice, facial expression, movements, and gestures.

Despite such a frequent, almost natural, use of nonverbal signals, and therefore despite an implicit skill in using them, it is not easy to describe in detail and systematically the nonverbal communicative repertoire that we have at our disposal and be fully aware of it.

Nonverbal communication has a great many functions: It can be considered as a "relation language," the primary means for signaling changes in quality in interpersonal relations (interpersonal attitudes); it can be considered as the main means for expressing and communicating emotions; it has a special symbolic value that expresses, in simple body language, attitudes about self-image and one's body and contributes to presenting oneself to others; it sustains and completes verbal communication and performs a meta-communicative function, as it provides elements for interpreting the meaning of verbal expressions; it acts as a "dispersion channel," as, given that it is less subject to the conscious control or unconscious censure than language, it allows the profound content of the experience of the individual to emerge more easily; it regulates the interaction, by contributing to synchronize the turns and sequences, provide feedback, and send attention signals; and, finally, it also replaces verbal communication in situations that do not allow the use of language.

For the purposes of this chapter, more in-depth information has to be given on some of the communicative functions carried out by nonverbal behavior in face-to-face interaction; in particular, the interpersonal (or expressive) function, the regulation and synchronization of the interactive sequence, and the meta-communicative function need to be analyzed.

A verbal message is never solely a neutral transmission of information to the surrounding world. It is always also a communication that concerns the relationship between interlocutors. Indeed, whatever the subject of a conversation may be, the people confirm or discuss the relationship between them. The world to which the messages refer in this case, whether directly or otherwise, is the world of social status and power, love and "solidarity," hostility and affectivity. In this case, we can speak of "presentation function" as opposed to "representation" (or referential) function. Both imply a relationship between a signifier and something that is signified but in a very different way. Phrases are an explicit representation of their semantic content, but, at the same time, when they are spoken in a given interpersonal context, they present requests whose reference is the relationship between the interlocutors. For example, the request for superiority is not expressed with explicit statements such as "I am superior to you, so I give you orders," but it can be transmitted implicitly with the tone of voice, a glance, or standing at a certain distance. These are significant signals, even though no dictionary gives their meanings. The information exchanged therefore concerns many aspects relating to the participants in the interaction and to the relationships existing between them, and can be grouped into three main classes: (a) social and personal identity; (b) temporary emotional states and interpersonal attitudes; (c) social relations.

How a person speaks and acts, how he or she moves and dresses, leaves clues as to some sides of his or her personality (extrovert, shy, etc.) and some social-demographic characteristics (age, place of origin, social ranking, etc.). These are partly signals that a person is able consciously to use to present him/herself; i.e., by proposing a certain image to others, the person can obtain the desired result (for example, to appear eccentric or of high social status) by manipulating his or her outer appearance, nonlinguistic aspects of the exchange (accent, tone of voice, rhythm), or the style of nonverbal behavior. The expression of emotional states can be explicit, i.e., declared verbally (for example, "I'm happy today"), or expressed through nonverbal signals (for example, a smile, a relaxed facial expression, a dreamy look). This is also true for communicating interpersonal attitudes to the interlocutor (kindness, courtesy, hostility, refusal, etc.). In all these cases, nonverbal signals seem to be more effective communicators than words.

The most common emotions are expressed clearly by the exterior behavior. For example, an anxious state can be identified by the tone of voice, facial expression, gestures, and glances. Certain common body movements, seemingly without purpose, can indicate emotional activation just as particular gestures can indicate specific emotive states (for example, tightening the fists can reveal aggressiveness, scratching could be a sign of embarrassment, mopping the brow is a sign of tiredness).

During an interaction, not only are the attitudes toward the interlocutor expressed but also the attitudes toward the topic being discussed. A person may be interested, involved, bored, or disgusted by the topic of discussion, and this can be expressed by facial expressions. In each social encounter, information regarding the social (or role) relations existing between the participants is exchanged. Particular relationships of kinship, familiarity, and power are characterized by the right or duty to use determined linguistic forms associated with adequate nonverbal expressions.

This is not surprising because this is how everyday communication takes place on the basis of the conventions existing in any given culture and which are part of every individual possessing social skills.

In order for the exchange of information of any kind to take place, the interaction must obviously be set in motion, negotiated, and regulated. A central problem for understanding face-to-face communication lies in analyzing the rules that govern (or underlie) each interpersonal exchange. In order for communication to take place, and not a chaotic and incomprehensible mixture of gestures and words, the interlocutors must be aware of the rules for the use of symbols, as well as for a series of elements such as exchanging the roles of speaker and listener, saying hello and goodbye, and so forth. Nonverbal elements play a predominant role in this scenario, as they allow the exchange to be divided into hierarchically organized units, and make for easier synchronization between participants. The characteristic turn-taking in a conversation therefore requires each participant to send and receive a series of signals whose purpose is to regulate what is happening, so as both to maintain the present phase and allow the gradual passing to a subsequent phase. This is not, however, a simple distribution of roles; the conversation also implies a mutual coordination of movements, a veritable "synchrony of interaction."

As has already been said, there are two aspects to each communication, one relating to the "content" of the message, the news transmitted, and the other concerning the way in which this message must be understood and the "relation" existing between those communicating.

The relational aspect concerns communication about the communication; i.e., meta-communication. This is done both by means of verbal expressions and nonverbally. Nonverbal behavior has a meta-communicative function in providing the information necessary for interpreting the meaning of verbal expressions, and evaluating the real feelings or intentions of the speaker.

The videoconference via the internet: pros and cons

As has already been said, the videoconference via the internet is a type of synchronous CMC that allows several channels such as voice and image to be used simultaneously, files to be sent and received, a screen for writing or drawing to be shared, computer presentations to be prepared (e.g., slide projections), etc. It is characterized by multimedia, hypertextual, synchronous, and interactive aspects (Newhagen, 1996). It differs from and has many advantages over written CMC. First of all, it ensures the use, at least in part, of "meta-communication" aspects that characterize everyday conversation and that indicate how to understand the content of what is being communicated. Indeed, nonverbal signals (especially the tone of voice and facial expression) suggest which specific meaning should be attributed to the communication in progress. It also guarantees the identity of the interacting subjects through interpersonal perception processes and through these makes both subjects feel they are actually "present." As such, the concept of "social presence" has been proposed (Short *et al.*, 1976), understood as the capacity of the means of communication to transport the presence of the interacting subjects and give them the impression of being entirely within a communicative environment, thanks to the activation of many (if not all) sensorial channels and various mental processes for processing and integrating sensorial data. The realism and immediacy of the interaction is thus accentuated for those who are interacting long distance, and the actual distance between them seems to be reduced. It is also suggested that this "social presence" is encouraged not only by the quantity of information transmitted ("media richness"; Sproull and Kiesler, 1986), but also by the possibility of interacting with others about specific tasks (task-oriented communication).

The more the videoconference makes interlocutors feel that the communicative experience is not mediated and, even though the communication takes place long distance, it also occurs in a shared place, almost in the "same place," the more effective it is. As such, the "means" of communication is perceived as a sensitive tool that simplifies and brings people together.

The concept of presence is of vital importance in evaluating the efficacy of the videoconference, as, more than other forms of CMC, it should overcome the space–time limitations of the interaction, succeeding in transmitting the maximum number of verbal and nonverbal communicative cues, lessening the risk of ambiguous information being transmitted. Muhlbach *et al.* (1995) suggested replacing the concept of "social presence" with "telepresence," which means the experience of the remote environment made possible by a means of communication. Subjects perceive two environments simultaneously: the physical environment where each subject is located while interacting and the remote environment represented by the means of communication. Thanks to the telepresence aspect, the latter has prevalence over the former. The two components of telepresence are "spatial presence" (capacity to perceive visual and audible cues from the remote environment which is being contacted) and "communicative presence" (perception of verbal and nonverbal signals sent by remote interlocutors). The same authors also noted that the possible lack of success of the videoconference could be due above all to the poor level of telepresence caused by technological limitations: Indeed, the difficulty in using nonverbal signals of the face and body and the cues about the depth of the environment do not allow subjects to make full use of the interactions created in a videoconference or deal with and solve important issues successfully.

The videoconference would therefore be an effective means for guaranteeing the sense of presence to interlocutors who can use, with some modulation, nonverbal signals (facial expressions, gaze, gestures, posture) that contribute to defining many aspects of the interpersonal situation such as the immediacy of the communication and the degree of familiarity (trust) between the interlocutors, aspects which go beyond the meaning of words.

Another advantage of the videoconference over textual forms of CMC is the fact that it allows for a more precise definition of turntaking in communicative exchanges. It is indeed possible to obtain feedback in almost real time and the overlap can be sufficiently reduced.

The videoconference can be used in many different areas; we will consider just a few of the more important ones: in work (long-distance collaboration and meetings between people in different locations), long-distance education (teleteaching), health care (telemedicine, telehealth), legal contexts, etc.

In work situations, which aim to reach an objective within a relatively short and well-defined space of time, the main aim has been to evaluate the efficacy of the videomediated interaction in relation to the reaching of the envisaged result. To this end, comparative studies have been conducted on the efficacy of the "performance" in different conditions: face-to-face, audioconference, and videoconference. The results obtained did not show significant differences between face-to-face conditions and the videoconference (Olson *et al.*, 1995); it can be considered that the videoconference may therefore be effective for this type of use.

The videoconference is also widely used in long-distance teaching (teleteaching). It is perceived by reproducing, although long-distance, the interaction between one person (teacher) and many people (pupils), typical of a normal lesson at school. The teacher is a shared resource for geographically distant pupils, who can interact with the teacher in a collaborative learning logic. The studies conducted to evaluate the efficacy of this application are rather controversial. In some cases, the difficulty was found of "long-distance pupils" to maintain high attention levels in relation above all to the quality of the images; in addition, the users' satisfaction varies in relation to motivational factors and to previous experience (Kies *et al.*, 1996). If more systematic interaction between teachers and pupils is necessary, some difficulties are attributed to the problems of managing turn-taking and to the fact that it is not easy to send and receive feedback (attention, approval, etc.) about the communication in progress (Rettinger, 1995). Other studies show that long-distance teaching can lead to the same results as traditional teaching, and even that it develops pupils' autonomy (Robson *et al.*, 1991). It should be remembered, however, that videoconference teaching not only requires more commitment and attention from pupils, but also forces teachers to adapt their performance to a decidedly new interactive context (familiarization with the technology, optimization of timing and rhythm of the interaction, keeping pupils' attention, etc.).

A relatively recent application of the videoconference is telemedicine or telehealth (Nickelson, 1998), which means communicating via computer technologies to provide long-distance health services (diagnosis, treatment, consultancy, supervision, training). An interesting branch of telehealth is e-therapy (Castelnuovo *et al.*, 2001; Grohol, 1999), which includes strictly medical (e.g., telesurgery) and psychological (e.g., psychotherapy) applications (Castelnuovo *et al.*, 2001; Federico, 1999; Riva, 2001).

Some recent studies analyze the ways in which surgeons operate on a patient, connected in a videoconference both with an expert supervising the operation and with students learning surgical techniques; this highlights the strategy with which long-distance interlocutors share the "action space" in order to perform the operation correctly, but also to regulate the long-distance communication (Mondada, 2001a, 2001b).

The development of the videoconference has also produced applications in the mental health field. It is considered as a possible solution for providing services where direct (physical) contact between operators and patients may be problematic (Jerome and Zaylor, 2000). Various services may be provided in this way: consultations, diagnostic evaluations, and actual psychotherapeutic treatments. Patients show good acceptance of the videoconference as opposed to face-to-face encounters (Ghosh *et al.*, 1997).

The use of the videoconference in psychotherapy has already had positive results. Bouchard *et al.* (2000), for example, used the videoconference to subject patients suffering from PD (panic attack disorder) to cognitive behavioral therapy. The results were satisfying, even if patients may require a period of adaptation (Cook and Doyle, 2002).

The videoconference is also used in legal contexts. Performing court proceedings via videoconference avoids transferring the participants (defendants, witnesses, etc.) and the risks associated with it. This practice is already widespread in the USA, where, for example, there is a serious problem with defendants escaping during transfers; but this solution has also been used in Europe in particularly delicate cases (when defendants are considered to be particularly dangerous or in child abuse cases).

The largely positive considerations outlined above about the videoconference do, however, go against the fact that despite this means of communication having been available for several decades (since the 1970s, well before the internet), it has not been as successful as may have been expected, given the considerable investments in it.

The failure (or partial failure) of this type of long-distance communicative technology and strategy can be attributed to a multitude of factors, some of which are technical and others psychosocial. Some forecasts made in the 1970s about these new technologies suggested that within a decade the vast majority of meetings between institutions and organizations would take place via electronic means (Snyder, 1971). The available statistics, however, show a rather smaller-scale use of this means of communication. Videoconference systems became established and spread rather slowly only after the mid-1980s. Even after the advent of the internet, the development of videoconference systems was slowed by the difficulties in reaching the objective of taking into account all the needs and peculiarities of the different, numerous potential users (companies, enterprises, public institutions, scientific research centers, education/training institutions, etc.) by adapting the "videoconference product" to each of these. That is, it is not easy to design videoconference systems that meet the characteristics (organizational styles, decision-making processes, final uses, etc.) of the user, so as to guarantee full consistency with the communicative processes which the technology must actually serve. It has already been shown, for example, that the videoconference is more suitable for certain types of meetings than others. The introduction of the videoconference has not cut down the number of trips being made for meetings and appointments. In fact, paradoxically, numbers of face-to-face encounters have actually increased as a result of experiences in videoconference. It could be suggested that the long-distance videoconference is a stimulus; it arouses the curiosity and interest to arrange face-to-face meetings with one's interlocutors.

Another reason for the limited success of the videoconference is the lack of opportunity it provides for informal interaction, as it is well known that much significant information is exchanged and many important decisions taken during informal encounters (Mintzberg, 1973).

Laboratory tests have shown that when the long-distance communication by videoconference implies cooperative processes centered on relatively simple tasks, it is quite effective; however, when complex negotiations are in progress with interlocutors chasing contrasting objectives, videoconferences are more problematic (Williams, 1975, 1977). In this light, Egido (1990) maintains that in order to improve the efficacy of the videoconference, it is necessary to understand how this system modifies communicative processes and the working style of interlocutors. Improving the technological quality of the videoconference is not sufficient; we also need to understand the effects that it produces on people, on organizations, and on the interaction processes in which they are involved.

In any case, it is always useful to identify some problematic aspects that make interpersonal communication via the videoconference less than satisfying.

It is usually natural for participants to stare at the images of the interlocutors that appear on screen. As such, the gaze is not directed at the TV camera, thus disorienting the exchange of glances (e.g., eye contact) that is typical of face-to-face communication and that conveys important information and encourages synchronization of the exchanges. The most obvious effect of this phenomenon is a significant interference with the natural flow of communication. One possible solution to this problem may be a system where the TV camera and screen are in the same line, in order that when participants look at the screen, they are also looking at the TV camera.

During a conversation, the listener does not normally remain passive, but sends a multitude of feedback signals through the face, body movements, gestures, vocal signals, etc., in order that the speaker realize the level of comprehension and reactions of the interlocutor and modulate his or her behaviour accordingly. This exchange between the speaker and the listener is not wholly effective in a videoconference because the feedback signals are rather rapid and "subtle." The result is a partial loss of fluidity, and verbal or vocal signals can appear more frequently to replace those received via the visual channel, which are less accessible.

In face-to-face conversation, each participant regulates turn-taking in interpersonal exchanges via a multitude of strategies and signals (linguistic, paralinguistic, and intonational cues; direction of gaze; gestures; etc.); in a videoconference conversation, the regulation of turn-taking is more complex, generates more pauses and interruptions, and takes longer to convey the same amount of information as a face-to-face interaction.

During a conversation, the production and organization of body movements, and particularly gestures are closely related to the organization of the conversation. In particular, two categories of gestures can be observed: on the one hand, regulatory gestures aimed at maintaining the flow of conversation and facilitating turn-taking; on the other hand, co-verbal gestures that relate to the mental processes of the speaker and serve not only to represent shapes, objects, and actions (illustrators in the strict sense) but also to provide a punctuation system and represent more abstract characteristics of the conversation. The gestures that accompany speech are guided by the same control mechanism that organizes the conversation and perform a communicative function in that they add to and complete the information provided by speech, attracting the attention and facilitating the comprehension of the receiver. In a videoconference, as much for technical reasons (the amplitude of the TV camera field of vision) as for reasons associated with situational factors, both the quality and quantity of gestures are reduced; there is also a discrepancy between the transmission speed of audio information and video information (audio-video asynchrony), and movements are slowed such that they may make for an unpleasant "unnaturalness" in the interaction. This difficulty may interfere with the efficacy of the communication in exactly those situations, for example, when people of different cultures are interacting (see below), where interlocutors need as much information as possible in order to attain an acceptable degree of mutual comprehension.

Finally, a spatial factor should be pointed out regarding the organization of videoconferences involving several individuals in one or in both locations. The communication of the person occupying the center of the screen is more incisive and effective for the listener. To avoid these effects of spatial arrangement, which in face-to-face conversation are usually overcome thanks to the fact that the listener directs and centers his/her attention on whoever is speaking at the time, it is necessary either to use fixed shots that give equal emphasis to all persons present or prepare equipment that allows the shot to be systematically centered on the person currently speaking. This strategy, while also facilitating the possibility of exploring and getting to know the remote environment, further increases the sense of telepresence.

Intercultural implications (aspects) of nonverbal communication

Today's social reality leads to increasingly frequent interactions between individuals belonging to different cultures. Long-distance means of communication with new technologies, including textual and videocommunication via the internet, accentuate this tendency.

Encounters between people of different cultures are apparently not significantly different from those between individuals from the same culture; any difficulties or problems that occur in intercultural encounters can be considered as due to difficulties and problems inherent in interpersonal communication, verbal and nonverbal, as communicative processes in themselves represent an area of human behavior where considerable cultural differences can be encountered; in fact, precisely the observation of the interaction between individuals belonging to different cultures draws the attention and leads us to comprehend certain aspects of communicative processes that may otherwise be difficult to identify.

The verbal component of the interaction is clearly the most significant and important part of the encounter. It is relatively simple to grasp and understand cultural differences that distinguish verbal communication, as it is not difficult to recognize a language as "foreign"; it is not so easy to realize the differences, especially the more subtle ones, that concern aspects of nonverbal communication: vocal intonation, facial expression, gestures, posture, etc. It should also be noted that the difficulties and problems (incomprehension, misunderstandings, failures, etc.) encountered in intercultural exchanges should be put into relation with the rules, conventions, and habits that regulate and govern social interaction within various cultures and more markedly condition the use of nonverbal signals.

The expression of emotions and interpersonal attitudes, the means with which the spatial configuration of an encounter is structured (distance and orientation between speakers, posture, physical contact, etc.), gaze direction, and the way of implementing certain ritual behaviors (such as beginning and ending an encounter, or saying hello and goodbye) can throw up cultural differences and specificities that make the intercultural encounter more demanding. As mentioned, nonverbal signals transmit explicit and implicit messages and contribute to outlining the quality of the interpersonal relationship. It is therefore relevant that they are used consistently with social and cultural usages and expectations that the interlocutors adhere to. It is observed that nonverbal behavior consistent with cultural expectations is more effective and facilitates the interaction more than one's ethnic origins.

One difficulty emerges, for example, when a behavior felt to be adequate and effective in one culture can be considered inadequate, improper, or ineffective if evaluated in the light of shared behavioral usages, customs, and models in another culture.

Indeed, it is on the basis of certain beliefs, usages, and values shared within a certain culture that "social abilities" and therefore "socially competent and effective" individuals are identified. Cultural differences borne by numerous nonverbal signals have been highlighted that play an important role in face-to-face communication and that can therefore represent a source of misunderstanding and difficulty in interpersonal relations between individuals from different cultures.

The expression of emotions and interpersonal attitudes should be considered first of all. Systematic observation and experimental studies have highlighted the fact that although aspects universal and shared by humans do exist in emotional expression, differences can also be attributed to cultural specificity.

The well-known Ekman theory (1972) of neurocultural context in expressions of emotion attempts to distinguish between biologically determined expressive processes (neural facial affect program), which are activated at the same time as an emotive experience, and the intervention of culturally determined rules (cultural display rules) that are superimposed over expressive programs and modulate them, and that produce various consequences in individuals' behavior, determining variations that concern the expressive intensity (attenuation, intensification) as much as the emotional specificity of the expression (simulation, dissimulation, neutralization, etc.).

Numerous contributions (Matsumoto, 1990, 1991) have then attempted to explain the cultural influence on the expression of emotions, introducing a dimensional approach to the analysis of cultures on the pattern of Hofstede's model (1980, 1983), and also considering the typical dynamics of ingroup–outgroup processes.

Significant cultural differences, which considerably condition interpersonal perception, are also highlighted in the use of the direction of gaze and in particular eye contact (or mutual gaze) between the two interlocutors having a conversation.

It is observed, for example, that subjects belonging to Arab and Latin-American cultures use eye contact more frequently and for longer than northern European populations. Excessive eye contact can be viewed as "threatening," "insolent," or disrespectful; on the contrary, a person who avoids eye contact may be perceived as impolite, bored, or insincere.

In Europe, Latin-Mediterranean populations are very expressive and use a wide repertoire of gestures, whereas northern populations use a more limited range of gestures. But the difference lies not only in the quantity: The very meaning of some gestures may vary from culture to culture and cause incomprehension and misunderstandings. Pointing the index finger is, for example, considered impolite or rude in many Arab and Middle East countries (Morrison *et al.*, 1994), just as the thumbs up, used mainly in North America to mean "OK," can be taken as a sexual insult in Greece (Collett, 1982).

With regard to the spatial configuration adopted in social interaction, physical contact is more common in those cultures where physical closeness and a more delimited personal space are perceived (South American and Latin-American cultures). Thus, when subjects from "high-contact" and "low-contact" cultures meet, the former may appear intrusive or impolite, whereas the latter may appear cold and detached (Argyle, 1982). As for posture, cultural differences can be observed with regard to the fact of perceiving more "open" or "closed" body poses toward the interlocutor in public interaction (McGinley *et al.*, 1984). As has already been said, however, intercultural differences do not concern only the quantity and quality of the nonverbal signals, but also the rules and conventions that govern the social behavior, determine its meanings, and create the conditions for further difficulties in the interaction between individuals from different cultures.

The differences resulting from rules and conventions derive mainly from the values that distinguish various cultures. Of the four dimensions proposed by Hofstede (1980, 1983) for outlining the relational differences between cultures, individualism-collectivism and the power distance have often been considered to explain some important differences in behavioral styles in public interactions.

Individuals belonging to cultures with "high individualism" (North Americans, for example) prefer to adopt more explicit, direct behavior, talk loudly, and express even negative emotions if necessary, whereas collectivist cultures (Asian cultures, for example) prefer to maintain group harmony and avoid behavior that may break up the social cohesion; they always behave in a more controlled way, and less explicitly, and may thus appear to Westerners as rather inscrutable.

The differences also concern those behaviors that display the hierarchical or power subdivisions in social organization; in North American culture, individuals prefer to establish relationships on the same level, which are expressed in social interaction with rather informal communicative processes, whereas in cultures where a strong differentiation of social status and power exists (such as India, for example), people prefer forms of interaction that reflect and enhance status differences.

The picture that emerges from this brief overview of cultural differences in nonverbal communication in social interactions is considerably complex: if we maintain that, in any case, various difficulties can be shown in face-to-face interaction between individuals belonging to different cultures, these difficulties will be even more accentuated in situations such as a videoconference.

The technological constraints put in place by long-distance communication create, on the one hand, a more "artificial," less "easy-going" condition, but, on the other hand, can imply a loss of information that may accentuate the risk of incomprehension and failed communication. Nonetheless, this new opportunity to communicate long-distance with people from other cultures is a chance to overcome ethnic, racial, and cultural barriers.

It is understandable why many scholars place emphasis on the necessity to encourage all possible forms of "intercultural training" (Harrison, 1992; Landis, 1996; Ward et al., 2001) that favor the acquisition of specific skills to make communication more effective.

Getting to know and experiencing the differences that can occur in intercultural communication lessen the possibility of misunderstandings, reduce elements of dissatisfaction that characterize intercultural encounters, and favor sociocultural adaptation (Ward and Kennedy, 1999).

Conclusion

We can conclude our comments by stating that communication via videoconference represents the closest form of synchronous CMC to face-to-face communication; considering all the asynchronous forms of textual communication via the internet up to the videoconference, the latter certainly features the greatest number of characteristics of face-to-face conversation.

It is carried out in a situation that implies two typical elements of conversational processes: first, the participants' commitment to collaborate and the cooperation during the formulation of the message; second, the possibility of using feedback that allows the message to be processed immediately in terms of social meaning.

Communication via the videoconference also guarantees the identity of interacting subjects and implies a series of normative elements that ensure the efficacy of the interactive process. That is to say, it does not produce the typical "social void" found in textual CMC, where the personal identity of the other individuals involved tends to fade and even disappear, creating the conditions for impersonal, detached interactions. In this light, the videoconference, given that it transmits a considerable quantity of information, is able to sustain interpersonal relationships effectively, by exploiting a shared context that allows for mutual understanding.

When the videoconference is used for such purposes as collaborative work or teleteaching, it tends to reproduce, on a technological level, relationship and collaboration modalities similar to real life. The possibility of integrating further multimedia aspects into this work or study construct supported by the videoconference via the internet allows the involvement of various sensorial channels within a varied, complex communicative experience.

The videoconference via the internet therefore represents a new opportunity that opens new horizons in communication between people. In particular, this opportunity concerns the spatial aspects in terms of a "global network" that tends to do away with both the space that divides us and the time differences, encouraging communicative exchanges in real time; the power of the media used also allows a large quantity of data of any kind to be sent and received (text, sounds, icons).

A significant change is occurring which forces individuals to adapt habitual forms of communication, takes on considerable cultural relevance, and produces a significant impact on important social processes (in education, production, science, etc.).

References

Argyle, M. (1982). Intercultural communication. In S. Bochner (ed.), *Cultures in Contact: Studies in Cross-Cultural Interaction* (pp. 61–79). Oxford: Pergamon.

Bouchard, S., Payeur, R., Rivard, V., *et al.* (2000). Cognitive behaviour therapy for panic disorder with agoraphobia in videoconference: preliminary results. *Cyberpsychology and Behavior*, 3(6), 999–1007.

Castelnuovo, G., Gaggioli, A., and Riva, G. (2001). Cyberpsychology meets clinical psychology: the emergence of e-therapy in mental health care. In G. Riva and C. Galimberti (eds), *Towards Cyberpsychology: Mind, Cognition and Society in the Internet Age* (pp. 230–251). Amsterdam: IOS Press.

Collett, P. (1982). Meetings and misunderstandings. In S. Bochner (ed.), *Cultures in Contact: Studies in Cross-Cultural Interaction* (pp. 81–98). Oxford: Pergamon.

Cook, J. E. and Doyle, C. (2002). Working alliance in online therapy as compared to face-to-face therapy: preliminary results. *Cyberpsychology and Behavior*, **5**(2), 95–105.

Egido, C. (1990). Teleconferencing as a technology to support cooperative work: its possibilities and limitations. In J. Calegher, R. E. Kraut, and C. Egido (eds), *Intellectual Team Work: Social and Technological Foundations of Cooperative Work* (pp. 351–371). Hillsdale, NJ: Erlbaum.

Ekman, P. (1972). Universals and cultural differences in facial expressions of emotions. In J. Cole (ed.), *Nebraska Symposium on Motivation, 1971*, vol. 19, (pp. 207–283). Lincoln, NE: University of Nebraska Press.

Federico, P. A. (1999). Hypermedia environments and adaptive instructions. *Computers in Human Behavior*, **15**(6), 653–692.

Ghosh, G. J., McLaren, P. M., and Watson, J. P. (1997). Evaluating the alliance in video-link teletherapy. *Journal of Telemedicine and Telecare*, **3**, 33–35.

Grohol, J. M. (1999). Best practices in e-therapy. http://psychcentral.com/best/best3.htm.

Harrison, J. K. (1992). Individual and combined effects of behavior modelling and the culture assimilator in cross-cultural management training. *Journal of Applied Psychology*, **3**, 431–460.

Hofstede, G. (1980). *Culture's Consequences*. Beverly Hills, CA: Sage.

(1983). Dimensions of national cultures in fifty countries and three regions. In J. Deregowsky, S. Dziurawiec, and R. Annis (eds), *Explications in Cross-Cultural Psychology* (pp. 335–355). Lisse, The Netherlands: Swets & Zeitlinger.

Jerome, L. W. and Zaylor, C. (2000). Cyberspace: creating a therapeutic environment for telehealth applications. *Professional Psychology: Research and Practice*, **31**, 478–483.

Kies, J. K., Williges, R. C., and Rosson, M. B. (1996). *Controlled Laboratory Experimentation and Field Study Evaluation of Video Conferencing for Distance Learning Applications*. HCIL Hypermedia Technical Report HCIL-96–02. Human–Computer Interaction Laboratory, Department of Industrial and Systems Engineering, Virginia Polytechnic Institute and State University, Blacksburg, VA.

Landis, D. (1996). A model of intercultural training and behaviour. In D. Landis and R. Bhagat (eds), *Handbook of Intercultural Training* (2nd edn., pp. 1–13). Thousand Oaks, CA: Sage.

Matsumoto, D. (1990). Cultural similarities and differences in display rules. *Motivation and Emotion*, **14**, 195–214.

(1991). Cultural influences on facial expressions of emotion. *Southern Communication Journal*, **56**, 128–137.

McGinley, H., Blau, G. L., and Takay, M. (1984). Attraction effects of smiling and body position. *Perceptual and Motor Skills*, **58**, 915–922.

Mintzberg, J. (1973). *The Nature of Managerial Work*. New York: Harper & Row.

Mondada, L. (2001a). Intervenir à distance dans une operation chirurgicale: l'organisation interactive d'espaces de participation. *Bulletin Suisse de Linguistique Appliquée*, **74**, 33–56.

(2001b). Operating together through videoconference: members' procedures accomplishing a common space of action. *Proceedings of II EMCA Conference, Orders of Ordinary Action*, Manchester, July 9–11, 2001.

Morrison, T., Conaway, W. A., and Borden, G. A. (1994). *Kiss, Bow or Shake Hands: How to Do Business in 60 Countries*. Holbrook, MA: Adams Media.

Muhlbach, L., Bocker, M., and Prussog, A. (1995). Telepresence in videocommunication: a study on stereoscopy and individual eye contact. *Human Factors*, **37**(2), 290–305.

Newhagen, J. E. (1996). Why communication researchers should study the internet. A dialogue. *Journal of Communication*, **46**(1), 4–13.

Nickelson, D. (1998). Telehealth and the evolving health care system: strategic opportunities for professional psychology. *Professional Psychology: Research and Practice*, **29**, 527–535.

Olson, J. S., Olson, G. M., and Meader, D. K. (1995). What mix of video and audio is useful for small groups doing remote real-time design work? *Proceedings of CHI 1995, ACM Conference on Human Factors in Software*, pp. 362–368.

Rettinger, L. A. (1995). Desktop Videoconferencing: Technology and Use for Remote Seminars Delivery. Master's thesis, North Carolina State University, Raleigh, NC. http://pvprm.zesoi.fer.hr/1998-99-web/literatura/DVC4seminar.pdf.

Riva, G. (2001). Shared hypermedia: communication and interaction in web-based learning environments. *Journal of Educational Computing Research*, **25** (3), 205–226.

Robson, J., Routcliffe, P., and Fitzgerald, R. (1991). *Remote Schooling and Information Technology*. Canberra: Australian Catholic University.

Short, J., Wiliams, E., and Christie, B. (1976). *The Social Psychology of Telecommunication*. London: Wiley.

Snyder, F. W. (1971). *Travel Patterns: Implications for New Communication Facilities*. Bell Laboratories Memorandum.

Sproull, L. and Kiesler, S. (1986). Reducing social context cues: electronic mail in organizational communication. *Organizational Behavior and Human Decision Processes*, **37**, 157–187.

Ward, C., Bochner, S., and Furnham, A. (2001). *The Psychology of Culture Shock*. London: Routledge.

Ward, C. and Kennedy, A. (1999). The measurement of sociocultural adaptation. *International Journal of Intercultural Relation*, **56**, 1–19.

Williams, E. (1975). Medium or message: communications medium as determinant of interpersonal evaluation. *Sociometry*, **38**, 119–130.

(1977). Experimental comparisons of face to face and mediated communication: a review. *Psychological Bulletin*, **84**, 963–976.

CHAPTER 5

Video-linking emotions

Brian Parkinson and Martin Lea

Overview: How does video mediation influence communication of affective information? In the present chapter, we review the range of possible constraints associated with the video medium and consider their potential impact on transmission and coordination of emotions. In particular, we focus on the effects of transmission delays on interpersonal attunement. Results of a preliminary investigation of this issue are described. In the study, pairs of participants discussed liked and disliked celebrities via a desktop videoconferencing system. In one condition, the system was set up in its normal mode, producing a transmission delay of approximately 200 ms (high delay). In the other condition, transmission was close to instantaneous (low delay). Dependent measures included evaluative ratings of the celebrities and of the other party in the conversation and video-cued momentary codings of the interaction. Participants rated the extent of communication difficulties as greater in the normal than in the low-delay condition, but did not specifically focus on delay itself as the source of the problem. Low-delay pairs also showed greater accuracy and lower bias in their momentary ratings of attunement and involvement over the course of the conversation. Finally, there was greater convergence of affect when participants discussed mutually disliked celebrities, but greater divergence of affect when they were talking about celebrities liked by one party to the conversation but disliked by the other. These results are consistent with the view that the immediate interpersonal feedback provided by facial expressions facilitates the development of mutual rapport when attitudes are convergent, and may also facilitate nonverbal interpersonal influence when attitudes are discrepant. However, in another study in which interactants were friends rather than strangers, greater delay tended to result in amusement rather than lack of rapport, perhaps because of the attempted implementations of interaction repair strategies. The chapter concludes by arguing that the emotional consequences of using video-mediated communication (VMC) merit further research attention in order to complement the predominantly cognitive and performance-based focus of most previous studies of videoconferencing.

Theoretical background

How do we get someone to do something? Before beginning to answer such a question we would need to know much more about the specific nature of the situation. The first set of considerations relates to where we currently stand in relation to the other person (both physically and in terms of our respective roles, power differentials, and so on). There are obvious problems in exerting influence at a distance or when there are barriers between people (e.g., Parkinson, 2001). The second set of relevant considerations concerns the technical resources at our disposal for exerting interpersonal leverage. Of particular relevance to the present chapter are the means of communication that we can use to get our message across. As a general principle, we might suppose that the closer we are to the other person and the more resources we can draw on, the more impact we should have on the other person's actions (e.g., Rutter, 1987; Short *et al.*, 1976). However, remoteness and anonymity can also affect the relative salience of personal and social identity, and this factor may moderate or counteract this general tendency under many circumstances (e.g., Lea and Spears, 1991).

Many emotions may be seen as ways of getting someone else to do something (e.g., Parkinson, 1996). Someone gets angry with someone else to encourage that second someone to back down or apologize; people are frightened partly because their fear may encourage others to help them or go easier on them. Similarly, Fridlund (1994) has argued that facial movements are not expressions of pre-existing emotions but rather communications to particular real or imagined addressees and intended to influence their behavior (see Manstead, Lea, and Goh, this volume; Parkinson, 2005). For example, smiles may not be simple expressions of happiness but rather signals to others that one is ready to cooperate, play, or agree. From this perspective, the operation of some emotion presentations, like interpersonal influence attempts more generally, must depend on relative interpersonal location and available resources. In this chapter, we shall explore some of the implications of such an approach for understanding the impact of communication technologies on interpersonal affect.

For many readers, viewing emotions as strategic may seem to underestimate their apparently involuntary character. Further, the argument brings the unwanted implication that their causation derives from wholly individualized processes. To deal with these problems, we want to propose that strategic emotions derive developmentally from more implicit tactical adjustments operating between people rather than within each separable individual (cf. de Rivera, 1977). When emotion operates in this less articulated manner, relations are reconfigured as a function of interpersonally distributed cognition and emotion. Adult emotions represent variable combinations of these implicit and explicit interpersonal or individual processes (see also Parkinson *et al.*, 2005).

For example, work on caregiver–infant interaction suggests that humans are equipped to engage in communicative imitation from a very early age (e.g., Nagy and Molnár, 2004), and that they soon come to use specific emotion-like facial and postural adjustments to encourage or discourage another's attention (e.g., Reddy, 2000). Similarly, in adults, Kendon's (1973) careful observations of social interactions suggested that patterned and interpersonally attuned dynamic movements can serve to make or break contact with others, to signal readiness for conversational interruption, demonstrate mutual attentiveness to a common object, and so on. In our view, emotions represent a subset of these dynamic patterns of relation alignment, and apprehension of their conventional meaning within any given culture allows interactants to deploy them in the service of specific interpersonal projects. Thus, implicit modes of adjusting relative interactional positions become articulated and available for strategic deployment.

This chapter covers the effects of communication technology on both varieties of emotional process: the strategic and the tactical. In particular, we want to demonstrate how the technical characteristics of the medium of contact can alter the process of affective influence and the establishment of rapport. None of this should be taken to imply that psychological functioning is determined by the characteristics of technology. However, the tactics and strategies that are available for use partly depend on what there is to work with. People adjust their conduct to take account of what they can use.

Specific characteristics of video-mediated communication

The particular focus of this chapter is on video-mediated communication (VMC), wherein people engage in conversation remotely, using audio as well as visual channels. Perhaps the most familiar contemporary implementation is a Skype video chat across the internet. At first sight, it might appear that interacting with someone by this medium is very similar to interacting with someone face-to-face (FTF). However, a number of differences are apparent on closer consideration (see also other chapters of this volume). In this section, we catalog these differences, highlighting those that have been studied by previous investigators as well as those that have attracted less research attention. Some of the identified differences between VMC and FTF reflect necessary consequences of using these communication media, whereas others relate to potentially alterable features. Indeed, the ways in which VMC technology is currently used do not exhaust its possible implementations. Thus there may be technical as well as psychological solutions to some of its potential problems.

Restriction of movement and orientation
The use of a fixed camera in VMC means that interactants have to stay relatively still in order to be visible to each other. An alternative, more positive way of framing this characteristic of the medium as currently implemented, would be to say that users may have relatively more control over their mutual visibility. In either case, this fact tends to mean that interactants are unlikely to respond in the same way to cues relating to interpersonal distance when interacting via a VMC system. For example, Argyle and Dean (1965) imply that people regulate intimacy levels by choosing the distance at which they stand from one another. The removal of this possibility may mean that people interacting by video may resort to other means of adjusting their mutual psychological distance (cf. Patterson, 1996), both nonverbal (e.g., gestures, facial movements, vocal tone and speed, etc.) and verbal. If the cameras provide close-up images of the other person's face, this may produce a greater sense of immediacy and intimacy than is appropriate to interactants' current relationship (cf. Hall, 1966). Users may therefore seek to compensate by increasing social distance in other ways such as discussing less personal topics. Paradoxically, one consequence may be that VMC produces less intimacy than text-based or audio-only communication, because, in the latter cases, interactants may seek to increase rather than decrease the emotional relevance of the conversation itself when fewer alternative cues are available (see also Walther, Chapter 1, this volume). However, another possible response to apparent physical proximity is that interactants use the implied intimacy cues as a reference point, and adjust their conversation to match the perceived situational requirements.

Turning from interpersonal distance to orientation, most VMC inter-actions are conducted with users seeing a full-on visual image of the other's face on the monitor, thus simulating a FTF interaction in which participants face each other. Sommer's (1965) research suggests that this arrangement is more characteristic of competitive than coopera-tive interactions. When people are conversing or working together on a task, they tend to sit side-by-side or diagonally so that they can turn their head by less then 90 degrees in order to engage with the other. Thus, the usual implementation of videoconferencing may undermine the affiliative orientation of everyday interactions. However, there are obvious exceptions to the rule that FTF positioning implies competitiveness. For example, dating couples tend to sit opposite one another in a restaurant. Thus, interpretations of the implications of interpersonal orientations are likely to be flexible and context-specific.

Orientational movements as well as arrangements also take on a different quality in VMC. For example, gestures or sensory alignments directed either toward the other or at objects of common interest may be less visible or less possible when one remains fixed in a certain position. For example, leaning toward someone or something can convey something about future action and intention (cf. Fridlund, 1994) but may not carry the same weight when the signal is conveyed via a video channel. More generally, direction of attention as controlled by orientation of sensory organs cannot be altered to the same extent and does not convey the same information when the sender remains rooted to the spot (see also section "Being there," below).

Some of these effects are potentially alterable by using moving instead of static cameras. However, it is hard to envisage a future in which steadicam-style video signals are transmitted continuously as people go about their everyday business, moving from location to location. Indeed, such developments may sound rather undesirable anyway.

Sensory information
Although we are sometimes inclined to see life as a movie (or movies as real life), in fact the patterns of sight and sound that are transmitted by VMC technology differ from the sensory information sent and received in FTF encounters in several ways. The first and most obvious of these differences concerns the fact that some channels of sensory information go missing. Unless provided with scratch-and-sniff cards, we do not receive olfactory signals from the other when using VMC. Of course, this may be either a good or a bad thing. Similarly, we are unable to reach out and touch the other person directly even if provided with a virtual reality body suit equipped with appropriate transceivers. Some psychologists believe that subtle signals are transmitted through the olfactory channel (e.g., McCoy and Pitino, 2002). Regardless of the impact of such odors, it is certainly true that many people use manufactured scents to aid their self-presentations. Further, it is commonly accepted that holding someone's hand, kissing, or hugging carry emotional implications for people's interactions. For both of these reasons, the absence of sensory information beyond that

provided by visual and auditory channels is likely to make some difference to our emotional engagement with other people.

Even the sensory channels that are included in VMC may differ in several respects from their counterparts in everyday FTF conversations. The video screen provides a 2D display that does not usually provide perfect resolution, and the size of the picture may be either smaller or larger than the actual objects depicted. Although extreme close-ups may be available, it is not usually feasible to lean forward to get a different perspective on what one is looking at (see previous section). Control over camera angle and distance is limited in most contemporary systems, and even the incorporation of eye-movement-based adjustment does not yet fully match the dependence of what we normally see on the changing orientation of our sensory organs. Even greater problems are involved in devising systems that respond to how we move in relation to other people or objects of common attention.

Similar considerations also apply to audio channels. These may lack fidelity, and even full surround sound provides an imperfect representation of the localization of sounds and their correspondence to visually perceived objects. Tight modulation of volume may also be hard to achieve.

Most VMC systems are configured to provide full-face shots of the other person, and therefore explicitly exclude signals from other parts of the body, some of which may help to punctuate conversation (e.g., Goodwin, 1980, 1981; Kendon, 1967), contribute to the development of interpersonal rhythms as relationships unfold (e.g., Grammer *et al.*, 1998), or reveal a hidden emotion when it "leaks out" (e.g., Ekman and Friesen, 1969).

Other things, too, happen outside the frame of the video-screen during VMC. For example, the user's current affect may be partly shaped by something physically present but off-screen, to which verbal or nonverbal reference may be made. The receiver's lack of visual access to such an object or event means that the sender's attitude to it attains a different kind of significance or is relatively more ambiguous than it would otherwise be. Thus, social referencing whereby two parties calibrate their emotional responses to an object of mutual attention (e.g., Sorce *et al.*, 1985) may sometimes have a greater impact on appraisal of current events in VMC than FTF. Interactions may also be disturbed by "noises off" that have no direct bearing on the conversation but whose irrelevance may be less obvious to the person at the other end of the connection.

Although we have focused on the apparent limitations of the medium, VMC can also supplement the information that is normally available in FTF encounters. For example, it is possible to include users' own faces as well as those of their interaction partners on the screen, thus permitting careful self-monitoring of nonverbal presentation. Of course, whether the exertion of explicit control over what we show helps or hinders the process of interaction is by no means certain (e.g., Patterson, 1996). Morphing and animation software even potentially allow adjustment of one's visual or auditory image, subtly enhancing attractiveness or, in the extreme case, using avatars as idealized representatives of the self (e.g., Bente and Krämer, Chapter 8, this volume; Broglio and Guynup, 2003). Similarly, real or virtual objects of mutual interest may be displayed in ways that would not be normally possible (e.g., Brittan, 1992). The user may often select the perspective required and the degree of close-up.

Finally, even the apparent limitations of the medium may be exploited to the advantage of the user. For instance, sometimes it suits our purposes to restrict access to certain aspects of our presentation (Daft and Lengel, 1984; Markus, 1994; and see below), as happens when we use the telephone because we do not want the other person to sense the disapproval that might otherwise show on our face (or to notice that none of our smart clothes are clean enough to wear). Indeed, the presence of an attention-demanding visual signal may under some circumstances distract people from the content of the verbal information that is being exchanged (e.g., Matarazzo and Sellen, 2000; Short *et al.*, 1976).

Temporal parameters

Although virtually instantaneous transmission of video signals is now possible, many commonly used desktop VMC systems still have relatively low temporal resolution. Although the typical screen-refresh rate of computer monitors is 60 Hz or above, the frame rate of video systems is much lower (half the screen refresh rate under optimal circumstances but usually lower in practice). Often frames are lost during transmission due to bandwidth and processing limitations, introducing a jerky quality to the visual image. Any use of compression–decompression routines will also introduce a slight delay in transmitting the signal from one PC to another. Finally, synchronization of sound and vision is sometimes imperfect. All of these temporal factors may have an impact on the communication process.

Bruce (1996) speculates that slow VMC frame rates may reduce the discernibility of micro-expressions. Indeed, codecs (compression–decompression hardware or software) systematically delete frames containing small movement transitions in order to smooth out an otherwise jerky image. Some of these frames may be precisely those where a micro-expression occurred. It is therefore possible that inter-actants miss subtle cues of emotion when using VMC. Although people may not usually explicitly register these putative brief flashes of anger, contempt, suppressed happiness, or whatever (e.g., Ekman, 2001), it is still possible that their absence makes an implicit difference to social perceivers.

The jerkiness of the video image in some VMC systems may also lead to apparently sudden transitions between facial expressions that would have been smoother in FTF interaction. It is possible that this might sometimes lead to the impression of a micro-expression even when none had actually occurred. However, the significance and emotional meaning of these "leaked" movements is debatable (e.g., Fridlund, 1994). Excluding micro-expressions, the specific dynamic timing of facial movements may be sufficiently altered by some VMC systems to make a difference (Bruce, 1996).

Tang and Isaacs (1992) found that users prefer sound to be unde-layed even at the expense of losing its synchronization with visual signals in VMC. By contrast, other researchers (e.g., Bruce, 1996) have argued that speech perception is improved when sound and vision are synchronized even when there is a small delay in both. However, the introduction of a delay may bring unwanted effects for other aspects of interpersonal function.

One emotionally relevant temporal factor concerns the online attu-nement of nonverbal signals. Chartrand and Bargh (1999) provided experimental evidence of a "chameleon effect," whereby interactants automatically mimic specific nonverbal behaviors, especially if they are prone to perspective taking. Further, Chartrand and Bargh dem-onstrate that mirroring another person's movements results in smoother interaction and greater liking for the other person. It also seems to be the case that precisely matching the timing of the other can contribute to the development of shared affect. For example, Bernieri and Rosenthal (1991) have suggested that FTF interactants may estab-lish rapport by implicitly synchronizing their gestures and expressions with one another. Under these circumstances, the sensitivity of mutual attunement can be within a time frame of 50 ms (Condon, 1982), which is below the frame rate of many VMC setups. It seems likely therefore that the interpersonal processes for developing mutual rapport may operate differently in some kinds of remote communication.

Interactants may also rely on direct nonverbal feedback as a way of tracking the interpersonal impact of their messages. For example, a sender may intensify the display of enthusiasm whenever the receiver's attention seems to be drifting. Such processes, too, may operate implicitly and within very tight time frames. If interpersonal feedback is delayed, then the sender's nonverbal conduct will be attuned to the receiver's reaction to a momentarily earlier presentation, and the sender may have unduly intensified the display before registering the receiver's response. Clearly, such a process might undermine the success of the influence attempt because the respective presentations are sometimes misattuned or exaggerated.

To take a more directly emotional example, expressions of disapproval are normatively followed either by apology or acknowledgment of guilt, and any apparent delay in providing the appropriate interpersonal feedback may provoke intensified displays conveying irritation or anger (cf. Kiesler *et al.*, 1984). In other words, a sender may escalate the expression of anger if the message doesn't seem to be getting through to the receiver (Parkinson, 2001). To the extent that the required acknowledgment or appeasement feedback was already forthcoming (but not yet received because of transmission delay), such expressions may be read by their target as disproportionate, thus provoking retaliatory rather than mollifying responses. These responses in turn may evoke increasingly hostile responses from the initial sender. Such failures of interpersonal negotiation may lead to escalations in negatively toned nonverbal exchanges in a kind of vicious cycle.

Evidence that emotional displays are adjusted online to meet the demands of the communicative context has been provided by Bavelas *et al.* (1986), who showed how empathic winces of pain are precisely timed to coincide with eye contact from a person suffering a staged accident. Similarly, but on a broader time scale, Leary *et al.* (1996) have demonstrated that embarrassment continues to be expressed until its interpersonal function is fulfilled (when its face-saving message is known to have been received by the relevant addressee). In our view, dynamic attunement to addressees is a central feature of emotion presentations more generally, and the traditional emphasis on "expression" of private emotional meanings is overrestrictive when investigating communication in its everyday interpersonal and dynamic context (Parkinson, 1996, 2005).

In summary, antagonism, complementarity, and matching of emotional stances may operate differently when VMC systems with low temporal resolution are used. The study reported later in this chapter addresses some of these issues.

Being there

Many discussions of mediated communication have argued that different media vary in the range and extent of cues that can be transmitted from person to person (e.g., Rutter, 1987), or relatedly in the level of social presence that they afford (Short *et al.*, 1976). More recent discussions of virtual reality and embodiment have considered a more general notion of "presence" that includes the sense of unmediated perception of a remote physical as well as interpersonal environment (Lombard and Ditton, 1997). Such experiences of being somewhere other than the place where you are physically located are not new. Immersion in dreams, books, photographs, films, and so on is familiar to most of us. However, some commentators want to claim that new technology may ultimately offer something beyond this, an extended embodiment that allows direct registration of events occurring in cyberspace (see Biocca, 1997, 2001; Biocca and Nowak, 2001). The idea is that duplication of the active ingredients of the dynamic stimulus array may permit the perfect simulation of real perceptual experience in an actively negotiated physical environment. Although it is certainly possible that certain aspects of our everyday awareness of reality may be reproduced in this way, the resulting virtual world is unlikely to share all the features of the one that we normally inhabit. Perhaps the hardest kind of presence to recreate is social and emotional presence.

Perhaps the most obvious difference between FTF and VMC interactions is that people are physically co-present in the former but not in the latter. They share the same space and breathe the same air. This sense of being there together cannot entirely be reduced to differences in sensory stimulation. It is not simply that you can see the whole other person, orient your attention online to mutually accessible objects (e.g., Watts *et al.*, 1996), absorb the same smells, reach out and touch one another, and so on. It is also the fact that whatever you do carries direct consequences in the here-and-now for what the other person is doing, thinking and feeling. You could leave the location together or separately, the trajectories of your respective actions are for a time intimately interlinked.

Even the most elaborate virtual reality system seems incapable of reproducing this experience in all its aspects, including the histories of arriving and the future possibilities of leaving. Indeed, an argument might be made that VMC systems should not attempt to duplicate FTF experience but rather facilitate their own partially independent styles of relating to others (Lea and Giordano, 1997).

What difference does VMC make?

Despite its potential for supplementing normally available information, generally speaking, VMC is a more restricted medium than FTF with regard to sensory channels, temporal characteristics, and actual co-presence. The most obvious implications of its use, therefore, would be in terms of how the absences implied by remote communication interfere with, or otherwise disrupt, the normal processes of FTF interaction. Accordingly, Rutter (1987) argued that the cue limitations characterizing a medium (or its lack of "richness" or social presence, Daft and Lengel, 1994; Short *et al.*, 1976, see also Walther, Chapter 1, this volume) bring relatively direct negative consequences for the quality of interaction processes.

However, other commentators resist the implicit technological determinism of such a view, arguing that the impact of CMC depends on the context of its use. For example, Lea and Spears (1991) argue that normative behavior may be enhanced rather than reduced when social identity is made salient in internet conversations (see also Walther, this volume).

Although users may be influenced by organizational norms about the appropriateness of certain kinds of communication media for specific tasks (e.g., Fulk *et al.*, 1987), they also make their selection according to more strategic considerations. In particular, the perception that different communication channels work better for certain purposes may be based on personal experience in combination with received opinion (e.g. Markus, 1994; see Joinson, 2003 for an extensive review of these views). Finally, it is possible that users will learn to adapt to the characteristics of the medium (e.g., Isaacs and Tang, 1994), developing coping strategies that compensate for any initial deficiencies.

When and how do users' strategies override or compensate for the practical constraints of communication media? Certainly, not all aspects of VMC operate identically across all possible social and physical contexts. However, some of the affordances (e.g., Gibson, 1979) of the objects that we work with have direct and inescapable implications once we confront them. It is impossible, in principle, for example, to respond to interpersonal feedback that has not yet arrived. Of course, this does not mean that people cannot decide to avoid certain media because of their limitations, or even to exploit these limitations to their own advantage. But if some of these disadvantages are not consciously registered in the first instance, adjusting to them may require more intellectual time and effort. If the establishment of mutual rhythms of nonverbal interaction operates implicitly and outside awareness, it seems unlikely that we can directly correct for its absence. Nevertheless, our sense that something is missing may ultimately lead (by trial and error or otherwise) to the development of strategies that compensate even for something we did not realize was lacking.

Effects of transmission delay on interpersonal affect

In a study conducted at Brunel University (in collaboration with Nicola Start and Terry Davidson), we tested some of these ideas concerning the impact of transmission delay on interpersonal affect. An earlier study conducted by O'Malley and colleagues (1996) had already provided promising evidence that delay can influence inter-action. Their focus was on performance on a jointly attempted cogni-tive task (the map task). It was found that solution of this problem was more successful when immediate visual feedback was forthcoming in the low-delay condition. Part of this effect seems to have depended on the fact that conversational turn-taking was disrupted by the mis-timing of vocal and nonverbal signals.

From the present perspective, this earlier experiment had two basic limitations. First, the manipulation of delay was confounded with the characteristics of the technology used in the conditions that were compared. In particular, the low-delay condition used a higher-quality closed-circuit television system, whereas the high-delay condition used a "videophone" with relatively small screen size. It may be, therefore, that relatively poorer performance in the high-delay condi-tion arose not from delay per se, but from other limitations of the communication system (e.g., reduced social cues). Second and more importantly, there was no consideration of the possible emotional effects of transmission delay.

The current study deals with both of these issues. In particular, we wanted to test whether delayed interpersonal feedback interfered with the development of interpersonal rapport for the reasons outlined in the previous section. Our contention in this regard was that mutual attunement of dynamic nonverbal signaling would be disrupted if interpersonal cues were delayed even slightly. Second, if nonverbal presentations serve the emotional purpose of influencing the other's developing attitude online, then any delay in feedback should desynchronize feedback, leading to mistimed and wrongly targeted displays.

Method

In our study, 21 pairs of same-sexed participants who met for the first time in our laboratory conversed with one another from separate rooms using a desktop videoconferencing system (MeetingPoint 3.0 running on two PCs with webcams positioned on top of 17-inch color monitors and separate stick microphones; see Figure 5.1). Previous experience of VMC use among this sample was minimal, and many

Figure 5.1 Videoconferencing setup.

participants were fascinated to see how and how well the technology worked. In the low-delay condition, the camera for each PC was plugged directly in the back of the other participant's PC and the "view self" function was selected, using the software. This allowed simulation of videoconferencing but bypassed the usual compression–decompression routine, yielding a relatively short transmission delay (low-delay condition). In the high-delay condition, the conferencing system was run in its normal mode, producing a small but still barely noticeable lag (approximately 0.2 s) between the transmission and reception of any signal.

At the beginning of the procedure, participants were asked separately to rate their liking for 50 different celebrities. The experimenter then selected two of these celebrities to be the topic of discussion in separate 5-minute conversations via VMC. The discussed celebrities were selected on the basis of participants' ratings. One was disliked equally by both participants, and the other was liked by one of them, but disliked by the other. The intention of this agreement–disagreement manipulation was to assess the effects of lag on complementary as opposed to contrasting affect.

We used a range of measures to assess the impact of transmission delay. Participants rated the characteristics of the communication medium, and the extent to which they felt in tune with one another during the interaction, and their affect. Some of these measures were collected by a video-cued recall procedure (Gottmann and Levenson, 1985). This involved replaying a 2-min video excerpt from each conversation, and asking participants to make ratings of what they had been experiencing at various points during the original interaction. The experimenter stopped the tape every 10 s to allow participants to make these ratings. Our predictions were that increased transmission delay would lead to more negative judgments of the communication medium, more polarized affect in the disagreement condition, and lower levels of rapport throughout the procedure.

Results

Transmission delay had a number of effects on the various measures that we employed. In general, participants in the high-delay condition rated the characteristics of the medium in more negative terms (Figure 5.2). This effect applied even to factors that were apparently identical across the two conditions. Indeed, the lack of eye contact was thought to be more of a problem in the high-delay than in the low-delay condition, even though camera position made eye contact impossible across both. However, it might be argued that transmission delay made the lack of eye contact more noticeable because other speakers did not seem engaged in matters reflecting the conversation's common ground (Clark and Brennan, 1991) due to the momentary delay in nonverbal feedback. Relatedly, interactants may specifically seek out eye contact at moments when engagement is in doubt, and these may have been more frequent in the high-delay condition, making the absence of eye contact more noticeable.

In fact, the ratings of transmission lag in particular did not differ significantly between high-delay and low-delay conditions, suggesting that high-delay participants sensed that something was wrong with the interaction but could not always explicitly say what it was. The fact that an apparently underdetected transmission delay had an impact on other affect-related dependent variables seems to rule out any interpretation of our other findings based on demand characteristics.

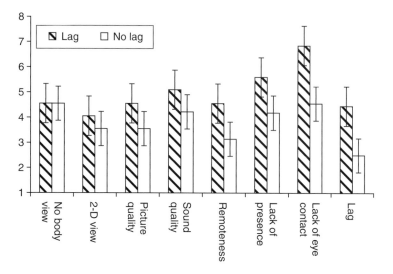

Figure 5.2 Rated extent of communication difficulties.

We next analyzed participants' perceptions of how much they felt "in tune" with the other participant (attunement) and how involved they felt in the conversation (involvement) as rated at 10-s intervals in the video-cued recall procedure. Mean scores were computed for each participant for each of the delay conditions. Ratings of attunement and involvement were significantly reduced by transmission delay. However, in both cases, the effect was stronger for the disagreement than the agreement conversation (Figure 5.3). In other words, lacking immediate interpersonal feedback seems to result in greater disengagement from interaction when a person does not share the other's opinion about a topic. This finding suggests that lag is more disruptive of interpersonal influence processes than processes underlying the establishment of mutual rapport.

Another interesting issue concerned the correspondence of feelings of rapport between interaction partners. If the sense of attunement and involvement is one-sided, this can lead to a failure of communication. Conceivably the fact that signals from the other party to an exchange are arriving too late may lead to sensing rapport when none is actually present (based on illusory correlations, for example; cf. Chapman and Chapman, 1967) or to not noticing attunement of the other person's responses when they are in fact reacting to you (but evidence of their reaction arrives too late for your purposes). For these reasons, we expected mutual rapport to be lower in high- than low-delay conditions.

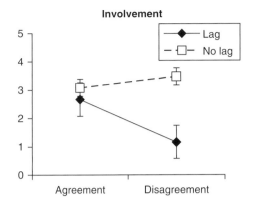

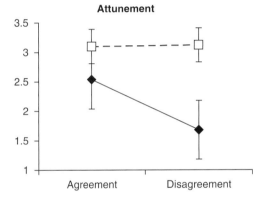

Figure 5.3 Mean ratings of involvement and attunement based on video-cued recall.

We calculated correspondence of rapport ratings during the video-cued recall procedure in two ways. First, we computed the difference between interactants' attunement and involvement scores at each 10-s interval and averaged these differences for each pair of participants. This procedure provides a crude index of the discrepancy between ratings over the dialog, usually referred to in the relationships literature as "bias" (e.g., Gagne and Lydon, 2004). Second, we computed correlations between the attunement and involvement ratings of interaction partners across all 10-s intervals for each pair. This procedure gives an estimate of the extent to which variations in attunement and involvement correspond over time between parties to an exchange (usually referred to as "accuracy"; see Gagne and Lydon, 2004).

The low-delay condition yielded closer correspondence of attunement and involvement ratings across measures of both accuracy and

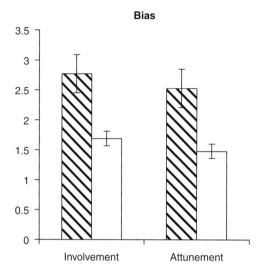

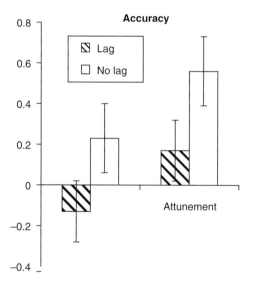

Figure 5.4 Mean correspondence of interaction partners' involvement and attunement ratings from video-cued recall procedure.

bias (Figure 5.4). Not only did participants rate their rapport at more similar levels to each other throughout their interaction in the low-delay condition (bias), but also the variations in perceived rapport tended to be more closely correlated (accuracy). Effects of transmission

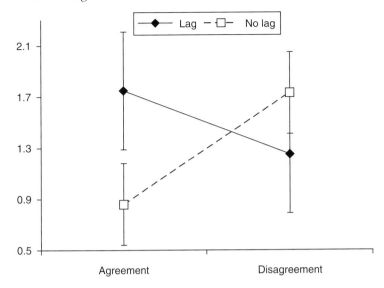

Figure 5.5 Mean discrepancy between interaction partners' happiness ratings.

delay on rapport therefore seem to operate at an interactional as well as an individual level. Attunement and involvement are more discrepant as well as generally lower across interactants when lags are longer.

A final issue concerns the effects of transmission delay on reported affect. Unlike attunement and involvement ratings, the levels of reported affect were relatively unaffected by transmission delay, although participants generally reported being happier in the agreement than in the disagreement condition. However, analysis of the correspondence between interaction partners' ratings of how happy they were feeling revealed an interesting pattern. Again, scores were based on the discrepancy between the affect ratings of parties to each conversation at every recorded 10-s interval (bias). When these scores were compared across delay and agreement conditions, we obtained a significant interaction effect, showing that high delay increased the difference between happiness ratings of the two interaction partners in the agreement condition, but decreased this difference in the disagreement condition (Figure 5.5).

Although we had not specifically predicted such an interaction effect, its nature is consistent with some of the reasoning behind our study. In particular, the agreement condition was intended to encourage the establishment of rapport and shared affect between interaction partners, while the disagreement condition was one in

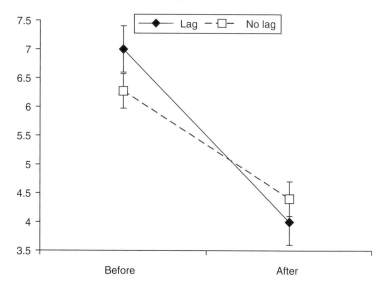

Figure 5.6 Differences between paired participants' liking ratings for celebrities before and after low- and high-delay conversations in study 2.

which participants were intended to have discrepant affective attitudes to the topic of discussion (a celebrity liked by one participant but disliked by the other). It therefore seems that the interaction task is best fulfilled if each partner's affect is similar to the other's in the agreement condition, but contrasts with the other's in the disagreement condition. Further, we had predicted that increased transmission delay would interfere both with the establishment of rapport in the agreement condition and with the exertion of mutual influence in the disagreement condition. In congruence with these predictions, participants were better able to synchronize their affective states during agreement and to maintain a contrasting affective stance during disagreement when the transmission delay was minimized.

A follow-up study (conducted in collaboration with Florian Vogt) focused only on the disagreement condition, and used acquaintances rather than strangers as interaction partners. In this study, we found that post-conversation ratings of discussed celebrities converged more in the low-delay than the high-delay condition. Participants' level of disagreement about their liking for the celebrities was lower following the conversation, and this effect was more pronounced in the low-delay condition (Figure 5.6). It therefore seems that under some circumstances mutual influence attempts can operate more successfully when immediate interpersonal feedback is available to allow online adjustment of one's own presentation.

However, many of the other effects reported in the first study were not replicated in the second study. We conclude, therefore, that many of the communicative limitations imposed by transmission delay may be circumvented if interaction partners are already familiar with one another and are consequently more able to anticipate and elaborate on the other's perceived reactions. Furthermore, many of the friends in the second study seemed to find the limitations of the medium a source of amusement rather than frustration. For participants who already know each other, the lack of attunement and online sensitivity is less likely to be attributed to lack of rapport, and attempts to resolve these problems in making contact may be improvised (some of them having surprising and potentially humorous consequences; e.g., repeated attempts to initiate a speech turn). Clearly, further work is required to determine the extent to which the results reported here depend on the specific characteristics of the relationship between interactants, their respective social identities, and their relative salience, as well as familiarity with the communication medium. As noted above, our prediction is not that there are inevitable negative consequences of transmission delay, but rather that its presence may invoke different strategies of interaction and different modes of coping.

Conclusions

Previous studies of the effects of temporal characteristics of VMC on communication processes have tended to focus on cognitive or performance-based measures (e.g., O'Malley *et al.*, 1996). The study reported here clearly suggests that the affective consequences of transmission delay are also worthy of research attention for both practical and theoretical reasons (see also Bruce, 1996). Indeed, we might argue that some level of mutual rapport is necessary before cooperation on practical tasks can be fully successful. The present study suggests that transmission delay may interfere to some extent with the establishment of rapport.

Because participants do not seem to be able to localize the source of any delay-induced trouble with interaction, their coping attempts may often be misdirected until experience teaches them what works and what does not. We found that participants felt less involved when interpersonal feedback was delayed, that their levels of involvement tended to correspond less well to those of their partners, and that they were less able to adjust their presentation to match the current demands of the interaction. However, we also found that for participants who already have rapport with one another, many (but not all) of these effects disappear.

Future research needs to address a number of limitations of the present studies. First of all, we need to establish the extent to which some of the apparent negative effects of transmission delay are mediated by its consequences for conversational turn-taking. Because giving up and taking the floor are conversational tasks facilitated by closely timed nonverbal signals (e.g., Goodwin, 1981; Sacks *et al.*, 1974; but see also Beattie, 1978, 1979), it would be unsurprising if participants found both of these tasks more difficult in the high-delay condition (see also O'Malley *et al.*, 1996), with potential deleterious consequences for rapport and affect. However, it might also be argued that these transitions themselves are based on changing patterns of attunement, involvement, and emotion. In either case, the relationships between these conversational and affect-related variables clearly require more attention than the current data permit.

The present results would also be substantiated by closer attention to the characteristics of the nonverbal and verbal conduct of interactants. Coding of higher-quality video-recordings by FACS (Ekman and Friesen, 1978) and conversation-analytic methods (e.g., Sacks *et al.*, 1974) would provide a wealth of data that might be capable of clarifying the dynamic processes of interpersonal negotiation and adjustment.

Another promising avenue for future research would be to explicitly assess the development of coping strategies based on continuing experience with communication technologies of this kind. Even if users are not always aware of the problems that they face, they may try various techniques for improving the consequences of their interaction and learn certain of these techniques simply on the basis of trial and error. There is already evidence that users of text-based CMC learn to deal with the informational restrictions of the medium by incorporating emoticons and other typographical interjections in their messages (Mallon and Oppenheim, 2002). The development of similar strategies in VMC has not yet been investigated to the same extent and is worthy of further attention. It would also be useful to explore the impact of explicit training about the limitations of the medium on communication success.

A final issue arises from our finding that transmission delay seems to have greater consequences for persuasion than for the establishment of rapport. One reason for this may be that the process whereby participants establish nonverbal synchrony in FTF interactions may not operate when only the other's face is presented as a 2D image on a video screen (or when the apparent distance from the other is too high or too low). For example, Heath and Luff (1992) suggest that the communicative functions of gestures partly depend on their appearance at the periphery of the visual field where our senses are more attuned to movement. In the VMC setup used in the present studies, attention was always explicitly directed at the image of the other's face, and therefore any automatic adjustments may have been undermined. For this reason, it would seem important to include FTF control conditions in future studies (e.g., Doherty-Sneddon *et al.*, 1997). However, any obtained differences between VMC and FTF might potentially relate to any of the possible differences between these communication modes outlined in the opening sections of this chapter.

Implications

Since the 1990s, the emphasis of nonverbal research has shifted from addressing the role of facial activity as a simple expression of underlying private emotions to a fuller appreciation of its interpersonal orientation and attunement (Parkinson, 1996; Russell and Fernández-Dols, 1997). Displays are specifically directed at real or imagined addressees (Fridlund, 1994), and their structure and timing depend on actual and anticipated responses from these audiences (e.g., Bavelas *et al.*, 1986). Nonverbal conduct therefore needs to be understood in its social and temporal context, as emerging from ongoing communicative acts which are attuned to mutually co-regulated conduct from the other party to the interaction (e.g., Fogel, 1993). Two modes of nonverbal coordination are particularly relevant to the present research:

1. *Temporal synchrony*: In our view, establishing an intersubjective frame of reference for communication (cf. Clark and Brennan, 1991) involves affective as well as informational grounding (e.g., Krauss and Fussell, 1990). In particular, during cooperative exchanges, interactants often develop mutual rhythms and synchronies in nonverbal conduct which are perceived in terms of rapport (Bernieri *et al.*, 1994) and which provide the basis for attaining an appropriate level of intimacy. Clearly there is a basic level of temporal resolution in signal transfer by VMC below which this kind of expressive coordination is unsustainable. However, as noted above, this by no means rules out the use of other means for attaining similar interpersonal consequences (as happens in extended text-based CMC interactions; Walther *et al.*, 1994). For example, it is possible that interactants learn to slow down or freeze expressive movements when using VMC technology in order to recreate or at least simulate the sense of interpersonal contact. Alternatively, more verbal cues

relating to the social relationship may be incorporated into the conversation to compensate for perceived inadequacies of nonverbal channels. The way that interactants deal with the tools at their disposal is itself an important topic for research.

2. *Temporal complementarity and conflict*: We propose that the business of persuasion and self-presentation requires tailoring of nonverbal presentations to the ongoing responses of others, and that limitations in immediate feedback (whether temporal or informational) can lead to inappropriate or mistimed displays. More generally, emotional expressions (like other communicative acts) have pragmatic functions whose satisfaction determines their modulation over time. Indeed, our suggestion is that nonverbal moves may form flexible and relationship-dependent adjacency pairs (cf. Sacks *et al.*, 1974), and any delays in the arrival of the preferred response may lead to renewal or intensification of the original display.

Again, however, it needs to be emphasized that there may be ways around the difficulties imposed by these forms of communication. Negative effects are neither uncontrollable nor inevitable. Further, there may be uncontrollable purposes that are served by the disruption of immediate interpersonal feedback that characterizes many currently operating VMC systems.

In summary, we propose that low temporal resolution of interpersonally provided nonverbal feedback can modify two kinds of nonverbal coordination during processes of emotion communication in videoconferencing: Levels of rapport will sometimes be reduced and pragmatically oriented displays sometimes intensified when the other party's expressive responses are less than immediate. Limitations of communicative media may therefore exacerbate negative emotion presentations in addition to undermining the development of mutual positive affect. Previous research has demonstrated that verbal communication increases cooperative behavior in social dilemmas (e.g., Bonas and Komorita, 1996) and that CMC can result in higher levels of hostility than FTF interaction (e.g., Kiesler *et al.*, 1984). The current studies have extended and developed these existing literatures by paying closer attention to real-time processes of nonverbal interaction.

References

Argyle, M. and Dean, J. (1965). Eye-contact, distance and affiliation. *Sociometry*, **28**, 289–304.

Bavelas, J. B., Black, A., Lemery, C. R., and Mullett, J. (1986). "I *show* how you feel": motor mimicry as a communicative act. *Journal of Personality and Social Psychology*, **50**, 322–329.

Beattie, G. W. (1978). Floor apportionment and gaze in conversational dyads. *British Journal of Social and Clinical Psychology*, **17**, 7–15.

(1979). Contextual constraints on the floor-apportionment function of speaker-gaze in dyadic conversations. *British Journal of Social and Clinical Psychology*, **18**, 391–392.

Bernieri, F. J., Davis, J. M., Rosenthal, R., and Knee, C. R. (1994). Interactional synchrony and rapport: measuring synchrony in displays devoid of sound and facial affect. *Personality and Social Psychology Bulletin*, **20**, 303–311.

Bernieri, F. J. and Rosenthal, R. (1991). Coordinated movement in human interaction. In R. S. Feldman and B. Rimé (eds), *Fundamentals of Nonverbal Behavior* (pp. 401–431). New York: Cambridge University Press.

Biocca, F. (1997). The cyborg's dilemma: progressive embodiment in virtual environments. *Journal of Computer-Mediated Communication*, **3**(2). www.ascusc.org/jcmc/vol3/issue2/biocca2.html.

(2001). Inserting the presence of mind into a philosophy of presence: a response to Sheridan and Mantovani and Riva. *Presence*, **10**, 546–556.

Biocca, F. and Nowak, K. (2001). Plugging your body into the telecommunication system: mediated embodiment, media interfaces, and social virtual environments. In C. Lin and D. Atkin (Eds.), *Communication Technology and Society* (pp. 407–447). Waverly Hill, VI: Hampton Press.

Bonas, K. S. and Komorita, S. S. (1996). Group discussion and cooperation in social dilemmas. *Personality and Social Psychology Bulletin*, **22**, 1144–1150.

Brittan, D. (1992). Being there: the promise of multimedia communications. *Technology Review*, **95**, 42–50.

Broglio, R. and Guynup, S. (2003). Beyond human: avatar as multimedia expression. *Virtual Storytelling, Proceedings: Lecture Notes in Computer Science*, **2897**, 120–123.

Bruce, V. (1996). The role of the face in communication: implications for videophone design. *Interacting with Computers*, **8**, 166–176.

Chapman, L. J. and Chapman, J. P. (1967). Genesis of popular but erroneous psychodiagnostic observations. *Journal of Abnormal Psychology*, **72**, 193–204.

Chartrand, T. L. and Bargh, J. A. (1999). The chameleon effect: the perception-behaviour link and social interaction. *Journal of Personality and Social Psychology*, **76**, 893–910.

Clark, H. H. and Brennan, S. E. (1991). Grounding in communication. In L. B. Resnick, J. Levine, and S. D. Teasley (eds), *Perspectives in Socially Shared Cognition* (pp. 127–149). Washington, DC: American Psychological Association.

Condon, W. S. (1982). Cultural microrhythms. In M. Davis (ed.), *Interaction Rhythms: Periodicity in Communicative Behavior* (pp. 53–76). New York: Human Sciences Press.

Daft, R. L. and Lengel, R. H. (1984). Information richness: a new approach to managerial behavior and organizational design. *Research in Organizational Behavior*, **6**, 191–233.

Daly-Jones, O., Monk, A., and Watts, L. (1998). Some advantages of video conferencing over high-quality audio conferencing: fluency and aware-ness of attentional focus. *International Journal of Human–Computer Studies*, **49**, 21–58.

de Rivera, J. H. (1977). *A Structural Theory of the Emotions*. Psychological Issues Monograph 40 (169 pp.). New York: International Universities Press.

Doherty-Sneddon, G., Anderson, A., O'Malley, C., Langton, S., Garrod, S., and Bruce, V. (1997). Face-to-face and video-mediated communication: a comparison of dialogue structure and task performance. *Journal of Experimental Psychology: Applied, 3*, 105–125.

Ekman, P. (2001). *Telling Lies: Clues to Deceit in the Marketplace, Politics, and Marriage* (3rd edn.). New York: W. W. Norton & Company.

Ekman, P. and Friesen, W. V. (1969). Nonverbal leakage and clues to deception. *Psychiatry, 32*, 88–106.

(1978). *The Facial Action Coding System (FACS): A Technique for the Measurement of Facial Action*. Palo Alto, CA: Consulting Psychologists Press.

Fogel, A. (1993). *Developing Through Relationships*. New York: Harvester Wheatsheaf.

Fridlund, A. (1994). *Human Facial Expression: An Evolutionary View*. San Diego, CA: Academic Press.

Fulk, J., Steinfield, C. W., Schmitz, J. A., and Power, J. G. (1987). A social information processing model of media use in organizations. *Communication Research, 14*, 529–552.

Gagne, F. M. and Lydon, J. E. (2004). Bias and accuracy in close relationships: an integrative review. *Personality and Social Psychology Review, 8*, 322–338.

Gibson, J. J. (1979). *The Ecological Approach to Visual Perception*. Boston: Houghton Mifflin.

Goodwin, C. (1980). Re-starts, pauses, and the achievement of a state of mutual gaze at turn-beginning. *Sociological Inquiry, 50*, 272–302.

(1981). *Conversational Organization: Interaction Between Speakers and Hearers*. New York: Academic Press.

Gottman, J. M. and Levenson, R. W. (1985). A valid procedure for obtaining self-report of affect in marital interaction. *Journal of Consulting and Clinical Psychology, 53*, 151–160.

Grammer, K., Kruck, K. B., and Magnusson, M. S. (1998). The courtship dance: Patterns of nonverbal synchronization in opposite-sex encounters. *Journal of Nonverbal Behavior, 22*, 3–29.

Hall, E. T. (1966). *The Hidden Dimension*. New York: Doubleday.

Heath, C. and Luff, P. (1992). Media space and communicative asymmetries: preliminary observations of video-mediated interaction. *Human–Computer Interaction, 7*, 315–346.

Isaacs, E. A. and Tang, J. C. (1994). What video can and cannot do for collaboration: a case study. *Multimedia Systems, 2*, 63–73.

Joinson, A. N. (2003). *Understanding the Psychology of Internet Behaviour: Virtual Worlds, Real Lives*. Basingstoke: Palgrave Macmillan.

Kendon, A. (1967). Some functions of gaze direction in social interaction. *Acta Psychologica, 26*, 100–125.

(1973). The role of visible behaviour in the organization of social interaction. In M. Von Cranach and I. Vine (eds), *Social Communication and Movement* (pp. 29–74). London: Academic Press.

Kiesler, S., Siegel, J., and McGuire, T. W. (1984). Social psychological aspects of computer-mediated communication. *American Psychologist, 39*, 1123–1134.

Krauss, R. M. and Fussell, S. R. (1990). Mutual knowledge and communicative effectiveness. In J. Galegher, R. E. Kraut, and C. Egido (eds), *Intellectual*

Teamwork: Social and Technological Foundations of Cooperative Work (pp. 111–145). Hillsdale, NJ: Lawrence Erlbaum Associates.

Lea, M. and Giordano, R. (1997). Representations of the group and group processes in CSCW research: a case of premature closure? In G. C. Bowker, S. L. Star, W. Turner, and L. Gasser (eds), *Social Science, Technical Systems and Cooperative Work: Beyond the Great Divide* (pp. 5–26). Mahwah, NJ: Lawrence Erlbaum Associates.

Lea, M. and Spears, R. (1991). Computer-mediated communication, de-individuation and group decision-making. *International Journal of Man–Machine Studies*, **39**, 283–301.

(1995). Love at first byte? Building personal relationships over computer networks. In J. T. Wood and S. Duck (eds), *Under-Studied Relationships: Off the Beaten Track* (pp. 197–233). Thousand Oaks, CA: Sage.

Leary, M. R., Landel, J. L., and Patton, K. M. (1996). The motivated expression of embarrassment following a self-presentational predicament. *Journal of Personality*, **64**, 619–636.

Lombard, M. and Ditton, T. (1997). At the heart of it all: the concept of presence. *Journal of Computer-Mediated Communication*, **3**(2). www.ascusu. org/jcmc/vol3/issue2/lombard.html.

Mallon, R. and Oppenheim, C. (2002). Style used in electronic mail. *Aslib Proceedings*, **54**, 8–22.

Markus, M. L. (1994). Finding a happy medium: explaining the negative effects of electronic communication on social life at work. *ACM Transactions on Information Systems*, **12**, 119–149.

Matarazzo, G. and Sellen, A. (2000). The value of video in work at a distance: addition or distraction? *Behaviour and Information Technology*, **19**, 339–348.

McCoy, N. L. and Pitino, L. (2002). Pheromonal influences on sociosexual behavior in young women. *Physiology and Behavior*, **75**, 367–375.

Nagy, E. and Molnár, P. (2004). Homo imitans or homo provocans? Human imprinting model of neonatal imitation. *Infant Behavior and Development*, **27**, 54–63.

Olson, J. S., Olson, G. M., and Meader, D. K. (1995). What mix of audio and video is useful for remote real-time work? *Proceedings of the Conference on Human Factors in Computing Science* (pp. 33–45). Denver, CO: Academic Press.

O'Malley, C., Langton, S., Anderson, A., Doherty-Sneddon, G., and Bruce, V. (1996). Comparison of face-to-face and video-mediated interaction. *Interacting with Computers*, **8**, 177–192.

Parkinson, B. (1996). Emotions are social. *British Journal of Psychology*, **87**, 663–683.

(2001). Anger on and off the road. *British Journal of Psychology*, **92**, 507–526.

(2005). Do facial movements express emotions or communicate motives? *Personality and Social Psychology Review*, **9**, 278–311.

Parkinson, B., Fischer, A. H., and Manstead, A. S. R. (2005). *Emotion in Social Relations: Cultural, Group, and Interpersonal Processes*. New York: Psychology Press.

Patterson, M. L. (1996). Social behavior and social cognition: a parallel process approach. In J. L. Nye and A. M. Brower (eds), *What's Social About Social Cognition?* (pp. 87–105). Thousand Oaks, CA: Sage.

Reddy, V. (2000). Coyness in early infancy. *Developmental Science*, **3**, 186–192.

Russell, J. A. and Fernández-Dols, J. M. (eds) (1997). *The Psychology of Facial Expression*. Cambridge University Press.

Rutter, D. R. (1987). *Communicating by Telephone*. Elmsford, NY: Pergamon.

Sacks, H., Schegloff, E., and Jefferson, G. (1974). A simplest systematics for the organization of turn-taking in conversation. *Language, 50*, 696–735.

Short, J., Williams, E., and Christie, B. (1976). *The Social Psychology of Telecommunications*. London: Wiley.

Sommer, R. (1965). Further studies of small group ecology. *Sociometry, 28,* 337–348.

Sorce, J. F., Emde, R. N., Campos, J., and Klinnert, M. D. (1985). Maternal emotional signaling: its effect on the visual cliff behavior of 1 year olds. *Developmental Psychology, 21*, 195–200.

Tang, J. C. and Isaacs, E. (1992). Why do users like video? Studies of multimedia supported collaboration. *Computer-Supported Cooperative Work, 1*, 19–34.

Walther, J. B., Anderson, J. F., and Park, D. (1994). Interpersonal effects in computer-mediated interaction: a meta-analysis of social and anti-social communication. *Communication Research, 21*, 460–487.

Watts, L., Monk, A., and Daly-Jones, O. (1996). Inter-personal awareness and synchronization: assessing the value of communication technologies. *International Journal of Human–Computer Studies, 44*, 849–873.

Wichman, H. (1975). Effects of isolation and communication on cooperation in a two-person game. *Journal of Personality and Social Psychology, 16*, 114–120.

CHAPTER 6

Impact of social anxiety on the processing of emotional information in video-mediated interaction

Pierre Philippot and Céline Douilliez

Overview: This chapter discusses whether various modes of internet communication affect differently socially anxious individuals as compared to nonanxious. It reviews the literature on the relationship between internet use and social adjustment, mainly, social anxiety and loneliness. Next, it develops the reasons why the mainstream modes of communication on the internet, i.e., chats and emails, are appealing to socially anxious and lonely individuals. It also reviews the literature showing that these individuals are indeed presenting different patterns of communication on the internet as compared to nonanxious individuals. Then, it examines whether the introduction of a video-channel in internet communication constitutes a difficulty for socially anxious people. It concludes by suggesting new directions for research at the applied or clinical levels as well as at the fundamental level.

Since the development of emailing more than 30 years ago, communication on the internet has impressively grown, in terms of quantity as well as technology (Pew Internet and American Life, 2002). It now allows various forms of communication: instant messages, chat, email, phone-mail, Skype, social networking sites, etc. From a psychological perspective, these different forms of communication have different implications in terms of the type of message conveyed and its emotional impact.

In this chapter, we will examine the relationship between social anxiety and internet communication. Our rationale is that these various modes of internet communication might affect differently people who are not at ease in the presence of others. We will first examine different hypotheses proposed in the literature to account for a relationship between internet use and social adjustment, mainly, social anxiety and loneliness. Next, we will develop the reasons why the mainstream modes of communication on the internet, i.e., chats and emails, are appealing to socially anxious and lonely individuals. We will also review the literature showing that these individuals are indeed presenting different patterns of communication on the internet as compared to nonanxious individuals. Then, we will propose that the introduction of a video channel in internet communication might constitute a difficulty for socially anxious people. As there is no research to date that has examined this possibility, we will ground our statement with proximal data: the research examining the processing of facial expression by socially anxious individuals. Finally, we will conclude the chapter by indicating possible new directions for research at the applied or clinical levels as well as at the fundamental level.

The relationship between internet use and social adjustment

The internet is widely used to communicate with others (Pew Internet and American Life, 2002). In this context, a debate has emerged regarding whether this new form of interaction promotes new types of social bonds, and whether it dampens daily social relationships in "normal life." Indeed, some data have suggested that the introduction of the internet in a household increases feelings of loneliness and depression (Kraut *et al.*, 1998). Other studies, however, have suggested that the deleterious effects of internet use on social relationships and emotional health are limited to a specific population of individuals who already present social deficits, independently of their use of the internet (McKenna and Bargh, 2000). Thus, two opposite hypotheses have been proposed to account for the potential relationship between internet use and social anxiety and loneliness (Morahan-Martin and Schumacher, 2003).

One hypothesis is that the internet is causing social anxiety and loneliness. The rationale developed to account for this relationship is that the internet isolates individuals from the real world and deprives them of real social contacts. The time spent on the internet is devoted to artificial and weak relationships at the expense of real-life social bonds that foster the sense of belongingness and connection. Further, the paucity of internet communication deprives individuals of the opportunity to practice social skills and to develop a sense of social competence. In line with this rationale, Kraut *et al.* (1998) report that, in their study, increases in loneliness and depression were related to decreases in family communication, social activities, and the size of the social network, which, in turn, were related to increased internet use. Similarly, in a large American survey (O'Toole, 2000), a quarter of the respondents regularly using the internet reported that it reduced their time spent with friends and family.

The opposite hypothesis is that lonely and socially anxious individuals are more likely to be drawn to the internet because of the very special type of social interactions it provides (Shepherd and Edelmann, 2001). Some authors have described online communication as an altered type of communication that might be particularly attractive to socially anxious individuals (e.g., Morahan-Martin and Schumacher, 2003; Turkle, 1995). Such individuals would feel protected by the anonymity of the interaction. Further, they would use the internet as a social relationships and identity "workshop" to work through sensitive interpersonal issues in the safety of the online environment (Turkle, 1995). Shepherd and Edelmann (2001) have suggested that the internet may fill a void for some individuals who have difficulty in establishing social bonds. Social isolation might thus lead to great internet use, and a cyclical relationship between social anxiety and internet dependence might develop.

Why the internet might be appealing to socially anxious individuals

As just suggested, several features of internet communication might be appealing to socially anxious individuals. Indeed, this population is especially sensitive to negative social evaluation and to its negative aftermaths: social humiliation and embarrassment (Clark and Wells, 1995), and, eventually, social rejection, isolation, and loneliness. As a consequence, socially anxious individuals avoid situations in which they are exposed to others and to potential social judgments. For instance, speaking in public is a situation typically feared by socially anxious individuals, but less exposed situations, such as writing in front of someone, can also raise anxiety to very high levels.

Internet communication, especially chats, instant messages, or emails, presents several characteristics that minimize expose to others or to being judged by others. First, partners of such interactions may remain totally anonymous and present themselves under a nickname. There is experimental evidence showing that anonymity on the internet diminishes social anxiety. Joinson (1999) tested participants' responses to various questionnaires on the internet under an anonymous and a nonanonymous condition: People reported lower social anxiety and social desirability, as well as higher self-esteem, when they were anonymous than when they were nonanonymous. Beyond anonymity, in actuality, people on the internet are totally free to construct for themselves the character or personae they wish. As formulated by Reid

(1993, p. 63), "users can be, quite literally, whoever they wish." Socially anxious people report that the anonymity of internet is liberating (Morahan-Martin and Schumacher, 2003). Thus, on the internet, socially anxious individuals can present a more idealized version of themselves and role-play different online personae. Some individuals even end up feeling more themselves online than off (Bargh *et al.* (2002)).

Another important aspect of internet communication is the lack of physical presence and in particular of face-to-face contact. Being under the scrutiny of others is especially anxiety provoking for socially anxious individuals. They are afraid that their anxiety will be very apparent to their interaction partners, through the clumsiness of non-verbal behavior, blushing, and the like. Socially anxious individuals have often been described as feeling "transparent" to others (Savitsky and Gilovich, 2003): They believe that others can literally read their mind and their emotions. In internet communication, such fears do not apply, as one cannot be seen by others. A related aspect of this characteristic of internet communication is that it allows "lurking." In chat rooms, one can just observe communications, with no fear of being seen by others or of being asked to participate in the interaction.

A third characteristic of internet communication potentially appealing to socially anxious individuals is the online culture that promotes disinhibition, i.e., weakened social restraints, role constraints, and social expectations (Joinson, 1998). Exchanges are less formal and the possibility of a faux pas is minimized. The pressure of social norms is definitely weaker on the internet. Online disinhibition may thus counter social inhibition, anxiety, and self-consciousness.

A fourth characteristic of internet communication is that it allows a better control of the social interaction itself (Morahan-Martin and Schumacher, 2003). Online, much more than in real-life interactions, individuals not only can choose with whom and when to communicate but also have time to compose the message and they feel less pressure to immediately answer their partners. This issue is particularly sensitive for socially anxious individuals, who often fear being paralyzed in social interaction, not knowing how to respond immediately in social interactions (Clark and Wells, 1995).

Finally, internet communication requires simpler communication skills than real-life, face-to-face interaction (Schnarch, 1997). Internet exchanges are often characterized by stylized patterns of communicating which make self-presentation easier. This aspect is further reinforced by the fact that internet communication relies on one channel: written messages. It thus offers a limited confrontation to the social partners.

In sum, several characteristic of internet communication might reduce the anxiety felt by socially fearful people during social interactions. Some of these characteristics revolve around the notion that, online, people can escape the scrutiny of others by remaining anonymous, by creating an entirely fictitious persona, and by not being physically seen. In addition, internet culture promotes a disinhibited style while offering more control on what and how one chooses to communicate. Given these characteristics, one might expect socially anxious individuals to rely more on internet communication for their social interactions or, at least, that they use the internet differently from nonsocially anxious individuals.

Patterns of use of the internet by socially anxious individuals

Whatever the direction of the relationship between social adjustment and anxiety and the use of the internet, the ideas developed above suggest that socially anxious or maladjusted individuals develop a different use of the internet than socially adjusted individuals. Several recent studies have explored this issue.

For instance, Kim and Davis (2009) have observed in a large sample of students that low self-esteem and social anxiety predicted problematic internet use (i.e., addictive use of the internet). Similarly, Caplan (2007) found that social anxiety predicted problematic internet use and preference for online social interaction, as compared to live interaction. These observations also apply to clinical populations: Erwin *et al.* (2004) surveyed a sample of clinically socially anxious individuals seeking information on social phobia on the internet. They observed that those with the most severe social interaction anxiety and who spent the most time interacting on the internet endorsed positive effects of internet use. The authors concluded that the internet might be the home of a population of individuals with severe social anxiety disorder.

More specifically, Gross *et al.* (2002) have observed that socially anxious and lonely teenagers interact on the internet more often with unknown or distant partners than socially adjusted peers. They also tend to chat more to avoid being alone than to contact friends. In contrast, teenagers who feel comfortable and connected with school peers use the internet to develop additional opportunities to interact with them. In line with our proposal, Gross *et al.* (2002) concluded that the internet may serve distinct functions for socially anxious and lonely individuals.

In a study addressing a similar issue, Morahan-Martin and Schumacher (2003) compared the use of the internet by lonely university students (scoring above the 80th percentile of the UCLA Loneliness Scale; Russell, 1996) to nonlonely students. Not only did lonely students report greater internet use (average of 5.4 hours a week) than nonlonely students (average of 3.0 hours a week), but also their motivation and behavior on the internet differed. As compared to socially well-adjusted students, lonely students were more likely to use the internet to relax, to work, for emotional support, to talk to others, or to pass time. They were also more likely to prefer online communication to face-to-face interaction, to report that online anonymity was liberating, and often to lurk online. Given the strong relation between loneliness and social anxiety (Solano and Koester, 1989), one might generalize these conclusions to socially anxious individuals as well.

These conclusions are corroborated by a study of Sheldon (2008), who surveyed a sample of student. She observed that respondents who felt anxiety and fears in their face-to-face communication used Facebook to pass time and feel less lonely more than other respondents, but they had fewer Facebook friends.

However, people who are lonely and socially more anxious tend to be more vulnerable than others to developing problems in their life from internet use. For instance, the time they spent on the internet tends to disrupt their work or social life (Loytskert and Aiello, 1997; Morahan-Martin and Schumacher, 2000, 2003; Young, 1998). More specifically, they report feeling guilty about the time they spend online, and to have missed social or work engagements to be online. They find it difficult to stop thinking about going on the internet, and they try to hide how much time they spend online (Morahan-Martin and Schumacher, 2003).

This differential pattern of internet use as a function of social anxiety may appear early. For instance, Harman *et al.* (2005) observed that young adolescents with social anxiety were more likely to report faking behavior on the internet (e.g., pretending to be older).

In conclusion, socially anxious individuals seem to use the internet differently from nonsocially anxious individuals. Some studies have reported evidence that the former spend more time on the internet and rely more on it for their social interactions than the latter. Socially anxious individuals use internet communication to obtain social contacts and emotional support. They are also more likely to develop internet-related problems in their daily life, including interference with "off-line" social contacts.

Potential impact of the introduction of multichannel communication on the internet for socially anxious individuals

In the preceding section, we have developed reasons why internet communication might be appealing to socially anxious and lonely individuals. However, these reasons apply only to the extent that one cannot be seen or identified during the communication. Such appeal of the internet for the socially anxious might disappear and even reverse if a video and/or an audio channel is added to internet communication, as in multichannel internet exchanges. Indeed, Schooten *et al.* (2007) have observed in a large sample of Dutch adolescents that the absence (or controllability) of nonverbal cues encouraged feelings of disinhibition. In addition, adolescents' social anxiety was related to their perceptions of the relevance of reduced nonverbal cues and controllability, but did not directly influence online self-disclosure.

In actuality, being filmed is an acute social stressor for many people, even socially well-adjusted individuals. For instance, Boucsein and Wendt-Suhl (1980) have examined the anxiety response of normal male students who were preparing a speech. In one experimental condition, students were informed that they would be videotaped during the speech. These participants showed marked anxiety responses, both at the subjective and physiological levels, as compared to control participants who knew they would not be videotaped. Furthering such evidence, we propose that the nonverbal emotional information conveyed by an added video channel to internet communication might constitute an important source of difficulty for socially anxious individuals.

This notion is congruent with the main models of social anxiety (Clark and Wells, 1995; Rapee and Heimberg, 1997). One tenet of these models is that socially anxious individuals would represent their self as a social object. They would construct this representation on the basis of their perception of how others see them. This perception would be biased by negative expectations. In this process, socially anxious individuals would thus construct a distorted impression of themselves that often takes the form of a visual image of themselves seen from the perspective of an observer (Clark and Wells, 1995; Spurr and Stopa, 2002). During social interaction, this – negative – representation of "self as seen by the others" would be activated, thereby increasing anxiety and disturbing social performance. Poor social performance would feed back into the negative self-representation, further increasing anxiety.

Being confronted by a videocamera or webcam is a strong reminder of that image of being observed by another. It should thus raise important levels of self-focus and social anxiety. Indeed, the literature on social anxiety suggests that, for socially anxious individuals, being observed by others is one of the main sources of anxiety (Safren and Turk, 1998). Being filmed is thus a particularly stressing experience, as they unavoidably become the focus of attention of the viewer.

Further, there is evidence that, during social interactions, socially anxious individuals do process differently nonverbal information such as that conveyed by a video channel. Specifically, they seem to particularly focus their attention on the threatening features of the facial expression of their interaction partner (Mogg and Bradley, 1998). Such a bias increases their social anxiety and often results in avoidance of the anxiety-provoking situation (Clark, 1999). For the present concern, one might suspect that, for socially anxious individuals, adding a video channel to internet communication might change this medium from an appealing one to an avoided one.

In sum, internet video communication features a conjunction of many anxiety-provoking factors: being filmed, being in an unfamiliar environment, being directly confronted by nonverbal messages of the partner, etc. (Heimberg *et al.*, 1992). To date, no research has been conducted to evaluate the impact of a video channel in internet communication, in terms of anxiety during the interaction. However, a whole body of research has investigated the relationship between social anxiety and nonverbal information processing. In the next sections, we will review this body of research, before drawing inferences for video communication on the internet.

Nonverbal facial information processing in socially anxious individuals

The study of biases and deficits in the processing of nonverbal interpersonal information has stimulated a wealth of research on anxiety in general (e.g., Williams *et al.*, 1999) and social anxiety in particular (Clark and McManus, 2002). Most of this research focuses on *attentional biases*; i.e., the fact that attention to nonverbal signals, such as facial expression, is differently allocated by socially anxious individuals as compared to nonanxious ones. For example, socially anxious individuals might have their attention more readily attracted to faces expressing threat than to other faces. Surprisingly little research has been devoted to evaluative biases and deficits, despite a strong belief among many clinicians that socially anxious individuals overestimate the intensity of threat in social signals (e.g., Beck *et al.*, 1985). We speak of an *evaluative deficit* in the case of generally poor performance in the identification of signals conveyed by a partners' nonverbal behavior. It is important to distinguish this situation from the situation in which one wrongly and *systematically* attributes a specific meaning or emotion (e.g., disgust) to a face, while it is actually a different meaning or emotion (e.g., sadness) that is expressed. In this latter case, we will speak of an *evaluative bias*.

In their cognitive-motivational model of anxiety, Mogg and Bradley (1998) have examined attentional and evaluative biases. Their model relies on two different systems: the valence evaluation system and the goal engagement system. The valence evaluation system assesses the stimulus threat value according to the relevance of the stimulus to the person's current concerns and past learning experiences. The goal engagement system allocates attention as a function of the output of the former system. If a stimulus in the environment is evaluated as threatening, the goal engagement system interrupts ongoing activities and orients attention to the threat stimulus. This model postulates that attentional biases in anxious individuals result from a negative and unbalanced appraisal of social situations (Mogg and Bradley, 2002).

Attentional biases

A wealth of studies has evidenced an attentional bias in socially anxious individuals' processing of threatening stimuli (see Musa and Lépine, 2000, for review). However, the direction of these attentional biases is the object of a controversy. On the one hand, several cognitive models of anxiety (e.g., Mogg and Bradley, 1998; Williams *et al.*, 1999) propose that anxious individuals preferentially attend to threatening information (Beck *et al.*, 1985).

Several studies have demonstrated such a bias in vigilance toward threat words by social phobics (Asmundson and Stein, 1994; Maidenberg *et al.*, 1996; Mattia *et al.*, 1993). Although some authors have argued that responses to words may index worry rather than an actual response to social stimuli (Chen *et al.*, 2002), the same findings have been replicated with more ecological material – faces – in social phobics (Gilboa-Schechtman *et al.*, 1999) and in a nonclinical sample with high fear of negative evaluation (FNE) (Mogg and Bradley, 2002; Watson and Friend, 1969).

On the other hand, some researchers predict the opposite attentional bias. Clark (1999) has proposed that avoidance of threatening information may play an important role in the maintenance of social anxiety. For instance, for social phobics, actively avoiding social stimuli (e.g., faces) constitutes a form of cognitive escape from anxiety-provoking situations (e.g., avoiding looking at others' faces makes conversation less likely; Clark and Wells, 1995). Studies using a probe detection task found that social phobics (Chen *et al.*, 2002) and socially anxious individuals (Mansell *et al.*, 1999) avoid emotional (negative and positive) faces.

In an attempt to reconcile these divergent findings, Amir *et al.* (2002) have proposed a two-stage model of information processing. According to this view, anxious individuals should show an initial hypervigilance for threat-relevant stimuli. This hypervigilance would be the consequence of automatic processes, and it could be observed without conscious perception of threat-relevant information (Mogg and Bradley, 1999). However, at further and less automatic stages of information processing, people should actively turn away from threatening information. Thus, this model postulates a dynamic shift of attention allocation from initial threat hypervigilance to later threat avoidance. For instance, while speaking to other people, socially anxious individuals would have their attention automatically attracted to frowns more readily than would nonanxious individuals. Because of this perception bias, socially anxious individuals are likely to automatically overactivate a state of social anxiety. However, as soon as a frown is detected, they would turn their attention away from it – and, more generally, from others' faces – to avoid the threatening stimulus and the discomfort associated with it. Unfortunately, in doing so, they are likely to maintain their anxiety: Not only are they likely to behave socially inappropriately, but they will also be unable to determine whether the frowns were a sign of actual social threat or, for instance, simply a sign of perplexity.

Two studies (Amir *et al.*, 1996, 2002), manipulating strategic control in the Stroop task, suggested that social phobics are able to use strategic processes to modulate their attention to threat. However, this "vigilance-avoidance" hypothesis was not supported in a sample of individuals with nonclinical anxiety (Mogg *et al.*, 1997).

In an experiment using the "dot prime" paradigm (Mogg *et al.*, 2004), we examined the time course of attentional biases for faces in order to evaluate further the vigilance-avoidance hypothesis. Social phobics and matched controls completed a probe detection task with facial expressions as stimuli. In order to observe whether or not the focus of attention changed over time, the stimulus duration was manipulated (either 500 or 1,250 ms). It was predicted, and observed, that social phobics would initially focus their attention on the threatening face, but that this attentional bias rapidly disappears. In contrast, nonphobics showed the opposite pattern. Similar results, using a different paradigm (the "homograph" paradigm), were reported by Amir *et al.* (1998). They fit nicely with the prediction of an initial automatic vigilance for threatening information, followed by a protective voluntary attempt to redirect attention away from the threatening stimulus.

Evaluative deficits and biases

In the previous section, we emphasized a strong belief that attentional biases result from evaluative biases. However, few studies have tested this hypothesis. In a study by Merkelbach *et al.* (1989), social phobics and controls were asked to evaluate angry, neutral, and joyful faces with respect to their pleasantness. Contrary to the cognitive-motivational model's prediction (Mogg and Bradley, 1998), no differences were observed between the two populations.

We recently replicated this intriguing result (Douilliez and Philippot, 2003): Socially anxious and control participants were asked to evaluate the degree of threat in fearful, joyful, and neutral faces. In addition, we extended the study to include two other types of stimuli – words and pictures – and manipulated the valence and social relevance for both of these. Our rationale was that faces are potent innate stimuli (Öhman and Soares, 1993), and, as such, the processing of faces should not be influenced by social anxiety. In contrast, words and scenes depicted in the pictures require an interpretation and can therefore be influenced by experience, including social anxiety. As predicted, replicating Merkelbach *et al.* (1989), no differences between anxious individuals and controls were observed for the evaluation of faces. In contrast, anxious individuals evaluated negative pictures and words as more threatening than did normal controls.

A possible limitation of the study by Merkelbach *et al.* (1989) and our studies is that prototypical facial expressions were used that displayed full-blown emotions. Not only do these extreme stimuli have little ecological validity, but they are also easy to decode, and the use of such a material is likely to produce ceiling effects (Hess *et al.*, 1997). To avoid ceiling effects and to incorporate material reflecting real-life expressions, we designed a study in which stimuli varied in emotional intensity (Philippot and Douilliez, 2005). Specifically, we used a series of emotional facial expressions constructed by Hess and Blairy (1995), in which two actors portray five emotions (happiness, anger, sadness, disgust, and fear) at four intensity levels: 0 percent (i.e., neutral), 30 percent, 70 percent, and 100 percent. These stimuli were presented in random order on a computer screen. Finally, to increase the sensitivity of our measures, participants rated each facial expression on 7-point scales for a large profile of eight emotions (happiness, sadness, fear, anger, disgust, surprise, shame, and contempt).

This decoding task was completed by 21 outpatients diagnosed with social phobia according to DSM-IV criteria; 20 outpatients diagnosed with another anxiety disorder (agoraphobia, general anxiety) according to DSM-IV criteria; and 39 controls who were matched for sex, age, and level of education. The analysis of the data revealed no differences among the three groups in terms of intensity ratings, accuracy, or systematic biases, nor did they differ in their estimation of the difficulty of the task.

Conclusions and implications for multichannel internet communication

Even if the "vigilance–avoidance" model of anxiety is not fully supported in social anxiety, socially anxious individuals have demonstrated initial attentive biases toward threatening stimuli, including facial expressions, in a number of empirical studies. However, socially anxious individuals do not seem explicitly to over- or underestimate the intensity of an emotion present on the face, and they accurately identify the emotions conveyed by the face. Clearly, further research is needed to investigate the possibility of implicit evaluative biases in socially anxious individuals and to examine the relationship between possible implicit evaluative biases and attentional biases.

In any case, the attentional biases for threatening facial expression evidenced in socially anxious individuals are consistent with Clark's (1999) proposal that anxiety is maintained by specific patterns of attention allocation to social information. In the present case, being automatically more attracted to threatening nonverbal information is very likely to raise the anxiety of socially anxious individuals during social interaction. In such contexts, social contacts might thus become more aversive and, ultimately, avoided. It is thus plausible that, for socially anxious individuals, adding a video channel to internet communication, especially one focusing on the most informative nonverbal channel, the face, might change this situation from a secure anonymous one to an aversive exposure.

Conclusions and future directions

Like any new technology, multichannel internet communication will be used by individuals according to their capabilities, needs, and goals. In this chapter, we have demonstrated that socially maladjusted individuals, in particular ones who are lonely and socially anxious, are using internet communication differently. As claimed by McKenna and Bargh (2000, p. 59), "there is no simple main effect of the Internet on the average person." For socially anxious and lonely individuals, many characteristics of internet communication via instant messages, chats, or emails, have made this mode of social exchanges a safer one than direct, face-to-face interaction. In particular, as there is no physical presence, it requires less social skill and allows more control in the exchange, and one can remain anonymous or even create for oneself a totally fictitious persona.

Our proposal is that the safety of the internet social arena might be threatened by the introduction of a video channel. As reviewed in the chapter, socially anxious individuals are very sensitive to being filmed. It makes them particularly self-conscious by activating the negative self-picture that they have constructed for themselves. As a consequence, their feeling of self-efficacy in such situations is likely to be very low. Further, adding a video channel also means being exposed to others' nonverbal messages and facial expressions. As reviewed, a wealth of evidence shows that socially anxious individuals allocate their attention to facial expression in a different manner than nonanxious individuals. In particular, they seem to be automatically attracted by potential signs of threat and rejection. This constitutes a second reason why adding a video channel to internet communication is likely to cause difficulty to the socially anxious.

However, the proposal that adding a video channel to internet communication will constitute a difficulty for socially anxious individuals is still a speculation, and no research to date has investigated this possibility. Such research, though, would present much interest, both at the applied level and at the fundamental level. At the applied level, one must be cognizant that, on the one hand, the internet is now more and more used to communicate with others (Pew Internet and American Life, 2002), in the private domain, but also in the work domain, and in contacts with the government. On the other hand, social anxiety is a prevalent condition (Barlow, 2002) that affects a significant number of people. It is estimated that 2 to 14 percent of the population suffer from a clinically significant social phobia (Pélissolo *et al.*, 2000; Weiller *et al.*, 1998). It is thus important to determine whether a part of the population might be excluded from an important means of communication because of its anxiety-causing condition.

At the fundamental level, multichannel internet communication offers an interesting "naturalistic" situation in which one can experimentally disentangle the respective contributions of different aspects of the communication from its emotional impact. In particular, by including or excluding the audio, or the video channel, one can study the specific impact of prosody, or of nonverbal visual information. Useful scientific information could be obtained by examining the impact of these channels on different variables such as social anxiety, desirability, or self-esteem (Joinson, 1999).

Finally, in a clinical perspective, one has to investigate how the new technological possibilities of the internet might be used as therapeutic tools. Very recent studies have reported experimental treatments for social phobia in virtual environments. These experimental treatments have used virtual characters (James *et al.*, 2003) or movies (Lee and Ku, 2002). Although virtual reality has the advantage of offering great control of the environment, it has several limitations. In particular, it is not as interactive as a real audience, and the participants are perfectly aware that they are interacting with a virtual entity and not with a real social partner. The fear of negative evaluation might thus be minimal in such situation. In contrast, on the internet, one does interact with actual people, and the possibility of social evaluation is thus much more real. However, control of the amount of social exposure can be exerted by filtering the channels used for communication. At the bottom of the hierarchy, one can imagine an anonymous exchange via written messages, while at the top, there is the possibility of an audio and video communication, with many possibilities between.

To conclude, multichannel communication on the internet might a priori constitute a difficulty for socially anxious individuals. This hypothesis, however, needs to be empirically tested. On the other hand, this new technology offers new possibilities for the study of the emotional impact of various channels of communication in social interaction, and for the treatment of social anxiety.

Acknowledgments

The writing of this chapter has been facilitated by grants from the Fonds National de la Recherche Scientifique de Belgique, 8.4510.99 and 8.4510.03. The authors appreciate the helpful comments of Céline Baeyens on earlier drafts of this chapter.

References

Amir, N., McNally, R. J., Riemann, B. C., Burns, J., Lorenz, M., and Mullen, J. T. (1996). Suppression of the emotional Stroop effect by increased anxiety in patients with social phobia. *Behaviour Research and Therapy*, *34*, 945–948.

Amir, N., Foa, E. B., and Coles, M. E. (1998). Automatic activation and strategic avoidance of threat-relevant information in social phobia. *Journal of Abnormal Psychology*, *107*, 285–290.

Amir, N., Freshman, M., and Foa, E. (2002). Enhanced Stroop interference for threat in social phobia. *Journal of Anxiety Disorder*, *16*, 1–9.

Asmundson, G. J. G. and Stein, M. B. (1994). Selective processing of social threat in patients with generalized social phobia: evaluation using a dot-probe paradigm. *Journal of Anxiety Disorders*, *8*, 107–117.

Bargh, J. A., McKenna, K. Y., and Fitzsimons, G. M. (2002). Can you see the real me? Activation and expression of the "true self" on the Internet. *Journal of Social Issues*, *58*(1), 33–48.

Barlow, D. H. (2002). *Anxiety and Its Disorders: The Nature and Treatment of Anxiety and Panic* (2nd edn.). New York: Guilford Press.

Beck, A. T., Emery, G., and Greenberg, R. L. (1985). Cognitive structures and anxiogenic rules. In A. T. Beck, G. Emery, and R. L. Greenberg (eds), *Anxiety Disorders and Phobias* (pp. 54–66). New York: Basic Books.

Boucsein, W. and Wendt-Suhl, G. (1980). An experimental investigation of elements involved in the anticipation of public speaking. *Archive für Psychologie*, **133**, 149–156.

Caplan, S. (2007). Relations among loneliness, social anxiety, and problematic internet use. *Cyberpsychology & Behavior*, **10**, 234–242.

Chen, Y. P., Ehlers, A., Clark, D. M., and Mansell, W. (2002). Patients with social phobia direct their attention away from faces. *Behaviour Research and Therapy*, **40**, 677–687.

Clark, D. M. (1999). Anxiety disorders: why do they persist and how to treat them. *Behaviour Research and Therapy*, **37**, 5–27.

Clark, D. M. and McManus, F. (2002). Information processing in social phobia. *Biological Psychiatry*, **51**, 92–100.

Clark, D. M. and Wells, A. (1995). A cognitive model of social phobia. In R. Heimberg, M. Liebowitz, D. A. Hope, and F. R. Schneier (eds), *Social Phobia: Diagnosis, Assessment and Treatment* (pp. 69–93). New York: Guilford Press.

Douilliez, C. and Philippot, P. (2003). Biais dans l'évaluation explicite de stimuli verbaux et non-verbaux: effet de l'anxiété sociale. *Revue Francophone de Clinique Comportementale et Cognitive*, **8**, 12–18.

Erwin, B., Turk, C., Heimberg, R., Fresco, D., and Hantula, D. (2004). The internet: home to a severe population of individuals with social anxiety disorder? *Journal of Anxiety Disorders*, **18**, 629–646.

Gilboa-Schechtman, E., Foa, E. B., and Amir, N. (1999). Attentional biases for facial expressions in social phobia: the face-in-the-crowd paradigm. *Cognition and Emotion*, **13**, 305–318.

Harman, J., Hansen, C., Cochran, M., and Lindsey, C. (2005). Liar, liar: internet faking but not frequency of use affects social skills, self-esteem, social anxiety, and aggression. *Cyberpsychology & Behavior*, **8**, 1–6.

Heimberg, R.-G., Mueller, G. P., Holt, C. S., Hope, D. A., and Liebowitz, M. R. (1992). Assessment of anxiety in social interaction and being observed by others – the Social Interaction Anxiety Scale and the Social Phobia Scale. *Behavior Therapy*, **23**, 53–73.

Hess, U. and Blairy, S. (1995). *Set of Emotional Facial Stimuli*. Montreal, Canada: Department of Psychology, University of Quebec at Montreal.

Hess, U., Blairy, S., and Kleck, R. E. (1997). Intensity of emotional facial expression and decoding accuracy. *Journal of Nonverbal Behavior*, **21**, 241–257.

James, L. K., Lin, C. Y., Steed, A., Swapp, D., and Slater, M. (2003). Social anxiety in virtual environments: results of a pilot study. *Cyberpsychology and Behavior*, **6**, 237–243.

Joinson, A. (1998). Causes and implications of disinhibited behavior on the internet. In J. Gackenbach (ed.), *Psychology and the Internet* (pp. 43–60). San Diego, CA: Academic Press.

  (1999). Social desirability, anonymity, and internet-based questionnaires. *Behavior Research: Methods, Instruments, and Computers*, **31**, 433–438.

Kim, H. and Davis, K. (2009). Toward a comprehensive theory of problematic internet use: evaluating the role of self-esteem, anxiety, flow, and the self-rated importance of internet activities. *Computers in Human Behavior*, **25**, 490–500.

Kraut, R., Patterson, M., Landmark, V., Kiesler, S., Mukophadhyay, T., and Scherlis, W. (1998). Internet paradox: a social technology that reduces social involvement and psychological well-being? *American Psychologist*, **53**, 1017–1031.

Lee, J. M. and Ku, J. H. (2002). Virtual reality system for treatment of the fear of public speaking using image-based rendering and movie pictures. *Cyberpsychology and Behavior*, *5*, 191–195.

Loytskert, J. and Aiello, J. (1997, April). *Internet addiction and its personality correlates*. Paper presented at the 68th meeting of the Eastern Psychological Association, Washington, DC.

Maidenberg, E., Chen, E., Craske, M., Bohn, P., and Bystritsky, A. (1996). Specificity of attentional bias in panic disorder and social phobia. *Journal of Anxiety Disorders*, *10*, 529–541.

Mansell, W., Clark, D. M., Ehlers, A., and Chen, Y. P. (1999). Social anxiety and attention away from emotional faces. *Cognition and Emotion*, *13*, 673–690.

Mattia, J. I., Heimberg, R. G., and Hope, D. A. (1993). The revised Stroop color-naming task in social phobics. *Behaviour Research and Therapy*, *31*, 305–313.

McKenna, K. Y. A. and Bargh, J. A. (2000). Plan 9 for cyberspace: the implications of the internet for personality and social psychology. *Personality and Social Psychology Review*, *4*, 57–75.

Merckelbach, H., Van Hout, W., Van den Hout, M. A., and Mersch, P. P. (1989). Psychophysiological and subjective reactions of social phobics and normals to facial stimuli. *Behaviour Research and Therapy*, *27*, 289–294.

Mogg, K., Bradley, B. P., de Bono, J., and Painter, M. (1997). Time course of attentional bias for threat information in non-clinical anxiety. *Behaviour Research and Therapy*, *35*, 297–303.

Mogg, K. and Bradley, B. P. (1999). Some methodological issues in assessing attentional biases for threatening faces in anxiety: a replication study using a modified version of the probe detection task. *Behaviour Research and Therapy*, *37*, 595–604.

(2002). Selective orienting of attention to masked threat faces in social anxiety. *Behaviour Research and Therapy*, *40*, 1403–1414.

Mogg, K. and Bradley, B. V. P. (1998). A cognitive-motivational analysis of anxiety. *Behaviour Research and Therapy*, *36*, 809–848.

Mogg, K., Philippot, P., and Bradley, B. (2004). Selective attention to angry faces in a clinical sample with social phobia. *Journal of Abnormal Psychology*, *113*, 160–165.

Morahan-Martin, J. and Schumacher, P. (2000). Incidence and correlates of pathological internet use among college students. *Computers in Human Behavior*, *16*, 2–13.

(2003). Loneliness and social uses of the internet. *Computers in Human Behavior*, *19*, 659–671.

Musa, C. Z. and Lépine, J. P. (2000). Cognitive aspects of social phobia: a review of theories and experimental research. *European Psychiatry*, *15*, 59–66.

Öhman, A. and Soares, J. J. F. (1993). On the automatic nature of phobic fear: conditioned electrodermal responses to masked fear-relevant stimuli. *Journal of Abnormal Psychology*, *102*, 121–132.

O'Toole, K. (2000). *Study offers early look at how internet is changing daily life*. Standford News. http://news.standford.edu/pr/00/000216internet.html.

Pélissolo, A., André, C., Moutard-Martin, M. F., Wittchen, H. U., and Lépine, J.-P. (2000). Social phobia in the community: relationship between diagnostic threshold and prevalence. *European Psychiatry*, *15*, 25–28.

Pew Internet and American Life Project (2002). Teenage life online: the rise of instant message generation and the internet's impact on friendships and family relationship. www.pewinternet.org/reports/2001/Teenage-Life-Online.aspx.

Philippot, P. and Douilliez, C. (2005). Social phobics do not misinterpret facial expression of emotion. *Behaviour Research and Therapy*, **43**(5), 639–652.

Rapee, R. M. and Heimberg, R. G. (1997). A cognitive-behavioral model of anxiety in social phobia. *Behaviour Research and Therapy*, **35**, 741–756.

Reid, E. (1993). Electronic chat: social issues on the Internet Relay Chat. *Media Information Australia*, **67**, 62–70.

Russell, D. W. (1996). UCLA Loneliness Scale (Version 3): reliability, validity, and factor structure. *Journal of Personality Assessment*, **66**, 20–40.

Safren, S. A. and Turk, C. L. (1998). Factor structure of the Social Interaction Anxiety Scale and the Social Phobia Scale. *Behaviour Research and Therapy*, **36**, 443–453.

Savitsky, K. and Gilovich, T. (2003). The illusion of transparency and the alleviation of speech anxiety. *Journal of Experimental Social Psychology*, **39**, 618–625.

Schnarch, D. (1997). Sex, intimacy, and the internet. *Journal of Sex Education and Therapy*, **22**, 15–20.

Schouten, A., Valkenburg, P., and Peter, J. (2007). Precursors and underlying processes of adolescents' online self-disclosure: developing and testing an 'internet-attribute-perception' model. *Media Psychology*, **10**, 292–315.

Sheldon, P. (2008). The relationship between unwillingness-to-communicate and students' Facebook use. *Journal of Media Psychology: Theories, Methods, and Applications*, **20**, 67–75.

Shepherd, R. M. and Edelmann, R. J. (2001). Caught in the web. *Psychologist*, **14**, 520–521.

Solano, C. and Koester, N. (1989). Loneliness and communication problems: subjective anxiety or objective skills? *Personality and Social Psychology Bulletin*, **15**, 126–133.

Spurr, J. M. and Stopa, L. (2002). Self-focused attention in social phobia and social anxiety. *Clinical Psychology Review*, **22**, 947–975.

Turkle, S. (1995). *Life on the Screen: Identity in the Age of the Internet*. New York: Simon & Schuster.

Watson, D. and Friend, R. (1969). Measurement of social-evaluative anxiety. *Journal of Consulting and Clinical Psychology*, **33**, 448–457.

Weiller, E., Bisserbe, J.-C., Maier, W., and Lecrubier, Y. (1998). Prevalence and recognition of anxiety syndromes in five European primary care settings: a report from the WHO study on Psychological Problems in General Health Care. *British Journal of Psychiatry*, **17**, 18–23.

Williams, J. M. G., Watts, F. N., MacLeod, C., and Mathews, A. (1999). *Cognitive Psychology and Emotional Disorders* (2nd edn.). Chichester: Wiley.

Young, K. (1998). *Caught in the Net. How to Recognize Signs of Internet Addiction and a Winning Strategy for Recovery*. New York: Wiley.

CHAPTER 7

Facing the future: emotion communication and the presence of others in the age of video-mediated communication

Antony S. R. Manstead, Martin Lea, and Jeannine Goh

Overview: Video-mediated communication is about to become a ubiquitous feature of everyday life. This chapter considers the differences between face-to-face and video-mediated communication in terms of co-presence and considers the implications for the communication of emotion, self-disclosure, and relationship rapport. Following initial consideration of the concepts of physical presence and social presence, we describe recent studies of the effect of presence on the facial communication of emotion. We then delve further into the different social psychological aspects of presence, and present a study that investigated how these various aspects independently impact upon self-disclosure and rapport. We conclude by considering how the absence of co-presence in video-mediated interaction can liberate the communicators from some of the social constraints normally associated with face-to-face interaction, while maintaining others and introducing new constraints specific to the medium.

Video-mediated interpersonal interactions are set to become a ubiquitous feature of everyday life. Recent advances in communication technologies, such as affordable broadband access to the internet and the appearance of third-generation mobile phones, mean that the much-heralded advent of the videophone is about to become reality. As video becomes ubiquitous, it places the face center-stage for the communication of emotion on the internet, much as it is in our normal "face-to-face" interactions. Of course the big difference between the face-to-face interactions that we take for granted today and the face-to-face interaction of the future is the absence of physical co-presence. In this new form of visual interaction, actors are separated by distance, communicating via webcams and computers or mobile phones.

In this chapter, we consider some of the social psychological implications of interacting face-to-face without physical co-presence. What does the absence of co-presence remove from the interaction? What might it add to the interaction? Does psychological presence necessarily imply physical co-presence? How does presence change the expression and communication of emotion, and how do these changes impact upon the rapport between two people in the context of developing new relationships or maintaining existing ones? Does lack of co-presence constrain the interaction or can it free the communicators from the normal constraints associated with face-to-face interaction, to create greater intimacy? What are the implications for the tens of millions of people who already share their intimate disclosures with others on the internet through self-help groups (Gackenbach, 1998), and the even larger number of people who use it to form new relationships and maintain existing ones (Lea and Spears, 1995), for whom video-mediated communication is about to become an everyday reality?

Technological considerations

Although video technology will, in a sense, bring face-to-face communication to the internet, there are of course important differences between "normal" face-to-face co-present interactions and video-mediated interactions over the internet. Many of these relate to technological features of the communication, and in particular some of the technically imposed constraints resulting from an as yet immature technology. These include transmission delays due to the limited bandwidth capacity of the internet and local networks (considered by Parkinson and Lea, Chapter 5, this volume), display delays due to the immense processing requirements for displaying moving faces, slow frame rates, and low-resolution images (Wallbott, 1991). But let us assume that these technical problems can be overcome with time. After all, processing power and typical bandwidth for accessing the internet have been increasing rapidly year on year, so we can probably safely assume that these technical constraints on internet videotelephony are temporary. However, other technical constraints are likely to remain for some time to come. Notwithstanding the development of teleimmersive environments (e.g., Raskar *et al.*, 1998), which promise a 3D experience of computer-mediated communication (CMC), video-mediated communication is essentially a 2D experience in contrast with the 3D experience of normal face-to-face interaction. The use of display screens, whether they are on the desk or in the hand, means that interpersonal distance is changed (often reduced) compared to normal co-present interactions.

The use of optical and digital zoom on cameras also means that interpersonal distance norms are changed in the video-mediated environment. Angles of view are also different. All these factors in turn mean that patterns of gazing are likely to be changed and that opportunities for mutual eye gaze are different from face-to-face interaction.

In this chapter we are going to put these technical issues and their impacts to one side and consider what is arguably the most profound difference between normal face-to-face interaction and video-mediated face-to-face interaction: the issue of co-presence. Specifically, we are going to consider the implications of co-presence, or its absence, on the communication of emotion, self-disclosure, and relationship rapport. The structure of the chapter is as follows. First, we will discuss the concept of presence and distinguish between physical presence and social presence. Next we will describe some recent studies that have examined the effect of presence on the facial communication of emotion. We will then attempt to decompose presence further into its different social psychological aspects, and describe a study that investigated how these various aspects independently impact upon self-disclosure and rapport. We will conclude by considering how the absence of co-presence in video-mediated interaction can liberate communicators from some of the social constraints normally associated with face-to-face interaction while maintaining others and introducing new constraints specific to the medium.

The concept of presence

The origins of the concept of presence are closely linked to the communication bandwidth considerations noted above (Lea and Giordano, 1997). Anxieties and concerns about the social consequences of reduced communication bandwidth were raised following the introduction of the telegraph and telephone more than 100 years ago. Anecdotal accounts of dire consequences (such as betrayal, fraud, and abuse) which befell those who naively treated full and attenuated bandwidth as if they were socially equivalent fueled debates among professional engineers as to what constituted sufficient presence for a medium to be judged as equivalent to face-to-face communication (Marvin, 1988, pp. 86–96).

The modern formulation of communication bandwidth in information theory and its application to communication by either humans or machines (Frick, 1959) provided the conceptual foundations for social evaluations of different media based on a mechanistic analysis of communication capacity. The corollary of this approach is that maximum "social presence" is found in normal face-to-face interaction where full physical presence pertains.

Thus, research into telephone communication in the 1970s (Short, Williams, and Christie, 1976) and CMC in the 1990s (Rice, 1993) attempted, with varying success, to map the bandwidth of different media onto communicators' subjective evaluations of social presence during interaction. Short *et al.* defined social presence as "the salience of the other in a mediated communication and the consequent salience of their interpersonal interactions" (p. 65). In practice, it is operationalized by dimensions such as unsociable–sociable, insensitive–sensitive, cold–warm, and impersonal–personal. Short *et al.* argued that restrictions on the ability to send nonverbal signals in certain media would reduce the immediacy of mediated communication, and thereby its quality. Immediacy in turn refers to the "degree of the intensity and directness of interaction between a communicator and the object of his communication" (Mehrabian, 1967, p. 414). Like social presence, immediacy was also held to enhance closeness, and a range of verbal and nonverbal immediacy behaviors that promoted affiliation were quickly adduced. Nonverbal cues such as voice, posture, facial behavior, and eye gaze have long been regarded as the essential lubricants and regulators of social interaction, as well as contributing to impression formation, rapport, and acquaintanceship development. First and foremost, they provide an important channel for communicating emotional intimacy in relationships (e.g., Altman and Taylor, 1973; Argyle and Dean, 1965; Patterson, 1973; Reis and Shaver, 1988). Thus, bandwidth and other constraints that prevent or limit the capacity of certain media to communicate nonverbal cues are considered to be the crucial factors underlying reduced social presence in various communication media relative to the ideal of face-to-face interaction. The social presence approach therefore predicts that the telephone, for example, would be rated lower than face-to-face communication in social presence, and numerous rating studies generally bear this out. However, a problem for the presence approach is that it cannot explain why in certain situations emotional communication and intimacy can be achieved in spite of using a medium supposedly low in social presence (Salem *et al.*, 1997). Indeed, the success of telephone crisis lines and help lines, such as the Samaritans, and their computer equivalents seems to depend very much on the *absence* of nonverbal cues and identifiers in the medium (Greist *et al.*, 1973).

Arguably, however, this conceptualization of social presence conflates two aspects of presence, the physical and the social dimensions. It might be more useful to treat these as distinct in order to analyze their psychological impacts (Biocca *et al.*, 2003; Ijsselstein, de Ridder, Freeman, and Avons, 2000; Rogers and Lea, 2005). The physical aspect of presence refers to the sense of being physically located somewhere, and physical co-presence more accurately refers to the sense of being located in the same place as another. Lack of co-presence then refers to the awareness of not being in the same location as another. Thus, one can have the sense of physically being in the same room as another, or of being in different nearby rooms, or of being separated by great physical distance. As the distance between the two locations increases, the likelihood of any communication being mediated by technology also increases, and media differ in the extent to which they can "transport" someone, psychologically, to the same place as another. Teleimmersive environments, for example, are considered to provide the closest psychological approximation to actual physical presence, and many have argued that videoconferencing, and to a lesser extent the telephone, can partially create a sense of "being there."[1]

Social presence, on the other hand, refers to the extent to which the situation is made social through the communication setting and the norms associated with it, the nature of the interpersonal relationship between the communicators, common group membership, shared social identities, and the unfolding communication itself. A sense of physical presence therefore refers to one's awareness of the *capacity* to relate to another in the physical space or the technology – for example, the capacity to see and/or be seen by another, or the capacity to communicate verbally or nonverbally. Social presence, on the other hand, refers to the social meaning that is given to these capacities, depending on the interpersonal (and group-based) relations between the communicators that are defined both prior to and during the unfolding social interaction, together with the social norms that prevail in the situation. Thus, one can experience physical presence through the sense of being, say, in a church or a library with another, but whether one experiences social presence depends on some degree of actual or implied social interaction – by participating in a communal activity, for example, rather than praying or reading alone. Furthermore, the precise nature of the experience of social presence will depend upon the kinds of social bonds described above. Thus, the capacity to communicate nonverbally will often be given a social meaning that can be portrayed as sociable, warm, and personal – the usual descriptors of social presence – when the interaction is with a friend or with a stranger with whom one is motivated to develop a positive relationship. But, equally, one can conceive of a high social

---

[1] Virtual reality systems in which interactants are represented by avatars may also provide a sense of presence (Biocca *et al.*, 2001).

presence situation being described as more unsociable, colder, or impersonal than a low presence situation precisely because the situation is capable of revealing more of, in the case of dislike, for example, the negative relationship between two interactants, and because positive communications are being withheld or responded to negatively.

The latter point is significant because, although social presence was originally defined by Short *et al.* in terms of salience of person and interaction, the way in which it has been operationally defined in many empirical studies (including those by Short himself) means that high social presence has become practically synonymous with sociability and intimacy, and the notion that rejecting, threatening, and hostile communication can be highly salient, and therefore just as indicative of high social presence, has been all but ignored. Similarly, immediacy – originally defined by Mehrabian to reflect interaction intensity – has coalesced with affiliation/rapport behaviors in many papers and studies (e.g., O'Sullivan *et al.*, 2004; Witt *et al.*, 2004). This conflation of social presence and immediacy as processes with desirable outcomes such as intimacy, affiliation, and rapport appears to reflect a pro-social bias or ideology of intimacy prevalent in communication research (Adams, 2001; Parks, 1982).

In short, two crucial aspects of presence are (1) awareness of another and of the capacity to relate to them – that is, the sense of physical presence; and (2) the social meaning given to the relating situation, which is often, but not necessarily, described in positive terms – that is, the sense of social presence. The degree of physical presence of a communication medium is therefore defined by its capacity to support relating to others – the kind of social cues it transmits, for example – as well as the social norms associated with the use of the communication medium, but the degree of social presence in a communication medium is essentially a matter of social meaning (often involving an evaluative component) that is necessarily unfixed and influenced by the social context of the communication.

With these conceptual refinements in mind, we now move on to review some of the social contextual factors surrounding emotion communication and how they relate to physical presence. In particular we will focus on how the *implied* presence of another – the awareness that another is nearby (in another room, for example) even though one is not in fact communicating with them – can affect facial behavior during emotional stimulation. We will be examining some research that suggests that even in these minimal presence conditions, facial communication of emotion or motivation takes place and is influenced by the social meaning of the situation.

Facial communication of emotion under minimal physical presence

As we have seen, much of the argument concerning media presence turns on the notion that nonverbal channels are reduced relative to face-to-face communication, which in turn implies a reduced capacity for emotion communication with consequent impacts upon the quality of social interaction. The notion that emotion is a vital part of everyday social communication has been cogently expressed by Zajonc (1980):

> There are practically no social phenomena that do not implicate affect in some important way. Affect dominates social interaction, and it is the major currency in which social intercourse is transacted. The vast majority of our daily conversations entail the exchange of information about our opinions, preferences, and evaluations. And affect in these conversations is transmitted not only by the verbal channel but by nonverbal cues as well – cues that may, in fact, carry the principal components of information about affect. It is much less important for us to know whether someone has just said 'You are a friend' or 'You are a fiend' than to know whether it was spoken in contempt or with affection. (p. 153)

It follows that if one strips away some or all of the nonverbal cues, the quality of communication will in some sense be degraded.

Interestingly, while researchers concerned with the impact of the internet on the communication process have been debating and researching the importance of social presence, there has developed a quite separate line of research in the psychology of emotion on the effects of social presence on emotional expression and experience, which we refer to here as *social context research*. Social context research has a variety of ancestors. One of the most important of these is ethology. Ethologists who study expressive behavior have long been aware of the ways in which this behavior is affected by social context. A frequently cited paper grounded in this ethological tradition is the one by Kraut and Johnston (1979). In one of the studies reported in this paper, Kraut and Johnston observed tenpin bowlers in two sorts of context, the first being when they knew what they had just scored but were still facing the pins, and the second being when they turned around to face their playing partners. The bowlers were observed to remain relatively inexpressive when facing the pins, even after scoring a spare or a strike, but to smile when facing their playing partners. The perhaps reasonable assumption of Kraut and Johnston was that there was no difference in the emotional state of the bowler between the moment that he or she scored a spare or a strike and the moment that he or she faced the fellow players. So the variation in facial behavior cannot be explained in terms of the underlying emotional state. Instead, they argued, on the basis of this and the other studies they reported, that *social involvement* is a major cause of smiling, independent of the individual's emotional state. Conceptually similar findings have been reported by Fernández-Dols and Ruiz-Belda (1995).

Such findings provide a potential challenge to what might be called the "textbook" view of facial expression of emotion, which holds that – other things being equal – so-called "basic emotions" are expressed in the face in rather invariant ways. An extensive program of research conducted by Ekman and Friesen (e.g., 1971), for example, shows that Western judges show a high degree of consensus in assigning still photographs of facial expressions to a prescribed set of emotion categories; and that members of preliterate cultures, such as the Fore of New Guinea, also exhibit above-chance agreement with these Western classifications. It is argued that such pancultural consensus reflects a fundamental consistency in the way in which subjective emotion is outwardly expressed in the face. How else is the consensus in reading facial expressions to be explained? These cross-cultural findings are supported by within-culture studies of the association between subjective emotion and spontaneous, covertly recorded facial behavior (e.g., Ekman *et al.*, 1980; Rosenberg and Ekman, 1994).

However, there are some limitations to this research program. With regard to the cross-cultural research, Russell (1994) has identified a number of problems, some methodological and some empirical in nature. With regard to the within-culture studies, the evidence concerning associations between subjective emotion and overt facial behavior is offset to some extent by other studies that failed to find such an association (e.g., Fernández-Dols *et al.*, 1997). A further line of work that raises questions about the "textbook" view of the relation between emotion and facial behavior is one in which facial behavior – but not emotion – is shown to vary as a function of social context. It is this line of work that is most relevant to our present concerns.

What makes this line of research relevant is not so much the finding that an expression generally thought to be expressive of, say, happiness or amusement is imperfectly related to how happy or amused people subjectively feel, as the evidence that facial displays vary systematically as a function of how social the situation is. How social the situation is, moreover, depends not simply on the physical presence of other people. A friend who is physically absent but who is engaged in the same task can also increase the sociality of the situation and thereby influence facial displays. The best-known evidence for this conclusion is the experiment reported by Alan Fridlund (1991). Participants in this study viewed a pleasant videotape under one of four conditions: alone; while believing a friend who accompanied them to the laboratory to be performing a different task (completing a questionnaire) in another room; while believing their friend to be viewing the same pleasant tape at the same time as the participant, but in a different room; and together with the friend in the same room. These conditions progress from least to most social. Fridlund's key findings were (1) that smiling increased as a function of sociality and (2) that subjective happiness did *not* vary as a function of sociality.

Important for our present concern is that even the *implicit* presence of the friend was sufficient to increase smiling behavior, especially when the friend was engaged in the same task as the participant. Fridlund explains this finding in terms of a "social role analysis." Friends who are sharing a pleasant experience, whether this sharing is face-to-face or physically remote, are in a role that calls for the frequent reciprocation of affiliative smiles. It is worth considering carefully the implications of these findings for internet communications. Friends watching the same amusing stimulus but who were physically remote from each other and were not even directly communicating with each other smiled nearly as much as friends who were watching the same stimulus in the same room. It seems reasonable to gloss the finding by saying that friends doing the same thing as oneself at the same time are socially present – at least, if the thing that is being done by the friend and oneself is affectively pleasant. One of the factors that underlies this social presence effect is probably the anticipation by friends that they will at some point have the opportunity to share their experience of the pleasant film. This suggests that the quality of the relationship between interaction partners moderates the impact of losing nonverbal cues, such that CMC has a greater impact on the quality of communication between nonfriends than between friends.

Our own research extends Fridlund's line of thinking by showing that the impact of social context on facial behavior is associated with and almost certainly mediated by two variables. The first is what we call *social motivation*. This is a construct borrowed fairly directly from Fridlund's (e.g., 1994) theoretical arguments concerning the evolutionary function served by facial displays. In brief, his argument is that the capacity to signal our social motives and intentions in a given set of circumstances, together with other people's capacities to notice these signals and take appropriate action, have survival value. Among other things, these capacities help individuals to establish social bonds and to avoid potentially deadly conflicts. The primary function of facial displays, on this analysis, is to signal our social motives. So-called "happy" faces are not expressing the individual's happiness per se but rather this person's motivation to affiliate with those around him or her by sharing a pleasant experience. So-called "sad" faces are not expressing the individual's sadness per se but rather this person's motivation to seek comfort and reassurance from those around him or her.

What we and others (e.g., Hess *et al.*, 1995) have shown is that if a person is exposed to a pleasant or humorous emotional stimulus and believes that a friend is being exposed to the same stimulus at the same time, he or she will smile more than if that other person is a stranger. Furthermore, the effects of the intensity of an emotional stimulus on facial behavior are often weaker or even nonexistent if the other person is a stranger, a finding first reported by Hess *et al.* (1995). Such findings are by no means limited to film stimuli. In one study (Jakobs *et al.*, 1999), we used humorous stories as the stimulus material, and had participants listen to these stories as told by a friend or a stranger in one of three ways: on a tape-recording, via a telephone, or face-to-face. Two stories were told, one of which had been shown in pretesting to be consistently funnier than the other. Facial behavior while listening to the stories was covertly video-recorded and subsequently scored, using the facial action coding system (FACS; Ekman and Friesen, 1978), a system for classifying all visible facial movement into one of 44 action units (AUs). Some of these AUs are especially relevant to smiling. AU12 is called the "lip corner raiser," and it raises the corners of the mouth upward, into what we colloquially call a smile; it corresponds largely to activation of the zygomaticus major muscle. AU6 is called the "cheek raiser," and it raises the cheeks by contracting the muscle that encircles the eye socket; it therefore corresponds largely to activation of this orbicularis oculi muscle. The combination of AU12 and AU6 is thought to produce an "enjoyment" or "Duchenne" smile, one that reflects the subjective experience of pleasant affect.

Mean AU12 and AU6 scores found in the Jakobs *et al.* (1999) study are shown in Figure 7.1. There were main effects of story, identity, and communication channel. As expected, the strong story elicited more smiling than did the moderate story. Also, more smiles were observed in the friend conditions than in the stranger conditions. Finally, there were significant interactions between story and identity and between identity and communication channel. These can best be summarized by saying that measures of facial activity were facilitated (1) if the storyteller was a friend and if the story was a strong one, and (2) if the storyteller was a friend and was also physically present.

Turning now to social motives, we had three measures: social motivation, motivation to express, and awareness of the storyteller. Mean scores on these scales are shown in Figure 7.2. There was a significant main effect of identity. Participants were more aware of the storyteller if he or she was a friend rather than a stranger. A main effect of

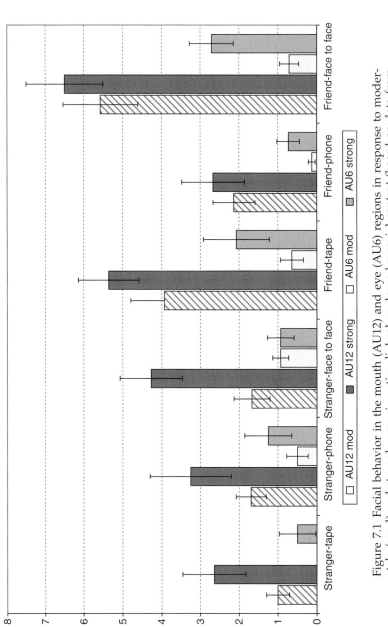

Figure 7.1 Facial behavior in the mouth (AU12) and eye (AU6) regions in response to moderately (mod) and strongly amusing stimuli, broken down by social context (based on data from Jakobs *et al.*, 1999).

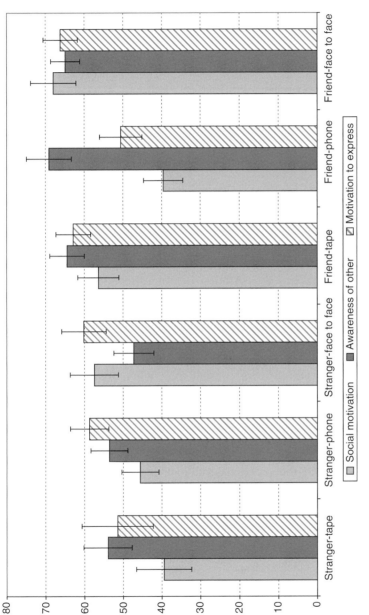

Figure 7.2 Mean scores for measures of social motivation, broken down by social context (based on data from Jakobs et al., 1999).

communication channel was also found. Social motivation scores were lower in the tape-recorder and telephone conditions than in the face-to-face condition. With regard to the issue of mediation, *motivation to express* proved to be a significant covariate. Although the main effects of identity and communication channel remained significant after the introduction of motive to express as a covariate, the interactions between story and identity, and between identity and communication channel were no longer significant. So although we can only speak here of *partial* mediation, it is interesting that at least some of the effects of varying the social context disappeared when controlling for one of the measures of social motivation.

The second variable that we believe to be crucial in determining how expressive people are in these sorts of situations is the *perceived appropriateness* of showing emotion in a given situation. Ekman and Friesen (1969) used the term "display rule" to refer to culturally variable norms governing expressive behavior in social settings. Although there is remarkably little by way of direct evidence that such norms influence facial behavior, there are good reasons to think that they do so. Consider the following experiment (Jakobs *et al.*, 2001). Participants viewed sad film clips that differed in strength under conditions that varied with respect to two key features of the social context, namely physical presence (explicit present, implicit present, alone), and identity of the other person (friend versus stranger). When we analyzed facial behavior, we found a main effect of condition on *frequency of sad expressions* and on *frequency of smiles*. Sad expressions were less frequent when others were present than when the participant was alone (see Figure 7.3). However, smiles were more frequent when a friend was present.

So social context effects on facial displays were found in this study, but there was no evidence that displays of sadness were more frequent in the implicit or explicit presence of friends. On the contrary, by comparison with the alone condition, there were *fewer* displays of sadness in all conditions in which another person was implicitly or explicitly present. As in our previous research, friends elicited stronger awareness of and motivation to communicate with the other than did strangers. However, of the two types of facial behavior influenced by social context (i.e., sad expressions and smiles), only smiling was related to social motives. What was responsible for the marked absence of sad facial displays in the social conditions of this experiment? Although we have no direct evidence for the operation of display rules in this study, it seems reasonable to assume that displays of sadness were regulated, consciously or unconsciously, by a norm that prescribes that as a Western adult one should not exhibit "weak"

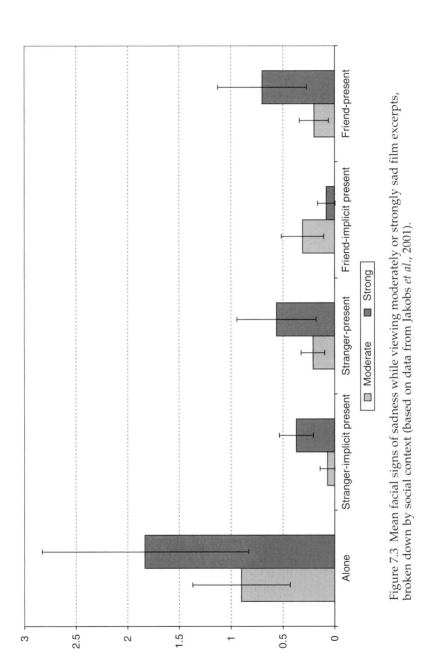

Figure 7.3 Mean facial signs of sadness while viewing moderately or strongly sad film excerpts, broken down by social context (based on data from Jakobs *et al.*, 2001).

emotions (at least not in response to a "mere" movie) in a social context – even if others are not physically present to observe those expressions. In subsequent research we have examined the role of display rules more directly (Zaalberg *et al.*, 2004).

What conclusions can we draw from this line of research on the impact of social context on facial displays? First, the *psychological* presence of others plays a key role in shaping facial displays. When others are psychologically present, there is some sense in which we communicate with them through facial behaviors, even if we are not directly interacting with them. So the fact that the person with whom you are communicating is in another room, another city, or, indeed, another continent does not mean that one does not smile "at" him or her, especially if he or she is a friend, or is someone with whom you would like to be a friend.

Second, although these facial behaviors are certainly affective in nature, it would be incorrect simply to characterize them as expressive (or not expressive) of emotion. Rather, they are used (especially when the interactants are friends) as ways of maintaining or strengthening their relationship. When we exchange smiles in everyday life, we communicate not so much the fact that we are happy as such, but rather that we are positively disposed to the other person. Quite how positive this disposition is will be reflected in the nature of the smile. A briefly flashed AU12 may simply acknowledge the other's presence, rather than ignoring him or her, which at least provides the basis for a relationship. A longer or more intense Duchenne smile may reflect happiness with the relationship or a desire to strengthen the relationship. Think of such smiles as a mixture of social lubricant and social glue: They smooth social interaction and help people to stick to each other.

Third, these facial behaviors can be (and often are) regulated for social purposes. Regulation does not of course necessarily mean that the behaviors are masked, minimized, or neutralized. They can also be enhanced, as when we smile or laugh at jokes that are not inherently amusing, or admire hairstyles that are not inherently attractive, or applaud performances that are not inherently impressive. Such regulation need not be "insincere." The expression of such positive emotion (or the suppression of negative emotion) may be a genuine reflection of our valuation of our relationship with the other persons concerned. In our view, regulation emerges from two sets of factors, one of which is what we have called social motivation, and is specific to the relationship(s) entailed in the setting, and the other of which is display rules, which are more general social norms about the appropriateness of expressing affect in a given social situation.

Let us summarize our observations so far about facial behavior and the communication of emotion in relation to presence. To begin with, it is clear that the complete absence of physical presence does not preclude facial expressions of affect.[2] Even a condition of implied presence, where the expresser is merely aware of the presence of another nearby, in another room, engaged in a similar task, but there is no possibility of actually communicating with the other, is sufficient to produce emotion expression. Moreover, the relationship between the two "communicators" influences the degree of awareness of the other communicator – that is, the sense of the social presence of the other – and this, combined with the capacity to communicate, influences the motivation to express emotion and in turn the amount of facial behavior. Thus the influence of physical presence upon facial behavior is dependent on the relationship between the interactants, their degree of social motivation, and their motivation to express. Secondly, and regardless of the communicators' capacity to communicate, cultural norms associated with display rules for emotion, together with the social norms associated with the personal relationship between communicators, combine to influence facial behavior. In short, social presence can be high and influence facial behavior during emotion even when physical presence is low, and this in turn suggests that a categorization of presence in terms of the different kinds of communication media that the internet supports is likely to yield no fixed relation to the quality of communication as shown by the face. Instead we need to consider carefully which factors underlie presence, how they map onto the different kinds of media that the internet supports, and how their impacts are affected by the social bonds and other aspects of the social context that pertain in the communication situation.

Although the distinction between friends and strangers is useful to demonstrate the influence of relational context on emotion communication even in the absence of physical co-presence and actual facial communication, it is difficult to identify the important aspects of these differences and how they interact with the features of presence to create their social psychological effects. After all, strangers and friends differ from one another on a number of dimensions, including identifiability, similarity, intimacy, history of interaction, likelihood of future interaction, shared norms for communication, and so on. For

---

[2] Of course, the fact that affective expressions occur in the physical absence of others is exactly what proponents of a neurocultural (Ekman, 1972) or "readout" (Buck, 1994) perspective on facial behavior during emotional experience would predict: When an individual is alone, facial behavior is not "contaminated" by the influence of display rules, and should therefore be a pure reflection of emotional stimulation.

example, friends are more similar on a range of attributes, including attitudes and values (Lea and Duck, 1982), and are aware that they are likely to agree in their interpretation of social stimuli (Funder and Colvin, 1988). Friends and strangers also differ with respect to the degree of other-focused attention, and this affects accurate understanding of emotion communication (Trommsdorff and John, 1992).

To explore these issues further, we adopted a different approach in the experiment described below, in which many of the features of the dyadic relationship were held constant and physical presence was decomposed into its underlying features, which were then systematically manipulated. The results revealed some surprising evidence of the social constraints on emotion communication produced, not always as one might expect by the absence of co-presence in internet communications, but also by those aspects of presence that are inherent in our normal face-to-face communications.

Decomposing physical co-presence

As noted earlier, it is generally accepted that nonverbal cues form an important channel for communicating emotion, intimacy, and rapport, and that the face is a particularly relevant aspect of nonverbal communication in this regard. However, nonverbal cues serve several other functions, one very important aspect of which is the communication of visual identity. Similarly, we have noted that a crucial determinant of presence is the capacity to communicate nonverbal cues, and it is reasonable to suppose that both the identity and emotion communication functions of nonverbal cues contribute to our sense of presence.

In our experiment (Goh, 2004), we created a scenario that maximized the salience of facial communication of affect for participants. Each participant interacted with a stranger confederate following a carefully piloted procedure designed to encourage voluntary self-disclosure in an acquaintanceship exercise. The participant and confederate took turns to pose questions on different topics to one another from a prepared list that had been independently ranked for their intimacy value in a scenario similar to the experiment. The confederate was trained to respond with their previously prepared honest, open, and highly disclosing answers to these questions and also to pose questions from the list that consistently invited more intimate disclosures from the participant. However, the participant was free to answer (or not) as they wished and to choose questions that were more or less intimate to ask the confederate. Thus, the procedure relied upon acquaintanceship and reciprocity of disclosure norms (Altman and Taylor, 1973; Jourard and Jaffe, 1970) to encourage self-disclosure by participants. The participant and confederate were located in separate cubicles and interacted by means of a text-based computer conferencing system under one of three conditions. In the baseline *anonymity* condition, dyads were visually anonymous and interacted solely via the keyboard. In the second *identifiability* condition, the participant and confederate briefly saw one another while being led into separate cubicles, where their communication was solely text-based via the keyboard, as before. In the third *visual cues* condition, the procedure was exactly the same as in the second, except that text-based communication was augmented by the addition of a live silent videoconferencing link that displayed the faces of participant and confederate to one another in real time. Compared to the baseline condition, the second condition added the key component of visual identifiability to the situation, and condition three added both identifiability and nonverbal facial cues to the interaction. Independent coding of the transcripts of the discussions was used to quantify self-disclosure on two dimensions reflecting the distinction between breadth of self-disclosure (i.e., the number of different topics on which people self-disclose) and depth of self-disclosure (i.e., the extent to which people disclose intimate information; Altman and Taylor, 1973). Additional variables derived from self-report questionnaires measured trust in the confederate's openness, perceived disclosure reciprocity, private and public self-awareness, perceived similarity and rapport with the confederate, and perceived therapeutic value and enjoyment of the interaction.

The main comparisons between the anonymous and identifiable conditions can be summarized as follows (Figure 7.4). Introducing identifiability reduced the breadth and depth of self-disclosure; private self-awareness was also reduced, but public self-awareness and perceptions of partner openness increased. Rapport was unaffected, but the enjoyment and therapeutic value of the interaction were both reduced. Self-disclosure was perceived to be least reciprocal under anonymity, reflecting the participant's self-focus in this condition, which they also found to be of most therapeutic value. In sum, identifiability had a largely inhibitory effect upon self-disclosure, as well as directing attentional focus outwards.

Comparing the results of the identifiability and visibility conditions (Figure 7.5) allowed us to assess the effects of adding nonverbal cues to the interaction through the video link, independently of the effects of identifiability. The addition of nonverbal cues further reduced the breadth of self-disclosure, but *increased* the depth of self-disclosure to a level comparable with the anonymous condition. There were no effects on public self-awareness or partner trust, which were at similar

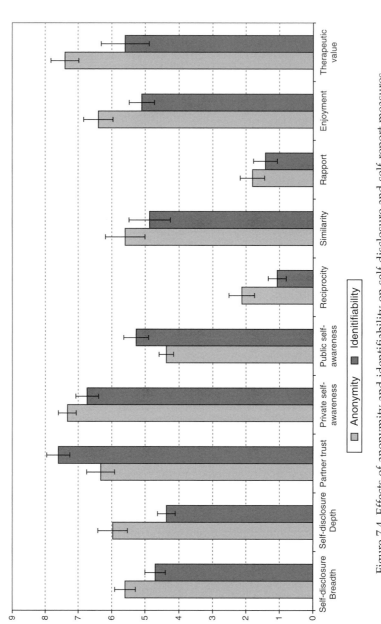

Figure 7.4 Effects of anonymity and identifiability on self-disclosure and self-report measures.

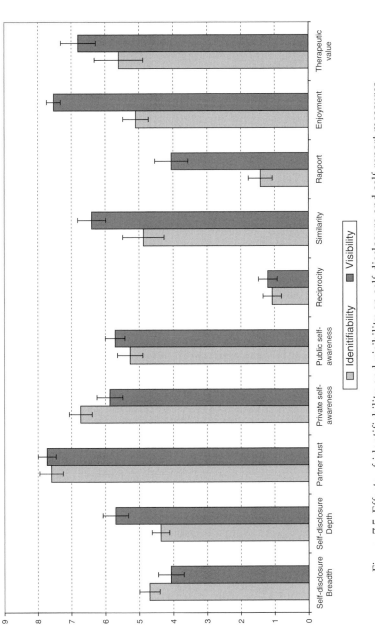

Figure 7.5 Effects of identifiability and visibility on self-disclosure and self-report measures.

levels to the indentifiable condition. However, perceived similarity and rapport with the partner were elevated, along with perceptions of therapeutic value and enjoyment of the interaction.

Our general interpretation of these comparisons is as follows. Visual identifiability has the effect of making the participant more generally aware of the presence of the other interactant, as reflected in increased trust in confederate openness and increased concerns about being evaluated by the confederate. This attention to the other is accompanied by a reduced focus on the private self, inhibiting the participant's own self-disclosure, and particularly intimate self-disclosures. Thus, one observes two functions of identifiability, a key component of presence, in this acquaintanceship situation: the first resulting from the identifiability of the self to the other, which has a generally inhibitory effect upon self-disclosure; the second resulting from the identifiability of the other to the self, which increases trust in the other. Identifiability does not in itself have implications for relationship development (perceived partner similarity and rapport remained at the levels found under anonymity), but seems to encourage a more superficial level of interaction, which is consequently experienced as having less therapeutic value.

The addition of nonverbal cues, the second key component of presence, has a markedly different effect, changing the nature of the encounter into a more personal interaction. There is greater intimacy in self-disclosure, and perceived similarity and partner rapport are at their highest levels in this condition, consistent with developing acquaintanceship. Thus, two key components of physical presence have opposing effects on self-disclosure. Facial cues function to increase the interpersonal quality of the interaction – which in this case means building rapport and encouraging self-disclosure, increasing acquaintanceship, and providing the foundations for relationship formation. However, visual identification is another powerful social psychological effect of physical presence that is not dependent upon online exchange of visual cues, but simply relies on the ability to notice and be noticed by another, if only for an instant. Despite the brevity of the visual exchange, this brings a different set of social psychological features to the interaction, such as legitimacy, accountability, and vulnerability, for which interpersonal and intergroup power relations are key (Spears and Lea, 1994). In the current mutual disclosure situation, being able to visually identify another is valued for the increased confidence it provides that the partner's self-disclosures are open and honest (because in some sense the partner could potentially be held accountable for them). For the same reason, being identified oneself increases feelings of personal vulnerability and accountability that lead to a more cautions approach to revealing the self to others – and this is reflected in reduced willingness to reciprocate self-disclosures.

Although identifiability and facial cues are two critical features of presence, it is unlikely that these are the only important aspects. Full presence adds a plethora of nonverbal cues, such as posture and gestures, which can combine with facial behavior to communicate emotion more powerfully (Flack *et al.*, 1999). Prolonged physical proximity during interaction also increases the potential implications of the communication for social action, and the potential for future interaction is greater than when interactants have only briefly met. For these reasons we might expect greater levels of intimate self-disclosure to accompany face-to-face interaction than video-mediated interaction. In short, the capacity for relatedness is increased in co-present face-to-face interaction, and this is precisely what the media comparison literature assumes (e.g., Rice, 1993; Rutter, 1987; Short *et al.*, 1976). Of course, there are further reasons why co-present face-to-face interaction might affect self-disclosure. Spontaneity and immediacy of feedback are highest in normal face-to-face interaction, meaning that closer coordination and social control of the interaction is possible (Edinger and Patterson, 1983; Kiesler *et al.*, 1984; Lea, 1991). However, the biggest difference is likely to arise from the oral mode of verbal interaction in normal face-to-face interaction, which allows more information to be exchanged in a given time, speeding the process of acquaintanceship, but confounding comparisons of co-present and distributed visual interaction with verbal communication modality (Lea *et al.*, 2001).

In order to compare the additional contribution of face-to-face co-presence over identifiability and nonverbal cues, we introduced a fourth condition to our experiment. Here the communicators were co-present in the same room, facing one another, but communicated verbally only by the text-based conferencing system, as in previous conditions, in order to eliminate any effects due to oral communication under co-presence. Furthermore, the physical constraints of the interaction situation, in which partners were seated in front of a monitor and typing at the keyboard, meant that additional cues that might have been provided through posture and gesture were also largely controlled for (e.g., Bull and Brown, 1977).

Surprisingly, the comparisons between the video-mediated and co-present conditions revealed significantly lower levels of breadth and depth of self-disclosure in co-present interaction (Figure 7.6). In fact, self-disclosure was lower than in any of the other three conditions. Perceived similarity and partner rapport were also reduced, along

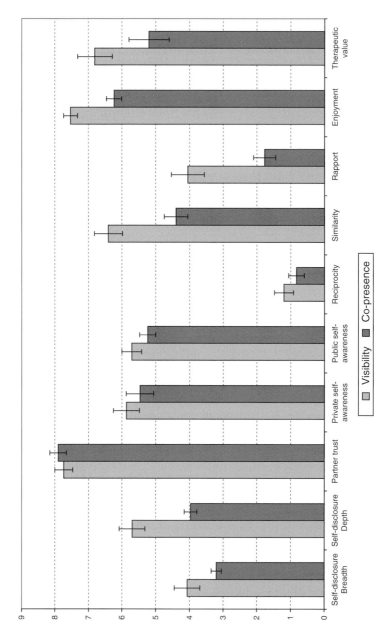

Figure 7.6 Effects of visibility and co-presence on self-disclosure and self-report measures.

with enjoyment of the interaction and its perceived therapeutic value. These findings are striking: Co-present interaction produced lower rapport and less intimate self-disclosure than video-mediated interaction. This is contrary to what media comparative approaches, such as social presence theory, predict. However, given the points we made earlier regarding definitions of social presence, we argue that this does not necessarily mean that our physically co-present condition had less social presence than video-mediated communication. Providing that one adheres to the original conception of social presence as *salience* of the person and the interaction, it is quite possible that under co-presence the interaction partners – or certain aspects of the partner/ interaction – were more salient, and yet (or rather precisely because of this) the interaction was lower in intimacy and rapport. So what factors are there in co-presence, over and above identifiability and nonverbal cues, that might increase interaction salience and yet explain this intriguing pattern of results? One answer is suggested to us by the markedly different patterns of eye gaze that were reported by the confederate in co-present and video-mediated interactions, with a much greater tendency for gaze avoidance under co-presence. We shall therefore briefly explore how eye gaze differs between co-present and video-mediated interaction as well as how these differences may affect self-disclosure and emotion communication.

The functions of eye gaze and its associated norms in co-present face-to-face interaction have been well documented (Argyle and Cook, 1976; Kendon, 1967; Kleinke, 1986; Rutter, 1984). In brief, according to Kleinke (1986), eye gaze functions to provide information, regulate interaction, express intimacy, exercise social control, and facilitate service and task goals, and the norms are to avoid prolonged staring in normal face-to-face situations because such behavior can signal disagreement, conflict, and aggression (Deutsch, 1976; Newton and Burgoon, 1990). We believe, however, that such norms may not apply as strongly in video-mediated communication. Here the gazer is not looking directly at the target, but at an image of the target on the computer screen, lessening the intensity (i.e., immediacy) of the gaze. At the same time, mutual eye gaze (eye contact) is harder to achieve due to the angle of view separating the camera from the video screen. Consequently, the target may be less aware of, and negatively influenced by, prolonged staring while self-disclosing. We suspect that this prolonged eye gaze allows the gazer to capture more of the emotional communication of their partner without contravening behavioral norms. However, staring has little or no effect upon interaction partly because gaze may be less closely coupled to conversation in text-based video interaction (Crown, 1991; Monk and Gale, 2002), but also because the content of the stare is not communicated as it is through mutual eye contact in face-to-face co-present interaction. Grayson and Monk (2003) have shown that videoconferencing system users quickly adapt to the vertical disparity between camera and monitor in desktop videoconferencing systems so that they can appropriately interpret a particular gaze direction as signaling that the other person is looking at them. However, knowing that you are being looked at is not the same as knowing *how* you are being looked at. Thus, if videoconferencing users can learn to recognize when they are being looked at, the lack of mutual eye contact means that they can nevertheless remain unaware of the emotional expression in the gaze, and this is a key difference from co-present interaction. Gaze without mutual eye contact may have positive benefits in video-mediated interaction. It is precisely when a participant can gaze uninterruptedly at the other without their eyes meeting that he or she can monitor the other person's facial behavior, thereby obtaining more affective information (Argyle and Kendon, 1967; Rutter, 1984, 1987). In addition to the face communicating the current emotions of the discloser, it can also provide affective enrichment of the self-disclosure being narrated in the text, concomitant with the emotional experience of the discloser (or another actor) in the reported situation (Merten, 1997). From the perspective of the target, being looked at during conversation is generally accepted as a display of interest, helping to build rapport during interaction and encouraging intimate self-disclosure (Duggan and Parrott, 2001; Ellsworth and Ross, 1975), and mutual gazing can also occur in videoconferencing without the mutual eye contact that typically breaks looking behavior. In contrast, the benefits of mutual eye contact characteristic of co-present interaction during self-disclosure are possibly more limited. Its general function in regulating turn-taking appears to be constrained (cf. Beattie, 1978, 1979; Kendon, 1967; Rutter *et al.*, 1978), but it does carry a strong evaluative component, powerfully signaling intimacy or dominance, while breaking eye contact can signal embarrassment in self-disclosure situations, as well as disinterest, detachment, disbelief, and dislike (Burgoon and Hale, 1987; Carnevale *et al.*, 1981; Edelmann and Hampson, 1981).

In short, mutual eye contact may be a particular aspect of interaction salience contributing to social presence, but capable of affecting the interaction in different ways depending on the social context. One explanation of our findings is that, compared to co-present interaction, videoconferencing provided opportunities for uninterrupted eye gaze, without the opportunities for eye contact (or breaking eye contact). This video gaze facilitated monitoring of the other's emotion communication, without the intensity and evaluative content of eye-to-eye contact, which led to more intimate self-disclosure and an increased sense of rapport between strangers.

An implication of this argument is that disclosure intimacy may depend not only on developing closeness and rapport but also, at a more basic level, on the absence of rejection cues. Indeed, a cluster of empirical findings suggests that fear of rejection and sensitivity to rejection cues predict whether intimate self-disclosure will occur, patterns of eye gaze and eye contact, and preferences for computer-mediated versus face-to-face environments (Ando, 1978; Gurtman, 1987; Horley *et al.*, 2003; Ksionzky and Mehrabian, 1980; Stritzke *et al.*, 2004; Wells and Kline, 1987). One possibility is that videoconferencing provides some immunization against the perception and impact of rejection cues – facial or otherwise – compared to co-present interactions, and that this, too, might account for our findings of reduced self-disclosure under physical co-presence. If so, the differences between videoconferencing and co-present interactions would have greater implications for shy or socially anxious individuals, who are more sensitive to cues of social threat and rejection. Philippot and Douilliez (Chapter 6, this volume) consider this issue in some depth and argue cogently that adding video to internet communications will be unattractive to those high in social anxiety. However, viewed from the other end of the social presence spectrum, we would argue that videoconferencing might be more attractive than physically co-present interaction for these individuals in certain circumstances, and that this might even offer some therapeutic advantage in the treatment of social anxiety.

Conclusions

It is obvious that more research is required to settle some of these specific claims. However, some of the more general implications of our studies for the facial communication of emotion over the internet are more straightforward. First, it is apparent that physical presence is not a necessary condition for facial communication of emotion to occur – emotion communication occurs even in the absence of any possibility to communicate it directly to another, and is more influenced by the quality of the relationship between the communicators and the cultural norms for the expression of emotions than by the kind of communication medium that is available. This is not to say that there is no increase in facial communication when the face is actually visible through video – facial communication provides important descriptive and coordinating information as well as emotion communication, and communicators will act upon this information – but as far as facial behavior during emotion is concerned, it appears that this will occur at least to some extent regardless of communication media. Moreover, we have shown that social considerations, such as the nature of the relationship between communicators – strangers or friends – and cultural norms for emotion communication, are likely to have as much systematic effect on emotion communication as the communication medium itself.

Secondly, communication of the face creates visual identifiability, which can reduce emotion communication and self-disclosure when the communication partner is a stranger. This highlights the importance of the power dimension in understanding the effects of facial communication on the internet. The "protective cloak" of anonymity (McKenna and Bargh, 2000, p. 62) that reduces the embarrassment and shame associated with intimate self-disclosure (Finn and Lavitt, 1994) probably only becomes relevant when the disclosure could potentially be acted upon by the audience to the detriment of the discloser. Our data suggest that a thorough analysis of the effects of visual identifiability needs to distinguish between the identifiability of others to the self, which increases feelings of trust in others, from its counterpart, the visibility of the self to others, which can increase feelings of vulnerability and accountability to others when communicating intimate emotions and self-disclosures.

Thirdly, the absence of physical presence in internet communications acts not only to constrain the face-to-face communication of emotions, but also to liberate communicators from some of the constraints associated with co-presence in normal face-to-face interaction. Communication of the face through videoconferencing and videophones increases the interpersonal dimension of internet interactions, relative to text, primarily, we believe, through the enhanced potential for online emotion communication, and concomitantly the ability to observe the emotions and relational affect of others. However, relative to co-presence, the lifting of some of the impacts, norms, and constraints associated with physically co-present social interaction, particularly concerning eye gaze, in videoconferencing can have a liberating effect upon participants.[3] Somewhat surprisingly, as we have seen, the result is that face-to-face communication via the internet can create more emotionally intimate conditions for interaction than normal face-to-face communication with physical co-presence.

---

[3] Note that the effects of video-mediated communication are not limited to the interpersonal dimension. Video can also cue social categorization when the group is capable of being visually cued (e.g., gender), and increase the sense of being immersed in a group, reflecting an intergroup dimension to social presence (in addition to the interpersonal) that has been largely ignored (Lea *et al.*, 2007; Rogers and Lea, 2005).

The implications of this are potentially very significant for counseling and therapeutic situations, as well as for the broader realm of interpersonal acquaintanceship and personal relationships in general.

References

Adams, C. H. (2001). Prosocial bias in theories of interpersonal communication competence: must good communication be nice? In G. J. Shepherd and E. W. Rothenbuhler (Eds.), *Communication and Community* (pp. 37–52). Mahwah, NJ: Lawrence Erlbaum Associates.

Altman, I. and Taylor, D. A. (1973). *Social Penetration: The Development of Interpersonal Relationships*. New York: Holt, Rinehart and Winston.

Ando, K. (1978). Self-disclosure in the acquaintance process: effects of affiliative tendency and sensitivity to rejection. *Japanese Psychological Research*, **20** (4), 194–199.

Argyle, M. and Dean, J. (1965). Eye-contact, distance and affiliation. *Sociometry*, **28**, 289–304.

Argyle, M. and Kendon, A. (1967). The experimental analysis of social performance. In L. Berkowitz (ed.), *Advances in Experimental Social Psychology* (vol. III, pp. 55–98). New York: Academic Press.

Argyle, M. and Cook, M. (1976). *Gaze and Mutual Gaze*. London: Cambridge University Press.

Beattie, G. W. (1978). Floor apportionment and gaze in conversational dyads. *British Journal of Social and Clinical Psychology*, **17**, 7–15.

(1979). Contextual constraints on the floor-apportionment function of speaker-gaze in dyadic conversations. *British Journal of Social and Clinical Psychology*, **18**, 391–392.

Biocca, F., Harms, C., and Burgoon, J. K. (2003). Towards a more robust theory and measure of social presence: review and suggested criteria. *Presence*, **12**, 456–480.

Biocca, F., Kim, J., and Choi, Y. (2001). Visual touch in virtual environments: an exploratory study of presence, multimodal interfaces, and cross-modal sensory illusions. *Presence*, **10**, 247–265.

Buck, R. (1994). Social and emotional functions in facial expression and communication: the readout hypothesis. *Biological Psychology*, **38**, 95–115.

Bull, P. and Brown, R. (1977). The role of postural change in dyadic conversations. *British Journal of Social and Clinical Psychology*, **16**, 29–33.

Burgoon, J. K. and Hale, J. L. (1987). Validation and measurement of the fundamental themes of relational communication. *Communication Monographs*, **54**, 19–41.

Carnevale, P. J., Pruitt, D. G., and Seilheimer, S. D. (1981). Looking and competing: accountability and visual access in integrative bargaining. *Journal of Personality and Social Psychology*, **40**, 111–120.

Crown, C. L. (1991). Coordinated interpersonal timing of vision and voice as a function of interpersonal attraction. *Journal of Language and Social Psychology*, **10**, 29–46.

Deutsch, R. D. (1976). An empirical investigation into the grammar of visual interaction: looks and stares. *Man–Environment Systems*, **6**, 163–173.

Duggan, A. P. and Parrott, R. L. (2001). Research note: physicians' nonverbal rapport building and patients' talk about the subjective component of illness. *Human Communication Research*, **27**, 299–311.

Edelmann, R. J. and Hampson, S. E. (1981). Embarrassment in dyadic interaction. *Social Behavior and Personality*, **9**, 171–177.

Edinger, J. A. and Patterson, M. L. (1983). Nonverbal involvement and social control. *Psychological Bulletin*, **93**, 30–56.

Ekman, P. (1972). Universals and cultural differences in facial expressions of emotion. In J. Cole (Ed.), *Nebraska Symposium on Motivation, 1971* (pp. 207–283). Lincoln, NE: University of Nebraska Press.

Ekman, P. and Friesen, W. V. (1969). The repertoire of nonverbal behavior – categories, origins, usage and coding. *Semiotica*, **1**, 49–98.

(1971). Constants across cultures in the face and emotion. *Journal of Personality and Social Psychology*, **17**, 124–129.

Ekman, P., Friesen, W. V., and Ancoli, S. (1980). Facial signs of emotional experience. *Journal of Personality and Social Psychology*, **39**, 1125–1134.

Ellsworth, P. C. and Ross, L. D. (1975). Intimacy in response to direct gaze. *Journal of Experimental Social Psychology*, **11**, 592–613.

Fernández-Dols, J. M. and Ruiz-Belda, M. A. (1995). Are smiles a sign of happiness? Gold medal winners at the Olympic Games. *Journal of Personality and Social Psychology*, **69**, 1113–1119.

Fernández-Dols, J. M., Sánchez, F., Carrera, P., and Ruiz-Belda, M. A. (1997). Are spontaneous expressions and emotions linked? An experimental test of coherence. *Journal of Nonverbal Behavior*, **23**, 163–177.

Finn, J. and Lavitt, M. (1994). Computer-based self-help groups for sexual abuse survivors. *Social Work with Groups*, **17**, 21–46.

Flack, W. F., Laird, J. D., and Cavallaro, L. A. (1999). Separate and combined effects of facial expressions and bodily postures on emotional feelings. *European Journal of Social Psychology*, **29**, 203–217.

Frick, F. C. (1959). Information theory. In S. Koch (ed.), *Psychology: A Study of Science* (pp. 611–636). New York: McGraw-Hill.

Fridlund, A. J. (1991). Sociality of solitary smiling: potentiation by an implicit audience. *Journal of Personality and Social Psychology*, **60**, 229–240.

(1994). *Human Facial Expression: An Evolutionary View*. New York: Academic Press.

Funder, D. C. and Colvin, C. (1988). Friends and strangers: acquaintanceship, agreement, and the accuracy of personality judgment. *Journal of Personality and Social Psychology*, **55**, 149–158.

Gackenbach, J. (1998). *Psychology and the Internet: Intrapersonal, Interpersonal, and Transpersonal Implications*. New York: Academic Press.

Goh, J. (2004). Self-Disclosure and Computer-Mediated Communication: Implications for Crisis Support on the Internet. M.Phil. dissertation, University of Manchester.

Grayson, D. M. and Monk, A. F. (2003). Are you looking at me? Eye contact and desktop video conferencing. *ACM Transactions on Computer–Human Interaction*, **10**, 221–243.

Greist, J. H., Klein M. H., and VanCura, L. J. (1973). A computer interview by psychiatric patient target symptoms. *Archives of General Psychiatry*, **29**, 247–253.

Gurtman, M. B. (1987). Depressive affect and disclosures as factors in interpersonal rejection. *Cognitive Therapy and Research*, **11**(1), 87–99.

Hess, U., Banse, R., and Kappas, A. (1995). The intensity of facial expression is determined by underlying affective state and social situation. *Journal of Personality and Social Psychology*, **69**, 280–288.

Horley, K., Williams, L. M., Gonsalvez, C., and Gordon, E. (2003). Social phobics do not see eye to eye: a visual scanpath study of emotional expression processing. *Journal of Anxiety Disorders*, *17*(1), 33–44.

Ijsselstein, W. A., de Ridder, H., Freeman, J., and Avons, S. E. (2000). Presence: concept, determinants and measurement. *Proceedings of the SPIE, Human Vision and Electronic Imaging V*, 3959–3976.

Jakobs, E., Manstead, A. S. R., and Fischer, A. H. (1999). Social motives and subjective feelings as determinants of facial displays: the case of smiling. *Personality and Social Psychology Bulletin*, *25*, 424–435.

(2001). Social context effects on facial activity in a negative emotional setting. *Emotion*, *1*, 51–69.

Jourard, S. M. and Jaffe, P. E. (1970). Influence of an interviewer's disclosure on the self-disclosing behaviour of interviewee. *Journal of Counselling Psychology*, *17*, 252–257.

Kendon, A. (1967). Some functions of gaze direction in social interaction. *Acta Psychologica*, *26*, 22–63.

Kiesler, S., Siegel, J., and McGuire, T. (1984). Social psychological aspects of computer-mediated communication. *American Psychologist*, *39*, 1123–1134.

Kleinke, C. L. (1986). Gaze and eye contact: a research review. *Psychological Bulletin*, *100*, 78–100.

Kraut, R. E. and Johnston, R. E. (1979). Social and emotional messages of smiling: an ethological approach. *Journal of Personality and Social Psychology*, *37*, 1539–1553.

Ksionzky, S. and Mehrabian, A. (1980). Personality correlates of self-disclosure. *Social Behavior and Personality*, *8*, 145–152.

Lea, M. (1991). Rationalist assumptions in cross-media comparisons of computer-mediated communication. *Behaviour and Information Technology*, *10*, 153–172.

Lea, M. and Duck, S. (1982). A model for the role of similarity of values in friendship development. *British Journal of Social Psychology*, *21*, 301–310.

Lea, M. and Giordano, R. (1997). Representations of the group and group processes in CSCW research: a case of premature closure? In G. C. Bowker, S. L. Star, W. Turner, and L. Gasser (Eds.), *Social Science, Technical Systems and Cooperative Work: Beyond the Great Divide* (pp. 5–26). Mahwah, NJ: Lawrence Erlbaum Associates.

Lea, M. and Spears, R. (1995). Love at first byte? Building personal relationships over computer networks. In J. T. Wood and S. Duck. (eds), *Understudied Relationships: Off the Beaten Track* (pp. 197–233). Thousand Oaks, CA: Sage.

Lea, M., Spears, R., and De Groot, D. (2001). Knowing me, knowing you: effects of visual anonymity on self-categorization, stereotyping and attraction in computer-mediated groups. *Personality and Social Psychology Bulletin*, *27*, 526–537.

Lea, M., Spears, R., and Watt, S. E. (2007). Visibility and anonymity effects on attraction and group cohesiveness. *European Journal of Social Psychology*, *37*, 761–773.

Marvin, C. (1988). *When Old Technologies Were New: Thinking About Electric Communication in the Late Nineteenth Century*. Oxford University Press.

McKenna, K. Y. A. and Bargh, J. (2000). Plan 9 from cyberspace: the implications of the internet for personality and social psychology. *Personality and Social Psychology Review*, *4*, 57–75.

Mehrabian, A. (1967). Attitudes inferred from neutral verbal communications. *Journal of Consulting Psychology, 31*, 414–417.

(1969). Some referents and measures of nonverbal behavior. *Behavior Research Methods and Instrumentation, 1*, 203–207.

Merten, J. (1997). Facial-affective behavior, mutual gaze and emotional experience in dyadic interactions. *Journal of Nonverbal Behavior, 21*(3), 179–201.

Monk, A. F. and Gale, C. (2002). A look is worth a thousand words: full gaze awareness in video-mediated conversation. *Discourse Processes, 33*, 257–278.

Newton, D. A. and Burgoon, J. K. (1990). Nonverbal conflict behaviors: functions, strategies, and tactics. In D. D. Cahn (ed.), *Intimates in Conflict: A Communication Perspective* (pp. 77–104). Mahwah, NJ: Lawrence Erlbaum Associates.

O'Sullivan, P. B., Hunt, S. K., and Lippert, L. R. (2004). Mediated immediacy: a language of affiliation in a technological age. *Journal of Language and Social Psychology, 23*(4), 464–490.

Parks, M. R. (1982). Ideology in interpersonal communication: off the couch and into the world. In M. Burgoon (ed.), *Communication Yearbook 5* (pp. 79–107). New Brunswick, NJ: Transaction Books.

Patterson, M. L. (1973). Compensation in nonverbal immediacy behaviors: a review. *Sociometry, 36*, 237–252.

Raskar, R., Welch, G., Cutts, M., Lake, A., Stesin, L., and Fuchs, H. (1998). The office of the future: a unified approach to image-based modeling and spatially immersive displays. In *Proceedings of ACM SIGGRAPH*, (pp. 179–188). New York: ACM.

Reis, H. T. and Shaver, P. (1988). Intimacy as an interpersonal process. In S. Duck (ed.), *Handbook of Personal Relationships: Theory, Research and Interventions* (pp. 367–389). New York: Wiley.

Rice, R. E. (1993). Media appropriateness: using social presence theory to compare traditional and new organizational media. *Human Communication Research, 19*, 451–484.

Rogers, P. and Lea, M. (2005). Social presence in distributed group environments: the role of social identity. *Behaviour and Information Technology, 24*, 151–158.

Rosenberg, E. L. and Ekman, P. (1994). Coherence between expressive and experiential systems in emotion. *Cognition and Emotion, 8*, 201–229.

Russell, J. A. (1994). Is there universal recognition of emotion from facial expression? A review of the cross-cultural studies. *Psychological Bulletin, 115*, 102–141.

Rutter, D. R. (1984). *Looking and Seeing: The Role of Visual Communication in Social Interaction.* Chichester: Wiley.

(1987). *Communicating by Telephone.* Elmsford, NY: Pergamon.

Rutter, D. R., Stephenson, G. M., Ayling, K., and White, P. A. (1978). The timing of looks in dyadic conversation. *British Journal of Social and Clinical Psychology, 17*, 17–21.

Salem, D. A., Bogat, A., and Reid, C. (1997). Mutual help goes on-line. *Journal of Community Psychology, 25*, 189–207.

Short, J., Williams, E., and Christie, B. (1976). *The Social Psychology of Telecommunications.* Chichester: Wiley.

Spears, R. and Lea, M. (1994). Panacea or panopticon? The hidden power in computer-mediated communication. *Communication Research, 21*, 427–459.

Stritzke, W. G. K., Nguyen, A., and Durkin, K. (2004). Shyness and computer-mediated communication: a self-presentational theory perspective. *Media Psychology*, **6**, 1–22.

Trommsdorff, G. and John, H. (1992). Decoding affective communication in intimate relationships. *European Journal of Social Psychology*, **22**, 41–54.

Wallbott, H. G. (1991). The robustness of communication of emotion via facial expression: emotion recognition from photographs with deteriorated pictorial quality. *European Journal of Social Psychology*, **21**, 89–98.

Wells, J. W. and Kline, W. B. (1987). Self-disclosure of homosexual orientation. *Journal of Social Psychology*, **127**, 191–197.

Witt, P. L., Wheeless, L. R., and Allen, M. (2004). A meta-analytical review of the relationship between teacher immediacy and student learning. *Communication Monographs*, **71**(2), 184–207.

Zaalberg, R., Manstead, A. S. R., and Fischer, A. H. (2004). Relations between emotions, display rules, social motives, and facial behavior. *Cognition and Emotion*, **18**, 182–207.

Zajonc, R. B. (1980). Feeling and thinking: preferences need no inferences. *American Psychologist*, **35**, 151–175.

CHAPTER 8

Virtual gestures: embodiment and nonverbal behavior in computer-mediated communication

Gary Bente and Nicole C. Krämer

Overview: Starting from an overview of the role of nonverbal channels in computer-mediated communication (CMC), a functional model of nonverbal behavior as a possible framework for future research is introduced. Based on this, several technologies and systems for avatar-based interaction are presented, and their impact on psychological aspects of the communication is discussed. The focus of the chapter lies on the discussion of methodological preconditions for the systematic analysis of avatar-based communication. An avatar-based communication platform is introduced that allows for real-time transmission of gaze, head movements, and gestures in net communication. Different research paradigms are discussed that might lead to a deeper understanding of the function of nonverbal cues in CMC.

Introduction

As we know from psychological research and also from our everyday experience, nonverbal behavior (NVB), such as facial expressions, gaze, gestures, postures, and body movements, has a strong impact on the process and the results of our communicative efforts. They help to structure the course of verbal exchange, they complement our speech activity, they determine our social impressions, and they affect the emotional climate of our conversations. In this sense we may consider our body as a natural communication tool that, in contrast to speech, is rarely used consciously and does not refer to an explicit semantic code. As Edward Sapir (1949 [1928]) pointed out, "We respond to gestures with an extreme alertness and, one might almost say, in accordance with an elaborate and secret code that is written nowhere, known to none, and understood by all" (p. 556). Concerning communication of interpersonal attitudes, nonverbal channels even seem to have clear advantages over the verbal channel. Argyle (1975) concluded

> We can now answer the question of why bodily signals are used, in preference to verbal, for interpersonal attitudes. These signals, and the associated bodily structures, were operating before language was developed, and language appears to have developed mainly for other purposes. While words can express attitudes to others, bodily signals have certain clear advantages; first they are stronger, and have a more immediate impact; secondly, negative signals can be used outside full conscious awareness; thirdly, signals negotiating relationships can be used subtly, again outside awareness, and can be easily withdrawn. (p. 132)

Thus, it is not surprising that the partial or complete lack of non-verbal signals within mediated communication – especially within text-based net communication – is considered a deficit that might be overcome by including visual real-time channels into the medium. Although this assumption appears rather plausible at first glance, it has been controversial within the psychological literature on computer-mediated communication (CMC), bringing up the point that lack of visual communication might also be beneficial, as, for example, by filtering out nonverbal cues with negative social effects (e.g., power and dominance cues) or by fostering the creative use of verbal and textual exchange (Kiesler *et al.*, 1984; Walther, 1996). As this discussion is still open, the plausibility of the deficit hypothesis still makes it a major guideline for the development of multichannel communication technologies for engineers and computer scientists. In this line, videoconference systems are promoted as one possibility to render telecommunication more natural and effective (Buxton *et al.*, 1997). Developers and researchers from the field of virtual reality (VR) suggested a different approach. As early as the 1980s, Jaron Larnier, founder of the legendary VPL, Inc., conceptualized the so-called RB2 system (Reality Built for Two) as a telecommunication medium, allowing two people to meet in a shared virtual world and to interact with virtual objects as well as with virtual representations of each other. Later he commented on this crucial aspect of VR:

> One intriguing implication of virtual reality is that participants must be able to see representations of one another, often known as avatars. Although the computer power of the day limited our early avatars to extremely simple, cartoonish computer graphics that only roughly approximated the faces of users, they nonetheless transmitted the motions of their hosts faithfully and thereby conveyed a sense of presence, emotion and locus of interest. (Larnier, 2001)

Meanwhile, various avatar communication systems have been introduced, which have overcome the technical restrictions of the early-stage VR and provide more realistic computer models and real-time facilities for the registration and transfer of nonverbal cues. But there is still more speculation than empirical knowledge about the psychological functions of avatars and their potential impact on CMC. Many reasons might apply to the disintegrated picture of the research literature in this field: (1) The technologies used are different and hard to compare (e.g., immersive VR vs. desktop systems); (2) the functional levels of NVB are not distinguished in a systematic approach; (3) the socioemotional effects as well as performance aspects are measured with ad hoc instruments referring to different theoretical concepts; and (4) the specifics of avatar systems as compared to videoconference systems are not systematically explored, thus neglecting potential interactions between the experience of immersion (Biocca, 1992; Pimental and Teixiera, 1993; Shapiro and McDonald, 1992), telepresence (Naimark, 1990; Steuer, 1992; Zeltzer, 1992), and social presence (Biocca *et al.*, 2001; Short *et al.*, 1976). The last point is crucial for the use of avatars in at least three ways: (1) In contrast to interlocutors in videoconferences, avatars can move in a shared virtual space where the actors might also have contingent impact on virtual objects. (2) Avatar representations transmit nonverbal information without disclosing the identity of the communicators or even giving the user the choice of his or her appearance. (3) The transmission of nonverbal cues is based on behavioral data and not on pixels; thus, specific cues (e.g., eye contact) or behavioral qualities (e.g., movement velocity) can be detected and influenced consciously either by the actors themselves, by a third-party observer (e.g., the experimenter), or by the computer system.

Not all the issues mentioned above can be discussed here in detail. We will briefly comment on the role of nonverbal channels in CMC and introduce a functional model of NVB as a possible framework for future research. In addition, we will summarize some technological determinants that might have a strong impact on those psychological factors. The focus of the chapter, however, lies on the discussion of methodological preconditions for the systematic analysis of avatar-based communication. An avatar-based communication platform is introduced that allows real-time transmission of gaze, head movements, and gestures in net communication. Different research paradigms are discussed that might lead to a deeper understanding of the function of nonverbal cues in CMC as well as the improvement of avatar conference systems.

The role of NVB in CMC

The role of NVB in CMC can be discussed from two perspectives: that of CMC research and that of face-to-face research. As most studies on CMC have focused on text-based internet encounters (email, chat), it is not surprising that there is a conceptual prevalence of so-called deficit models, which assume a loss of social context information in CMC. Within their model, Short *et al.* (1976) explicitly pointed out the relevance of contextual cues conveyed via the visual channel, differentiating between static (appearance, setting) and dynamic (NVB) aspects. Whether this information loss causes negative or positive effects is still a matter of discussion. For example, Sproull and Kiesler (1986) pointed to specific risks:

> When social context cues are weak, people's feelings of anonymity tend to produce relatively self-centered and unregulated behavior. That is, people are relatively unconcerned with making a good appearance. Their behavior becomes more extreme, more impulsive, and less socially differentiated. (pp. 1495–1496)

Consequently, critics of CMC concluded that mediated text-based communication not only leads to emotional impoverishment but also facilitates antisocial and deviant behaviors due to deindividuation (e.g., flaming; Sproull and Kiesler, 1986). This assumption of deindividuation, however, has been challenged by the SIDE theory (Spears and Lea, 1994; Spears *et al.*, 1990). There are also specific hypotheses within the deficit approach concerning the positive effects of reduced social context cues; for example, Kiesler *et al.* (1984) expected an equalization effect in a sense that missing status cues could lead to a better balance of participation and mutual attention in net-based communications (see also Rawlins, 1989).

In fact, the conditions of advantages and disadvantages of CMC with respect to face-to-face interactions have not yet been demonstrated. Further, it is not clear at all whether the deficits observed can be overcome by including nonverbal channels in CMC. Open questions are, for example, which aspects of NVB serve which interpersonal functions, and to what extent avatar technologies can help to convey this relevant information. The conceptual starting point for a future CMC research avatar platform thus can hardly be a global deficit hypothesis. Moreover, a differentiated model of the communicative potential of NVB is needed from which more specific research hypotheses and strategies for analysis can be derived. We suggest a functional model of NVB referring to social psychological theory and face-to-face communication research. Based on the relevant literature (Birdwhistell, 1970; Patterson, 1994), we suggest a distinction between four functional levels of NVB (Bente and Krämer, 2001; Bente *et al.*, 2001b):

(1) *Modeling functions* are connected to the fact that humans seem to have clear advantages in performing motor tasks when they can observe somebody else showing the required movements (e.g., when instructing someone how to handle a VCR).

(2) *Discourse functions* are closely related to verbal behavior. Pointing gestures, illustrative gestures, and beat gestures (such as waving a hand to structure the speech flow) belong to this functional category (Efron, 1941; Ekman and Friesen, 1969).

(3) *Dialogue functions* include turn-taking signals (e.g., eye contact) and back-channel signals (e.g., head nods), and they serve the smooth flow of interaction when exchanging speaker and listener roles (Duncan, 1972). For example, the listener signals with the help of a beginning gesture that he claims the turn, while the speaker signals that he is ready to yield the turn when he stops gesturing.

(4) *Socioemotional functions* are the least explored in nonverbal communication research. Although ample empirical evidence indicates that NVB has an enormous impact on our perception and evaluation of other people (how much we like them, whether they are trustworthy or not, etc.; e.g., Frey, 1999), little is known about the secret codes that actually lead to those interpersonal effects. As we will discuss later, the avatar technology can also be a valuable research instrument to unravel some of these secrets of NVB.

This is not the place to give a comprehensive overview of the large and heterogeneous field of nonverbal communication research (for an overview, see Krämer, 2001). However, some relevant research questions and results will be outlined referring to this functional differentiation. As the modeling function bears face validity and is certainly the least complex, we will focus here on discourse, dialogue, and socioemotional functions. The overview should enable the reader to get an impression of the numerous questions and some answers that characterize the research field.

Discourse functions of NVB

As stated above, nonverbal signals serving discourse functions are closely connected to speech and can supplement, complement, or even substitute for verbal utterances. Substitution is given especially in sign language for the deaf or so-called emblems (Ekman and Friesen, 1969; e.g., the emblematic signs and iconographic symbols used by divers).

Although these kinds of signals might be relevant when analyzing CMC, we will focus on gestures and facial expressions that merely accompany speech instead of replacing it. Some researchers have argued that gestures primarily fulfill functions for the speaker (e.g., with regard to assistance while formulating; Krauss and Chiu, 1998; Rimé, 1983), while others hold that the actual function of gestures is to affect the recipient in various ways (de Ruiter, 1998; Ekman and Friesen, 1969), as has been assumed for NVB in general (Frey, 1999; Fridlund, 1997). Gestures seem to play a crucial part in human interaction since they can serve each of the communicative functions that can be distinguished for nonverbal communication, sometimes even at the same time.

Ekman and Friesen (1969) termed gestures that accompany and clarify verbal information "illustrative" (Efron, 1941). Closely connected to paraverbal aspects such as intonation or loudness of voice, they frequently serve supplementing functions by symbolizing objects that the speaker refers to (iconic gestures), or by pointing at them (deictic gestures). Beat gestures, on the other hand, do not symbolize anything but underline the rhythm of speech. McNeill (1992) similarly distinguished iconic, metaphoric, and beat gestures. Cassell *et al.* (1999) used his assumptions on the relation of discourse structure and gestures for the implementation of embodied conversational agents.

Facial expressions can also serve discourse functions. Chovil (1991) empirically identified various facial illustrators. Especially raising and lowering of eyebrows is used for emphasizing specific syllables. Chovil differentiated four different linguistic categories: syntactic displays (27 percent of eyebrow movements), semantic speaker displays that are redundant with speech (21 percent), semantic speaker displays that are not redundant with speech (14 percent), and listener comments (14 percent). The most important category, syntactic displays, is related to the structure of speech or to emphasizing specific syllables. Actions like raising or lowering the eyebrows or widening the eyes are used as emphasizers, underliners, question markers, offers, sentence-change markers, end of utterance markers, or even commas. Moreover, these signals may indicate the organization of the story told (story announcement, story continuation, end of story or topic, topic change). Semantic speaker displays that are redundant with speech accompany verbal content with corresponding emotional displays and evaluations (e.g., depicting surprise, disgust, thoughtfulness), while nonredundant semantic displays are shown in addition to verbal aspects. Listener comments in most cases are back-channel behaviors. Chovil (1991) summarized:

The results of this study have shown that when facial displays were analyzed in terms of their relationship to linguistic features and the messages conveyed by the displays, they were found to have important discourse functions; they marked out various discourse features and illustrated or added semantic content. Both speakers and listeners were found to use facial displays in a variety of ways. The displays occurred both on their own and within spoken utterances. (p. 190)

Dialogue functions of NVB

Research concerning the dialogue functions of NVB virtually ended in the early 1980s as if all questions with regard to regulations of speaker–listener change had been answered. Actually, Duncan and his colleagues (Duncan, 1972; Duncan and Fiske, 1979) presented an impressive research program that focused on the nonverbal cues regulating turn-taking (whereas researchers like Sacks *et al.*, 1974, concentrated on verbal and paraverbal aspects). According to Duncan (1972; Duncan and Fiske, 1979), turn-yielding signals of the speaker are given by at least one of the following cues: (1) intonation ("terminal clause"), (2) prolongation of last syllable, (3) termination of gestures, (4) sociocentric sentences ("you know"), (5) decrease of loudness, and (6) completion of sentence. The more cues a speaker shows, the smoother is the turn-taking. Kendon (1967) further identified rotation of the head toward the listener as crucial; if the speaker does not look up at the end of his utterance, the answer is more frequently (71 percent compared to 29 percent when looking up) delayed or missing. Another signal is meant to prevent the listener from taking the turn: By gestures, the speaker shows that he intends to go on and simultaneously that turn-yielding cues are negated. The listener, on the other hand, shows by means of nodding, paraverbal feedback ("mm-hmm"), or short questions that he would like to continue listening. Yngve (1970) coined the term *back-channel signals* for these cues which are frequently shown when the turn is offered but is declined. If the listener eventually wants to take his turn, he indicates this via a so-called speaker-state signal that might consist of rotating the head away from the interlocutor, audible inhalation, beginning gesture, and/or overloudness. Kendon (1967) also emphasized the importance of gaze behavior (e.g., 70 percent of utterances are started by looking away). Duncan's as well as, to some extent, Kendon's results permit us to estimate the transition probabilities of specific nonverbal dialogue signals. However, data on the exact order and/ or timing of these cues are rather weak.

Despite these results, the importance of visual cues within the turn-taking process has been doubted (see Rimé, 1983) since interlocutors are still able to lead well-organized conversations when they do not see each other (e.g., during telephone conversations). However, Rutter and Stephenson (1977; see also Rutter *et al.*, 1978) demonstrated that this channel loss causes changes in the structure of the communication processes. They reported that in situations in which merely the audio channel is available, fewer interruptions and less simultaneous speech can be observed. According to Rutter and Stephenson (1977), this might be because the effect of an interruption (e.g., displeasure) cannot be observed directly. One´s own behavior cannot be corrected accordingly, and thus the danger that the conversation will collapse is increased. The decent flow of conversation also depends on cues that a person is not willing to yield the turn. In detailed analyses, Donaghy and Goldberg (1991) showed that the speaker who is interrupted reacts with an increase in activity as well as in complexity of head movements, which can be interpreted as signs of unwillingness to yield the turn.

Socioemotional functions of NVB

Socioemotional functions of NVB are not completely independent of dialogue and discourse functions. A smooth flow of the conversation will be likely to influence mutual person perception and interpersonal climate in a positive way. On the other hand, a restriction of NVB (e.g., in an avatar) to discourse and dialogue functions and a neglect of socioemotional aspects might lead to negative effects because the lack of movement or facial activity could be interpreted as negative social attitude rather than a consequence of technical restrictions or other context variables. Watzlawick *et al.*'s (1967) claim, "One cannot not communicate!" seems to cover this phenomenon perfectly. Displaying NVB without incorporating socioemotional cues will probably be interpreted as lacking communicative effort, friendliness, or worse. Although the literature on socioemotional aspects of NVB is rather diffuse, there seems to be a recurring model for classifying nonverbal cues along three basic production and reception dimensions. Mehrabian (1969) is most often quoted for his distinction between evaluation (immediacy cues), potency (dominance cues), and activity (responsiveness cues).

Evaluation (immediacy cues)
According to Mehrabian (1969), immediacy cues and proxemics (interpersonal distance) communicate interest and lead to positive

evaluations of others. Immediacy (or involvement; see Patterson, 1982) is signaled by touch, forward lean, eye contact, body rotation toward the interaction partner, increased speech rate, nodding, verbal reinforcements, few self-manipulators, frequent smiles, gestures, and relaxation (Haase and Tepper, 1972; LaCrosse, 1975; Mehrabian, 1969; Palmer and Simmons, 1995; Patterson, 1982; Rosenfeld, 1966; Schlenker, 1980). Smiling is also said to communicate submissiveness (appeasement pattern; Henley, 1977; Keating *et al.*, 1977; Patterson, 1994), but several studies show that the predominant effect is to convey friendliness and affiliation (Brunner, 1979; Carli *et al.*, 1993, 1995; Deutsch *et al.*, 1987; Graham and Argyle, 1975; Halberstadt and Saitta, 1987). In general, persons who smile are evaluated as more cheerful, successful, relaxed, and polite (Page, 1980, unpublished). Immediacy can also be communicated more subtly; for example, by means of head postures. Especially the lateral head tilt has been described as a powerful determinant of person perception (Frey *et al.*, 1983; Krumhuber and Kappas, 2005; Montagner *et al.*, 1977). It has been shown that a lateral head tilt can lead to attributions as friendly, relaxed, sympathetic, modest, sensitive, inviting, and likeable (Frey *et al.*, 1983; Signer, 1975, unpublished). These effects, however, are not limited to the evaluation dimension. Krämer (2001) found that that lateral head tilt can also affect the perception of dominance. Actually, the interpretation of immediacy cues and of most other NVB is very context dependent. In this context, Grammer (1990) commented with respect to laughter, "Laughter ... conveys messages that range from sexual solicitation to aversion, depending on which and how many different signals are present" (p. 209). Moreover, Frey *et al.* (1983) showed that the effects of a smile depend on the presence and extent of lateral head tilt. Therefore, it is crucial to transmit every bodily signal. Merely transmitting the smile but not the head tilt would lead to a different impression on the receiver.

Beyond the effects that can be assigned to more or less discrete signals, interpersonal evaluation can also be influenced by changes in general activity level (Bente and Krämer, 2008; Krämer, 2008). As Young and Beier (1977) demonstrated, an increase of head movements has positive effects in terms of evaluation and liking. Moreover, Bente *et al.* (1996) presented evidence that women are found to be more attractive by men when they show increased head movement activity. Grammer *et al.* (1997) also emphasized the importance of dynamic cues with regard to communication of interest and liking. The authors stated that the specific form or configuration of movement – for example, "raising an arm fast or slow, with fist clenched or not, the movement staying at the maximum flexion for a certain time and going back fast or slowly" – determines perception and interpretation. DePaulo and Friedman (1998) concluded that expressiveness is crucial since it is related to liking as well as influence, and it increases success. The activity level can also serve as an amplifier for specific immediacy cues. Mehrabian and Williams (1969) pointed out that "in particular, when a relatively high level of activity is combined with other cues which communicate liking ... activity may be seen as a vehicle for the communication of the intensity of liking" (p. 54).

Potency (dominance cues)
Aspects of dominance and status are ubiquitous in human relationships and are to a large extent regulated via nonverbal cues (DePaulo and Friedman, 1998; Millar *et al.*, 1984). Siegel *et al.* (1992) demonstrated that even in family communication 91 percent of the nonverbal signals shown were found to exercise control. Findings on dominance cues, however, are less consistent than those on immediacy cues. Remland (1982) distinguished actions degrading the physical presence of a person (touching, expansive gestures, rotating body away from the partner, interruptions) and actions degrading intellectual presence (e.g., make a fool of someone). Mehrabian (1969) especially focused on relaxation cues (asymmetry of arms, sideward tilt of body, asymmetry of legs, relaxed hands, leaning backward). He further mentioned increased leg and foot movements, self-manipulators, less nodding, less friendly facial expression, increased speed of speech, and increased loudness. Whereas some of these aspects could not be confirmed in other studies (Aguinis *et al.*, 1998; Carli *et al.*, 1993; Henley, 1977; Schlenker, 1980), leaning backward was consistently shown to affect dominance attributions (Carli *et al.*, 1993). Gaze behavior is also clearly connected to dominance. People are perceived to be dominant when they look at the interaction partner especially while speaking and less so when listening (Dovidio *et al.*, 1988; Exline, 1972; Exline *et al.*, 1975). DePaulo and Friedman (1998) concluded that dominant people "can stare more but have to look less" (p. 12). Schlenker (1980) presented findings that indicate that leaders who look frequently at their inferiors are evaluated less positively in terms of leadership. Consequently, he states, "Both apes and humans show greater visual attentiveness toward their superiors than their inferiors; the higher one's status, the less one has to look at others" (p. 244). Dominance is also attributed when specific facial expressions such as lowered brows and other forms of anger displays are shown (Camras, 1982; Edinger and Patterson, 1983; Friedman, 1979; Keating *et al.*, 1977; Schlenker, 1980). Even children who show a so-called *plus face* (which is similar to the anger display) are more likely to win a quarrel than children

showing a *minus face* (which shows submissiveness by avoiding gaze, lowering corners of the mouth). Touch also can be used to demonstrate and manifest dominance: When people differ in status, touch is non-reciprocal and shows dominance (Henley, 1977; Patterson, 1994). Further, there is weak evidence that raising or lowering of the head is connected to dominance (Argyle *et al.*, 1970; Kepplinger and Donsbach, 1983; Lanzetta *et al.*, 1986; but see Kappas *et al.*, 1994, for evidence that merely evaluation is affected). Dynamic cues can also have some influence. Richards *et al.* (1991) found that women who are evaluated as submissive show less expansive gestures than women perceived as dominant.

Of special importance with regard to mediated communications are findings showing that dominance cues also foster persuasion. Power of persuasion increases when loudness and frequency of speech are increased, when more gestures and facial expressions as well as more frequent nodding are shown, and when eye contact is prolonged (Mehrabian and Williams, 1969). Additionally, "rewarding" behaviors such as forward lean and eye contact lead to increased persuasiveness (Keeley and Hart, 1994; Patterson, 1994; Sieber, 1996).

Activity (responsiveness cues)
Higher levels of activity are said to communicate responsiveness (increased facial expressions, loudness of speech, etc.; see Mehrabian, 1969). It can be questioned, though, to what extent responsiveness represents a dimension of its own. Higher responsiveness and activity are correlated with evaluation (Bentler, 1969) in the sense that increased activity is connected to positive attitudes. DePaulo and Friedman (1998) summarized that responsiveness – or expressiveness as they call it – is related to likeability, empathy, charisma, and influence. Riggio and Friedman (1986) concluded that activity determines perception in the first place:

> We often quickly decide if a person is likeable and approachable. Although observers may use any available cues in making such judgments, people seem especially willing to make such judgments once they have seen the individual in action – that is, once they have observed movement, speech, and emotional expression. These impressions will in turn affect the nature of ensuring social interaction. (p. 425)

Women especially are evaluated by their facial activity. On the other hand, activity parameters can be used to communicate displeasure, as, for example, when defending the turn (Donaghy and Goldberg, 1991). An additional aspect of this dimension is the phenomenon that interaction partners adapt their NVB (speech parameter, postures, as well as movements) to each other while conversing (see reciprocity and compensation, Argyle and Cook, 1976; mirroring, Bernieri and Rosenthal, 1991; conversational adaptation, Burgoon *et al.*, 1993; simulation patterning, Cappella, 1991; synchrony, Condon and Ogston, 1966; congruence, Scheflen, 1964; motor mimicry, Lipps, 1907; Bavelas *et al.*, 1986; nonconscious mimicry, Chartrand and Bargh, 1999; and accommodation, Giles *et al.*, 1987). Wallbott (1995) defined the phenomenon as "the tendency to exhibit such nonverbal (and verbal) behaviors that resemble those of our interaction partners, when we evaluate them positively or when we want to be evaluated positively by them" (p. 93). In this sense, nonverbal communication seems to be an important means to "tune in" with the interaction partner. Grammer *et al.* (1998) demonstrated that these adaptations occur on a very subtle level that cannot be observed overtly.

This brief overview might have shown that NVB constitutes a complex communication system that – especially because of the context dependence – cannot be described in a deterministic way. Dynamic and static aspects are fused, and effects are multidimensional. As mentioned above, it can be assumed that providing nonverbal channels in CMC is not a question of yes or no, but more a matter of costs and benefits in certain contexts, which are defined by the characteristics of the technology, the task, and the people involved. It is evident that the availability of nonverbal cues might not be useful in every case. This is true for face-to-face communication and CMC as well. Hehl *et al.* (1998) showed that "normal" families benefit from the availability of the visual channel, while families with anorexic daughters, whose relationships presumably are detached, got along better when communication was restricted to the audio channel. Additionally, we have to consider that the processing of nonverbal information as a cognitive process could interfere with other cognitive tasks and thus lead to specific disadvantages. If cognitive resources are used for social judgment and person perception (Patterson, 1994), one might be distracted from other tasks. Moreover, social cues could automatically trigger social reactions even if those are not target-oriented or reasonable (Krämer and Bente, 2002; Rickenberg and Reeves, 2000). In this context, we must analyze in more depth the conditions under which socioemotional signals are necessary, convenient, irrelevant, or even disturbing in CMC.

Analyzing the effects of embodiment: setups and paradigms

As we mentioned above, the idea of avatar-based communication is not a very recent one. It emerged in the 1980s in the early stage of VR systems development as a means to extend the use of immersive VR to the area of interpersonal communication. Most of the current avatar platforms are based on this idea and were developed within the research area of VR once they were technically feasible. Avatar systems can also be seen in the tradition of broadband telecommunications, especially videoconferences and audiovisual net meetings. In fact, the current avatar systems take various forms due to these diverse origins. Thus, avatars can be static placeholders presented in a window on the desktop or fully interactive 3D representations of humans moving in a virtual space, which is provided via head-mounted display (HMD) or by a CAVE (immersive VR environment where projectors are directed to four, five, or six of the walls of a room-sized cube). Following Steuer's (1992) conception of telepresence, these systems can vary extremely with respect to interactivity and vividness. Within "social VR," these differences will not only have implications for a sense of "being there" but also for the interpersonal functionality of embodiment and the creation of social presence. We will describe a selection of avatar platforms and point to possible perceptual and socioemotional implications of their technical specifications, advantages, and shortcomings. Although likewise limited in some technical respects, our own setup at the University of Cologne, the so-called virtual communication environment (VCE), will be described in more detail. The VCE platform is the basis for a variety of experimental research paradigms that have been developed to study the effects of embodiment and computer-mediated NVB in virtual encounters. These research paradigms and exemplary results will be reported later in the chapter.

Technical specifications and psychological implications

In their least sophisticated forms avatars are static characters that can be navigated through simple virtual worlds. Interestingly, this has been the prevalent form of avatars with regard to the public for several years. During the 1990s, within countless chat systems and multiuser dungeons (MUDs) or virtual role-playing worlds, internet users picked avatars to represent themselves (Suler, 1999). Especially within MUDs, avatars were navigated through different rooms and places (e.g., castle, pub, or dragon cave), and by placing the avatar in relation to others, social structures and communicative acts were represented.

Nowadays, however, more sophisticated avatars are developed and used, as, for example, in more elaborate virtual worlds such as *Second Life* or *World of Warcraft*. Here, basic NVB has been preprogrammed and might be triggered. Doubtless, however, even the choice of rather

Figure 8.1 Virtual learning environment (Müller *et al.*, 2002).

static representations can have social-psychological implications by triggering specific stereotypes and setting up related interpersonal expectations (e.g., when changing gender). But it is evident that this type of embodiment can hardly serve specific communicative functions as connected to NVB. There are in fact different levels of sophistication at which dynamic aspects of visual communication can be included in avatar systems. Some of the systems are very selective, opening just those channels which have a clearly defined interpersonal or communicative meaning, – for example, raising the hand to get the turn. In most cases, these systems require a conscious decision by the user to launch the nonverbal cue by clicking a button or hitting a key (as in *Second Life* or *World of Warcraft*). Other systems do not require a conscious decision and transmit all behavior that can be detected by motion-capture devices. A system of the first type has been introduced by Müller *et al.* (2002). They presented a desktop-based learning environment that allows up to eight people (their respective avatars) to meet at a virtual table (Figure 8.1). Communication is text-based, and fundamental gestures like thumbs up and thumbs down or raising the hand can be displayed by pressing keys. Additionally, participants can indicate that they are puzzled by displaying a question mark above their head (see also Müller *et al.*, 2003). First evaluation studies show that learners were able to use gestures and symbols in a sensible way and that satisfaction as well as experience of social presence was increased compared to traditional chat or audio conferences. A similar system that was developed for the application area of acting rehearsals within a virtual environment by means of avatars is presented by Slater *et al.* (2000; see Slater and Steed, 2002). Participants are able to control navigation through a room, arm movements (up and down), and head rotations by keyboard, slide, and mouse control. Facial expressions are controlled by clicking on a smiley face. Speech is transmitted directly via headphones. Preliminary evaluations with actors showed that during its first use the system was not experienced as very helpful, but during the course of four interactions the actors somewhat accommodated to the situation. In consequence, presence (in the sense of "being in the environment") as well as social presence (in the sense of "being with another person") steadily increased.

Blascovich *et al.* (2002) introduced a system of the second type. They presented a fully immersive 3D avatar platform in which the participants can meet in a virtual room. Crucial for the immersive quality is an HMD that includes trackers to capture positions and rotation of the head (Figure 8.3). Data about head movements are used to calculate necessary changes concerning the graphical display and to render the environment accordingly. Users are consequently able to look around in the virtual room as they would in a real room – a phenomenon that is called sensumotorical feedback. Hence, with regard to spatial aspects, group interaction resembles interactions in real groups: If person B is seated on the right, one has to turn right to get him or her in view. One shortcoming, though, is the fact that only rotation of the head is captured and presented to the other participants. Gestures or even subtle body movements are not transmitted. Nevertheless, Blascovich *et al.* (2002) promised that "compared to other telecommunications media, [immersive virtual environment technology] offers the greatest sense of actual presence and also conveys important contextual cues" (p. 21). Furthermore, they described their system as a research tool of the future because it provides the opportunity to systematically control various parameters within a realistic setting. Thus, internal and external validity are ensured, replications are facilitated, and analyses of larger samples are possible.

Slater *et al.* (1998) also developed a virtual environment that can be experienced via immersive systems. Here, an HMD and two tracking devices are applied. One of the devices tracks head movements in a direct way while the other device is connected to the mouse, resulting in mouse movements being displayed as movements within the room.

Alternatively (and even simultaneously), participants can navigate through the virtual environment by means of a desktop-based system. Here, navigation is accomplished by using the keyboard arrow keys to produce forward and backward body movements as well as rotations. The virtual room is displayed on a conventional screen.

The technical differences described necessarily have implications for the psychological effects of avatar communication. The availability and means of production of nonverbal cues, as well as the immersive quality, are likely to affect production aspects of communication as well as perception and evaluation. To systemize psychological effects, we propose to employ Steuer's (1992) model of telepresence. He conceptualized effects of virtual environments in terms of the feeling of being "there" or "within" a virtual world as dependent on technology. He further distinguished *vividness* and *interactivity* as predominant dimensions:

> The first, vividness, refers to the ability of a technology to produce a sensorially rich mediated environment. The second, interactivity, refers to the degree to which users of a medium can influence the form or content of the mediated environment. (p. 80)

Vividness depends on sensory *breadth* (number of sensory modalities that are simultaneously addressed) as well as sensory *depth* (degree of differentiation or resolution concerning specific modalities). Interactivity is constituted by *speed* (rate with which the virtual world assimilates information), *range* (number of action alternatives available at a given point), and *mapping* (ability of the system to map possible reactions to input).

The systems depicted above certainly differ in terms of *vividness*. On the one hand, sensory *depth* varies due to different display resolutions. But because several studies have proved that quality of presentation has only minor effects on psychological experiences (see Bente *et al.*, 2001c; Petersen and Bente, 2001) we assume that resolution will not affect communication processes unless a critical limit is not met. Concerning *breadth*, on the other hand, differences between the setups are marginal: Within all systems visual and auditory channel are addressed.

Differences in the presentation of visual information (desktop vs. immersive systems) are connected with the question of whether one actually experiences oneself as present in a virtual room and whether sensumotorical feedback is provided. This seems to be rather a question of mapping. While some systems allow for sensumotorical feedback in the sense that one turns the head and addresses another participant, other systems do not permit any head rotation (due to the fact that the head has to be directed toward the screen). This difference becomes especially salient and psychologically meaningful when more than two persons are involved in the interaction. In this case eye contact and mutual addressing behavior cannot be simulated with a desktop-based system because only immersive systems permit three or more participants to capture and display actual addressing movements. Given the importance of addressing and gaze behavior for turn-taking processes, as well as the socioemotional aspects described above, it can be concluded that desktop-based systems have severe disadvantages for communication processes of groups, as demonstrated by the failure of early videoconferences. Additionally, the immersive quality seems to be a critical variable on its own. Evaluating their immersive avatar system, Slater *et al.* (1998) came to the conclusion that whether group members are provided with a more sophisticated VR technology or not affects group processes. Analyzing the cooperation of triads, they provided one of the participants with immersive technology, whereas the other group members used desktop systems with conventional screens. An important result was that the participants in the immersive condition were more often recognized as leader of the group (see also Slater and Steed, 2002).

In addition to the effects just described, there are also differences concerning production and perception of NVB (automatic transfer vs. conscious control). This is relevant with regard to the dimension of interactivity as defined by Steuer (1992). On the one hand, nonverbal signals may be captured and transmitted directly, allowing for a spontaneous and subconscious usage of nonverbal cues as in face-to-face interaction (see Blascovich *et al.*, 2002 for a reduced direct transmission and our system depicted below for a near complete transfer of movement data). On the other hand and distinct from face-to-face communication, there are systems that merely allow the volitional sending and receiving of NVB (respectively signals) by means of buttons, mouse clicks, etc. (e.g., the systems presented by Müller *et al.*, 2002, and Slater *et al.*, 2000). Psychologically, the way in which NVB is produced, transmitted, and displayed might influence communication processes in various ways. There are at least three conceivable implications of using the second form: (1) the sender will be more self-aware when consciously choosing what to display, (2) the number of signals sent at any time is restricted due to the fact that cognitive resources of the sender are limited, and (3) the receiver will not only get the message with a slight delay but will also come to different conclusions about the message knowing that the sender had time to consciously choose what to send (e.g., Slater and Steed, 2002). One potential advantage of this form, on the other hand, might be the fact that communication is restricted to necessary aspects. Current research cannot yet answer the question of whether potential advantages outweigh potential drawbacks (e.g., senders might be overstrained or communication might be too artificial and inefficient).

Additionally, other discriminating aspects can be identified that might affect psychological aspects beyond Steuer's (1992) dimensions. The availability of a shared workbench or shared objects might facilitate communication processes and foster the usage of nonverbal cues with regard to discourse functions (e.g., pointing). Also, whether participants actually are in the same virtual room (or are at least presented on screen within the same virtual room) might influence how far one experiences oneself as part of a group.

The virtual communication environment

The virtual communication environment (VCE) developed in our laboratory at the University of Cologne can be seen as a hybrid system that is based on desktop VR but also conveys a wide range of nonverbal cues in a fully interactive real-time mode (Petersen *et al.*, 2002). Interaction is therefore not only more immediate as compared to the avatar system described (e.g., by Müller *et al.*, 2002) but also more complete in the sense that all crucial aspects of NVB including subtle movements are conveyed. The interaction resembles face-to-face interaction or video-based communication. However, in contrast to a videoconference, it still allows masking of identity and experimental control of behavioral data flow. In particular, the VCE allows (1) the real-time interaction of up to three interlocutors, including nonverbal signals like head movements, body movements, gestures, and eye movement; (2) the experimental variation of the visual appearance of the interlocutors; (3) the online filtering of behavioral cues; (4) the recording of verbal and nonverbal behavior; (5) the interactive and/ or algorithmic modification of behavior protocols; and (6) the off-line rendering and display of interactions or selected behavior protocols. NVB is detected by means of cybergloves, Polhemus trackers, and a high-resolution eye-tracking system, which was developed for this purpose. Behavioral data are transmitted via intranet (TCP-IP) and are presented to the interaction partner by an animation program (e.g., Kayara Filmbox). The ability to record the behavior of the inter-acting persons permits post-hoc analyses of the participants' behavior. The movements of the individual or the dyad can be parameterized for graphical and statistical analysis. The data can also be used for experimental computer simulations to study the effects of NVB. Specific

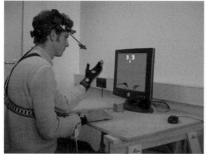

Figure 8.2 VCE I: virtual videoconference (VVC).

editors and algorithms allow the systematic variation of single cues or the whole movement dynamics in the data protocols. Further, the platform allows the use of different characters; not only can appearance be changed but also the number of channels transmitted. One avatar is reduced to crucial body aspects that display only fundamental nonverbal aspects such as head and eye movement as well as gestures. Another, machine-like avatar is provided with a face and a body. The body may be displayed or concealed, leaving merely hands and head visible. Additionally, there are three realistic, full-body models: one is male, one female, and one androgynous in appearance. The figures are chosen according to the goal of the specific study (see below). In the future, more different characters will be provided to avoid the confounding of realism, specific appearance, and displayed channels, although this can by definition never be ruled out completely.

Three setups can be distinguished within the VCE: (1) the virtual videoconference (VVC) presents the interaction partner's avatars on a separate monitor in full-screen mode (Bente *et al.*, 2008a, 2008b; Figure 8.2), (2) the integrated avatar workbench (IAW), developed for net-based cooperation, shows the avatar representations in a window inside a workbench (Cool Modes), (Bollen *et al.*, 2002); and (3) the extended desktop platform (EDP) projects the avatars on the wall behind the monitor. While the VVC and the IAW were configured for dyadic interactions, only the EDP can be extended to three or more people. In contrast to dyads, the interaction within small groups is much more dependent on nonverbal signals indicating mutual attention and addressing. The system forces more pronounced eye movements and even head rotations by placing life-size projections of the interaction partners at a larger distance from each other (Figure 8.3).

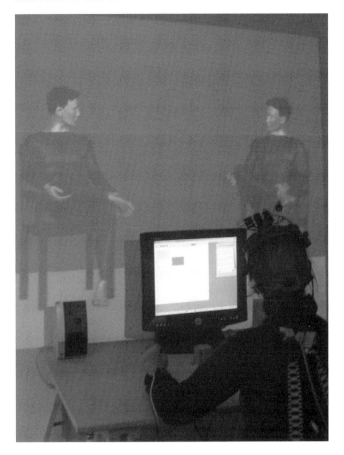

Figure 8.3 VCE III: extended desktop platform (EDV).

Research questions and paradigms

The VCE described above is a research platform rather than an avatar system for practical use. To feed real-time avatars with realistic non-verbal behavior still requires expensive hardware and software on the input side (motion capture devices, data gloves, eye trackers, etc.) as well as on the output side (HMDs, projection devices, modeling and animation tools, etc.). Certainly, technology will develop toward non-invasive, low-cost, video-tracking systems that can be placed on top of a PC monitor (or is even integrated), but it is not foreseeable when such systems will be commercially and affordably available. However, we see a unique chance to study the new medium in a, so to speak, prenatal stage by making systematic use of high-end VR components in our research laboratories in order to investigate the full range of imaginable future functionalities. In this context, Biocca (1992) suggested a decade ago:

> If virtual reality is likely to emerge as the next dominant medium – if not the 'ultimate medium' – should we not consider its implications now? Communication researchers rarely have a chance to observe the introduction, diffusion, and sociocultural presence of what may become the next dominant communication medium. (p. 9)

Actually, it is not clear whether optimal technical conditions (like fully immersive 3D environments with realistic avatars and full-range NVB) will be necessary for future practical applications in all respects, or whether restricted setups focusing on simple avatar representations and specific nonverbal cues can serve net communication in a sufficient or even a better way. To conduct the critical test, however, of under which conditions (task, interpersonal settings, context) what nonverbal aspects should be made salient, and which technical components are necessary to produce and to convey these cues, the experimental setups should provide variations across all levels of potential determinants. As described above, most systems under investigation exhibit specific technical restrictions and confoundings. Because they are focusing on different aspects of NVB and use different settings, the empirical results gained in various laboratories are hardly comparable, and comparative studies across avatar technologies are completely lacking. As shown above, the research questions are complex and divergent, and the same paradigms do not apply to all of them. Nevertheless, it seems worthwhile to develop common terminologies and a systematic view. Based on our own research experiences with the VCE, we suggest a distinction of three types of research paradigms. These are targeted at specific types of questions concerning the effects of embodiment and nonverbal avatar communication and, in consequence, have different technical requirements: (1) the *third-party observation paradigm*, (2) the *mixed-reality paradigm*, and (3) the *interaction paradigm*.

The third-party observation paradigm is defined by a passive observation situation. Prerecorded behavior of single persons or small groups is computer animated, using different types of avatars, and shown to observers, measuring their responses and asking for their impression ratings. As this is an off-line paradigm and thus not time-critical, computer animations can be done with standard 3D animation software. Animations can be based on motion-capture data or on time series protocols as generated by means of high-resolution coding procedures (see Bente, 2002; Bente and Krämer, 2002). There are some

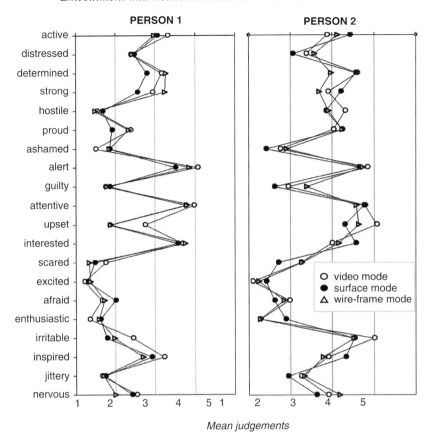

PERSON 1   PERSON 2

active
distressed
determined
strong
hostile
proud
ashamed
alert
guilty
attentive
upset
interested
scared
excited
afraid
enthusiastic
irritable
inspired
jittery
nervous

O video mode
● surface mode
△ wire-frame mode

Mean judgements

Figure 8.4 Impression profiles for video-recorded and reanimated behavior, using high- and low-fidelity computer models.

very relevant basic questions concerning embodiment and the use of computer characters that do not require interactivity at all. Questions include whether computer animations can convey nonverbal information to the same degree as video recordings and whether person-perception processes induced by videos and computer animations are equivalent. A further aspect that can be included in such media comparisons concerns the technical quality of the animations and the realism of the models that is necessary to generate a realistic impression. A series of studies has been conducted within the VCE showing that realistic reanimations of head and body movements alone can invoke the same impression as the original video recordings (see Bente *et al.*, 2001a, 2001c). Figure 8.4 shows an example of such a

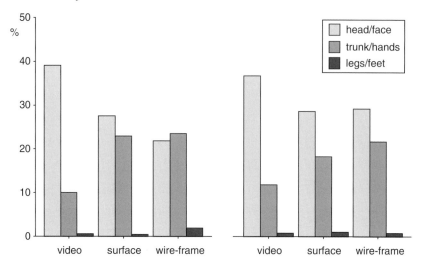

Figure 8.5 Focus of visual attention observing video-recorded and computer-animated nonverbal behavior in dyadic interactions.

media comparison. In fact, the sophistication of the computer models (wire frame vs. surface model) did not affect person perception at all.

Although very relevant with respect to the general issue of the potential socioemotional impact of embodiment, global media comparisons do not tell us anything about the communicative functions of particular nonverbal subsystems, activity patterns, or specific nonverbal cues. Answers to these questions are, however, very relevant not only to fundamental nonverbal research but also to the implementation of avatar systems. It might be necessary to decide upon the channels to include and the cues to transmit or to filter out. Many of the research questions in this context can be answered within simple, third-party observation setups also. As mentioned above, the VCE allows the systematic variation of computer models (sophistication, appearance, sex, etc.), the blending of behavioral channels (e.g., facial activity), and the interactive or algorithmic change of behavior (filtering out, inserting, or accentuating specific cues). In the study mentioned above (Bente *et al.*, 2001a, 2001c), for example, facial activity was not available in the computer animations. Although the visual attention of the observers shifted under these conditions from the face area to the hands of the actors as compared to the video (Figure 8.5), it was striking that the impressions reported were nearly identical (Figure 8.4).

In another study following this paradigm, we investigated the impact of very subtle nonverbal cues on the receiver's feelings toward the sender. We replicated real-life dyadic interactions and then tested impression effects of nonverbal variations. Lateral head position and general level of head movement were systematically varied. The results indicate that minor cues, such as activity and position of the head, have an immense impact on the receiver's evaluation of the sender. However, the effect of activity seems to be strongly context-dependent, since increased activity was only evaluated positively when the interaction was not conflict-laden (Krämer, 2001). Further studies that investigated the effects of gestures did not show similar differences (Krämer *et al.*, 2003). The data suggest that subtle head movements might even be more decisive for person perception than gestures (see also Krumhuber and Kappas, 2005). Provided that this assumption can be proven in further studies, it can be concluded that the accurate transmission of head movements is more important for CMC than the transfer and display of gestures or facial expressions.

The mixed-reality paradigm is in a way located between observation and interaction studies. In this paradigm the subject is a participating observer involved in communication with the experimenter or a confederate, who controls the avatar. Here, interactions can be analyzed without the potentially disturbing aspect that the participant has to wear motion tracker and data gloves (while the interaction partner does). The questions thus can be extended to spatial and temporal contingency phenomena, which are out of range in the mere observation studies. The participant is directly addressed, and thus eye contact and other relational nonverbal cues can be tested for their effects. It is further possible to study critical values in response delays, which seem to be crucial in turn-taking and back-channeling in face-to-face communications and thus also deserve attention within avatar-based CMC. Also, the effects of the character design can be studied under more realistic conditions – while at the same time exerting control over the interaction process to a certain extent (e.g., via instructing the confederate). Additionally, this paradigm can be used within research on human–computer interaction to investigate the effects of embodied conversational agents. For this purpose we suggested so-called Wizard of Oz studies, in which a computer agent is controlled by a hidden human expert without the user's knowledge (Bente and Krämer, 2001; Bente *et al.*, 2001b). This setting allows the evaluation of conversational agents under ideal conditions; i.e., with a fully functional social intelligence that cannot be implemented within a computer system at the present time.

The interaction paradigm is targeted at the usability and functionality of the avatar platforms within specific application scenarios. In this setting, all participants are connected to the tracking devices and interact with each other via the internet to solve specific cooperative or competitive tasks. As in the observation studies, media comparisons play a predominant role within this paradigm, focusing on the question of under which conditions avatar communication has advantages over other media and face-to-face communication. We conducted such a basic media comparison while varying task type (brainstorming vs. negotiation/problem solving) and interaction climate (cooperation vs. competition; Petersen, 2002; Petersen *et al.*, 2002). Results show that there were no effects on socioemotional outcome variables (such as variance of person perception). Significant media effects could be demonstrated for self-evaluation in the situation and rating of the interaction climate. Within avatar-based communication (and also video interactions), women experienced themselves as less dominant and in control than in face-to-face or audio-based communications, whereas men tended to experience it exactly the other way around. Concerning task performance, there were differences neither in production (number of ideas in brainstorming) nor in quality of arguments (in problem solving and negotiation tasks), indicating that users were able to adapt to the new medium without problems. For communication processes, however, several differences were observed. Structural aspects of interactions, such as turn-taking, were affected by the communication medium. The frequency of interruptions in avatar-based interactions was significantly lower than in face-to-face interaction and largely resembled the behavior in the audio condition. Thus, one could conclude that the thesis of Rutter and Stephenson (1977) that interaction partners do not dare to interrupt because effects are not observable (see above) is also true for avatar-based communication, hinting at the possibility that not all relevant cues are transmitted. Concerning the production of nonverbal parameters, there were no differences with regard to gestural activity; however, head movements differed considerably. The activity and complexity of movements was most pronounced in face-to-face interactions and, unexpectedly, least pronounced in avatar communication (Petersen, 2002; Petersen *et al.*, 2002).

Beyond mere media comparisons, the interaction paradigm provides all types of experimental variations as described above; i.e., variations of the physical appearance and experimental modifications of the behavior as well. Within a current project, female, male, and androgynous characters are used to determine which behavioral cues permit recognition of the sex of the interaction partner and how long identification takes when there is no hint from the physical appearance (Wortberg *et al.*, 2003). This paradigm provides an innovative possibility for research on stereotypes; for example, in order to study whether the effects of specific nonverbal dynamics vary depending on appearance (i.e., social role). Additionally, studies on the applied aspects of changing the appearance of CMC users might be conducted. The fact that, unlike in face-to-face interactions, one can choose one's own appearance augments the possibilities of communication and adds a new dimension with regard to impression management, which is already extensively used in chat and gaming communities. Women may present themselves as men and vice versa, attractiveness may be increased or scaled down, and other aspects such as race may be altered. But not only appearance can be changed. Variations in NVB can be introduced by blending particular channels (static filters) or modifying specific nonverbal cues (dynamic filters). For example, by providing and concealing specific channels (gestures, facial expression, head movements) in a systematic way, it can be determined which aspects and channels are necessary and efficient with regard to which tasks or situations. Additionally, fundamental results on the relative importance and specific functions of different channels can be derived. Using dynamic filters (i.e., specific algorithms), the experimenter can vary specific nonverbal signals within conversation. Thus, for example, smiles can be prolonged or removed and head movement activity can be increased by specific algorithms. This can be done right from the beginning of the conversation, introduced at a specific point, and applied to just one interaction partner or to both. One of the shortcomings of this approach is the fact that, once an experimental variation has been introduced, it develops its own dynamics. The approach therefore can be compared to an ecological experiment in which a specific perturbation is introduced in order to observe and analyze the adaptation and functioning of the system.

Conclusion

In this chapter, we demonstrated the potential of avatar-based communication for application as well as research. As we have shown, NVB serves important functions within interactions and heavily affects communication processes. Thus, by incorporating these additional cues, avatar communication provides new possibilities for CMC, compared, for example, to text- or audio-based interactions. But, as already discussed, the conclusion does not necessarily have to be that as many nonverbal cues as possible should be included in CMC. Depending on task or setting, it may be a more fruitful approach to select and transmit just specific channels or signals. In order to determine which channels or cues should be provided under which conditions, the avatar technologies can be employed as powerful research tools. Potentially, results will point out specific possibilities that might even mean an augmentation compared to face-to-face communication. Instead of conceptualizing CMC as deficit-laden, new insights could enable researchers as well as users to perceive and experience innovative and efficient modes of communication.

References

Aguinis, H., Simonsen, M. M., and Pierce, C. A. (1998). Effects of nonverbal behavior on perceptions of power bases. *Journal of Social Psychology*, **138**, 455–469.

Argyle, M. (1975). *Bodily Communication*. London: Methuen.

Argyle, M. and Cook, M. (1976). *Gaze and Mutual Gaze*. Cambridge University Press.

Argyle, M., Salter, V., Nicholson, H., Williams, M., and Burgess, P. (1970). The communication of inferior and superior attitudes by verbal and nonverbal signals. *British Journal of Social and Clinical Psychology*, **9**, 222–231.

Bavelas, J. B., Black, A., Lemery, C. R., and Mullett, J. (1986). I show how you feel: motor mimicry as a communicative act. *Journal of Personality and Social Psychology*, **50**, 322–329.

Bente, G. (2002). Entschlüsselung einer ungewissen Botschaft: zur Transkription und Analyse nonverbaler Kommunikationsprozesse [Decoding of an uncertain message: about the transcription and analysis of nonverbal communication processes]. In L. Jäger and G. Stanitzek (eds), *Transkribieren [Trancription]* (pp. 133–152). Munich: Fink.

Bente, G., Feist, A., and Elder, S. (1996). Person perception effects of computer-simulated male and female head movement. *Journal of Nonverbal Behavior*, **20**, 213–228.

Bente, G. and Krämer, N. C. (2001). Psychologische Aspekte bei der Implementierung und Evaluierung nonverbal agierender Interface-Agenten [Psychological aspects of implementation and evaluation of nonverbally operating interface agents]. In H. Oberquelle, R. Oppermann, and J. Krause (eds), *Mensch und Computer 2001 [Humans and the Computer 2001]* (pp. 275–285). Stuttgart: Teubner.

(2002). Virtuelle Gesten: VR-Einsatz in der nonverbalen Kommunikationsforschung [Virtual gestures: use of VR in nonverbal communication research]. In G. Bente, N. C. Krämer, and A. Petersen (eds), *Virtuelle Realitäten [Virtual Reality]* (pp. 81–107). Göttingen: Hogrefe.

(2008). Effects of nonverbal signals. In W. Donsbach (ed.), *The International Encyclopedia of Communication* (pp. 3334–3339). Oxford: Blackwell.

Bente, G., Krämer, N. C., and Eschenburg, F. (2008a). Is there anybody out there? Analyzing the effects of embodiment and nonverbal behavior in avatar-mediated communication. In E. Konijn, S. Utz, M. Tanis, and S. Barnes (eds), *Mediated Interpersonal Communication* (pp. 131–157). New York: Routledge.

Bente, G., Krämer, N.C., Petersen, A., and de Ruiter, J.P. (2001a). Computer animated movement and person perception: methodological advances in nonverbal behavior research. *Journal of Nonverbal Behavior*, *25*, 151–166.

Bente, G., Krämer, N.C., Trogemann, G., Piesk, J., and Fischer, O. (2001b). Conversing with electronic devices: an integrated approach towards the generation and evaluation of nonverbal behavior in face-to-face like interface agents. In A. Heuer and T. Kirste (eds), *Intelligent Interactive Assistance and Mobile Multimedia Computing* (pp. 67–76). Rostock: Neuer Hochschulschriftenverlag.

Bente, G., Petersen, A., Krämer, N.C., and de Ruiter, J.P. (2001c). Transcript-based computer animation of movement: evaluating a new tool for nonverbal behavior research. *Behavior Research Methods, Instruments, and Computers*, *33*, 303–310.

Bente, G., Rüggenberg, S., Krämer, N.C., and Eschenburg, F. (2008b). Avatar-assisted net-working. Increasing social presence and interpersonal trust in net-based collaborations. *Human Communication Research*, *34*(2), 287–318.

Bentler, P.M. (1969). Semantic space is (approximately) bipolar. *Journal of Psychology*, *71*, 33–40.

Bernieri, F.J. and Rosenthal, R. (1991). Interpersonal coordination: behavioral matching and interactional synchrony. In R.S. Feldman and B. Rimé (eds), *Fundamentals of Nonverbal Behavior* (pp. 401–432). Cambridge University Press.

Biocca, F. (1992). Communication within virtual reality: creating space for research. *Journal of Communication*, *42*, 5–22.

Biocca, F., Burgoon, J., Harms, C., and Stoner, M. (2001). *Criteria and Scope Conditions for a Theory and Measure of Social Presence*. East Lansing, MI: Media Interface and Network Design (M.I.N.D.) Lab. www.temple.edu/ispr/prev_conferences/proceedings/2001/Biocca1.pdf.

Birdwhistell, R.L. (1970). *Kinesics and Context*. Philadelphia: University of Pennsylvania Press.

Blascovich, J., Loomis, J., Beall, A.C., Swinth, K.R., Hoyt, C.L., and Bailenson, J.N. (2002). Immersive virtual environment technology as a methodological tool for social psychology. *Psychological Inquiry*, *13*, 146–149.

Bollen, L., Hoppe, U., Milrad, M., and Pinkwart, N. (2002). Collaborative modelling in group learning environments. In P.I. Davidsen, E. Mollona, V.G. Diker, R.S. Langer, and J.I. Rowe (eds), *Proceedings of the XX International Conference of the System Dynamics Society* (p. 53). Oxford: Wiley.

Brunner, L.J. (1979). Smiles can be back channels. *Journal of Personality and Social Psychology*, *27*, 728–734.

Burgoon, J.K., Dillman, L., and Stern, L. (1993). Adaptation in dyadic interaction: defining and operationalizing patterns of reciprocity and compensation. *Communication Theory*, *4*, 295–316.

Buxton, W., Sellen, A., and Sheasby, M. (1997). Interfaces for multiparty videoconferencing. In K. Finn, A. Sellen, and S. Wilber (eds), *Video-Mediated Communication* (pp. 385–400). Hillsdale, NJ: Erlbaum.

Camras, L. (1982). Ethological approaches to nonverbal communication. In R. Feldman (ed.), *Development of Nonverbal Behavior in Children* (pp. 3–28). New York: Springer.

Cappella, J.N. (1991). Mutual adaptation and relativity of measurement. In B.M. Montgomery and S. Duck (eds), *Studying Interpersonal Interaction* (pp. 103–117). New York: Guilford.

Carli, L. L., LaFleur, S. J., and Loeber, C. C. (1995). Nonverbal behavior, gender, and influence. *Journal of Personality and Social Psychology*, **68**, 1030–1041.

Carli, L. L., Martin, C., Leatham, G., Lyons, K., and Tse, I. (1993). Perceptions of nonverbal behavior. *Paper presented at the annual meeting of the American Psychological Association*, Toronto, Canada.

Cassell, J., Bickmore, T., Billinghurst, M., Campbell, L., Chang, K., Vilhjálmsson, H., *et al.* (1999). Embodiment in conversational interfaces: Rea. *CHI'99 Conference Proceedings* (pp. 520–527). New York: Association for Computing Machinery.

Chartrand, T. L. and Bargh, J. A. (1999). The chameleon effect: the preception–behavior link and social interaction. *Journal of Personality and Social Psychology*, **76**, 893–910.

Chovil, N. (1991). Discourse-oriented facial displays in conversation. *Research on Language and Social Interaction*, **25**, 163–194.

Condon, W. S. and Ogston, W. D. (1966). Sound-film analysis of normal and pathological behavior patterns. *Journal of Nervous and Mental Disease*, **143**, 338–347.

DePaulo, B. M. and Friedman, H. S. (1998). Nonverbal communication. In D. T. Gilbert, S. T. Fiske, and G. Lindzey (eds), *The Handbook of Social Psychology* (4th edn., vol. II, pp. 3–40). Boston: McGraw-Hill.

Deutsch, F. M., LeBaron, D., and Fryer, M. M. (1987). What is in a smile? *Psychology of Women Quarterly*, **11**, 341–352.

Donaghy, W. C. and Goldberg, J. (1991). Head movement and gender differences following the onset of simultaneous speech. *Southern Speech Communication Journal*, **56**, 114–126.

Dovidio, J. F., Ellyson, S. L., Keating, C. F., Heltman, K., and Brown, C. E. (1988). The relationship of social power to visual displays of dominance between men and women. *Journal of Personality and Social Psychology*, **54**, 233–242.

Duncan, S., Jr. (1972). Some signals and rules for taking speaking turns in conversations. *Journal of Personality and Social Psychology*, **23**, 283–292.

Duncan, S., Jr. and Fiske, D. W. (1979). Dynamic patterning in conversation. *American Scientist*, **67**, 90–98.

Edinger, J. A. and Patterson, M. L. (1983). Nonverbal involvement and social control. *Psychological Bulletin*, **93**(1), 30–56.

Efron, D. (1941). *Gesture and Environment*. New York: King's Crown Press.

Ekman, P. and Friesen, W. V. (1969). The repertoire of nonverbal behavior: categories, origins, usage and coding. *Semiotica*, **1**, 49–98.

Exline, R. V. (1972). Visual interaction: the glances of power and preference. In J. Cole (ed.), *Nebraska Symposium on Motivation* (pp. 163–206). Lincoln, NE: University of Nebraska Press.

Exline, R. V., Ellyson, S. L., and Long, B. (1975). Visual behavior as an aspect of power role relationships. In P. Pliner, L. Krames, and T. Alloway (eds), *Nonverbal Communication of Aggression* (pp. 21–52). New York: Plenum.

Frey, S. (1999). *Die Macht des Bildes [The Picture's Power]*. Berne, Switzerland: Huber.

Frey, S., Hirsbrunner, H.-P., Florin, A., Daw, W., and Crawford, R. (1983). A unified approach to the investigation of nonverbal and verbal behavior in communication research. In W. Doise and S. Moscovici (eds), *Current Issues in European Social Psychology* (pp. 143–199). Cambridge University Press.

Fridlund, A. J. (1997). The new ethology of human facial expressions. In J. A. Russell and J. M. Fernández-Dols (eds), *The Psychology of Facial Expression: Studies in Emotion and Social Interaction* (pp. 103–132). New York: Cambridge University Press.

Friedman, H. S. (1979). The interactive effects of facial expressions of emotion and verbal messages on perceptions of affective meaning. *Journal of Experimental Social Psychology*, *15*, 453–469.

Giles, H., Mulac, A., Bradac, J. J., and Johnson, P. (1987). Speech accommodation theory: the first decade and beyond. In M. L. McLaughlin (ed.), *Communication Yearbook* (vol. X, pp. 13–48). Beverly Hills, CA: Sage.

Graham, J. A. and Argyle, M. (1975). The effects of different patterns of gaze combined with different facial expressions on impression formation. *Journal of Human Movement Studies*, *1*, 178–182.

Grammer, K. (1990). Strangers meet: laughter and nonverbal signs of interest in opposite-sex encounters. *Journal of Nonverbal Behavior*, *14*, 209–236.

Grammer, K., Filova, V., and Fieder, M. (1997). The communication paradox and a possible solution: toward a radical empiricism. In A. Schmitt, K. Atzwanger, K. Grammer, and K. Schäfer (eds), *New Aspects of Human Ethology* (pp. 91–120). New York: Plenum.

Grammer, K., Kruck, K. B., and Magnusson, M. S. (1998). The courtship dance: patterns of nonverbal synchronization in opposite-sex encounters. *Journal of Nonverbal Behavior*, *22*, 2–29.

Haase, R. F. and Tepper, D. T. (1972). Nonverbal components of empathic communication. *Journal of Counseling Psychology*, *19*, 417–424.

Halberstadt, A. G. and Saitta, M. B. (1987). Gender, nonverbal behavior, and dominance. *Journal of Personality and Social Psychology*, *53*, 257–272.

Hehl, F. J., Eisenriegler, E., Jokiel, R., and Channon, S. (1998). The negative function of nonverbal communication in anorexic families: a family experiment. In D. H. Saklofske and S. B. Eysenck (eds), *Individual differences in children and adolescents* (pp. 50–62). New Brunswick, NJ: Transaction.

Henley, N. (1977). *Body Politics: Power, Sex, and Nonverbal Communication.* Englewood Cliffs, NJ: Prentice-Hall.

Kappas, A., Hess, U., Barr, C. L., and Kleck, R. E. (1994). Angle of regard: the effect of vertical viewing angle on the perception of facial expression. *Journal of Nonverbal Behavior*, *18*, 263–280.

Keating, C. F., Mazur, A., and Segall, M. H. (1977). Facial gestures which influence the perception of status. *Social Psychology Quarterly*, *40*, 374–378.

Keeley, M. P. and Hart, A. J. (1994). Nonverbal behavior in dyadic interactions. In S. Duck (ed.), *Dynamics of Relationships. Vol. IV: Understanding Relationship Processes* (pp. 135–162). Thousand Oaks, CA: Sage.

Kendon, A. (1967). Some functions of gaze-direction in social interaction: some examples described. *Acta Psychologica*, *26*, 22–63.

Kepplinger, H. M. and Donsbach, W. (1983). Der Einfluß von Kameraperspektiven auf Anhänger und Gegner eines Politikers [The influence of camera perspectives on supporters and opponents of a politician]. In W. Schulz and K. Schönbach (eds), *Massenmedien und Wahlen [The Mass Media and Elections]* (pp. 406–423). Munich: Ölschläger.

Kiesler, S., Siegel, J., and McGuire, T. W. (1984). Social psychological aspects of computer-mediated communication. *American Psychologist*, *39*, 1123–1134.

Krämer, N.C. (2001). *Bewegende Bewegung: Sozio-emotionale Wirkungen nonverbalen Verhaltens und deren experimentelle Untersuchung mittels Computeranimation [Moving Movement: Socioemotional Effects of Nonverbal Behavior and Their Experimental Investigation with Computer Animation]*. Lengerich, Germany: Pabst.

(2008). Nonverbal communication. In J. Blascovich and C. Hartel (eds), *Human Behavior in Military Contexts* (pp. 150–188). Washington, DC: National Academies Press.

Krämer, N.C. and Bente, G. (2002). Virtuelle Helfer: embodied conversational agents in der Mensch-Computer-Interaktion [Virtual helpers: embodied conversational agents in human–computer interaction]. In G. Bente, N.C. Krämer, and A. Petersen (eds), *Virtuelle Realitäten [Virtual Reality]* (pp. 203–225). Göttingen: Hogrefe.

Krämer, N.C., Tietz, B., and Bente, G. (2003). Effects of embodied interface agents and their gestural activity. In R. Aylett, D. Ballin, T. Rist, and J. Rickel (eds), *4th International Working Conference on Intelligent Virtual Agents* (pp. 292–300). Hamburg: Springer.

Krauss, R.M. and Chiu, C.Y. (1998). Language and social behavior. In D.T. Gilbert, S.T. Fiske, and G. Lindzey (eds), *The Handbook of Social Psychology* (4th edn., vol. II, pp. 41–81). New York: McGraw-Hill.

Krumhuber, E. and Kappas, A. (2005). Moving smiles: the role of dynamic components for the perception of the genuineness of smiles. *Journal of Nonverbal Behavior, 29*, 3–24.

LaCrosse, M.B. (1975). Nonverbal behavior and perceived counselor attractiveness and persuasiveness. *Journal of Counseling Psychology, 22*, 563–566.

Lanzetta, J.T., Sullivan, D.G., Masters, R.D., and McHugo, G.J. (1986). Emotional and cognitive responses to televised images of political leaders. In S. Kraus and R.M. Perloff (eds), *Mass Media and Political Thought: An Information Processing Approach* (pp. 85–116). Beverly Hills, CA: Sage.

Larnier, J. (2001). Virtually there: three-dimensional tele-immersion may eventually bring the world to your desk. *Scientific American, 284*(4), 66–75.

Lipps, T. (1907). Das Wissen von fremden Ichen [The knowledge of foreign egos]. In T. Lipps (ed.), *Psychologische Untersuchungen [Psychological Research]* (pp. 694–722). Leipzig: Engelmann.

McGrath, J.E. and Hollingshead, A.B. (1993). Putting the "group" back in group support systems: some theoretical issues about dynamic processes in groups with technological enhancements. In L.M. Jessup and J.S. Valacich (eds), *Group Support Systems: New Perspectives* (pp. 78–96). New York: Macmillan.

McNeill, D. (1992). *Hand and Mind: What Gestures Reveal About Thought*. Chicago: University of Chicago.

Mehrabian, A. (1969). Significance of posture and position in the communication of attitude and status relationships. *Psychological Bulletin, 71*, 359–372.

Mehrabian, A. and Williams, M. (1969). Nonverbal concomitants of perceived and intended persuasiveness. *Journal of Personality and Social Psychology, 13*, 37–58.

Millar, F., Rogers, L.E., and Bavelas, J. (1984). Identifying patterns of verbal conflict in interpersonal dynamics. *Western Journal of Speech Communication, 48*, 231–246.

Montagner, H., Henry, J. C., Lombardot, M., Benedini, M., Restoin, A., Bolzoni, D., *et al.* (1977). Études étho-physiologiques de groupes d'enfants de 14 mois à l'école maternelle [Physiological studies on a group of 14-month-old children in a nursery]. *Psychologie Médicale*, *9*, 2075–2112.

Müller, K., Kempf, F., and Leukert, S. (2002). Besser Kollaborieren durch VR? Evaluation einer VR-Umgebung für kollaboratives Lernen [Better collaboration through VR? Evaluation of a VR environment for collaborative learning]. In U. Beck and W. Sommer (eds), *Learntec 2002* (vol. II, pp. 475–482). Karlsruhe, Germany: Karlsruher Messe- und Kongress-GmbH.

Müller, K., Troitzsch, H., and Renkl, A. (2003). Der Einfluss nonverbaler Signale auf den Kommunikationsprozess in einer kollaborativen virtuellen Umgebung [The influence of nonverbal signals on the communication process in a collaborative-virtual environment]. *Zeitschrift für Medienpsychologie*, *15*, 24–33.

Naimark, M. (1990). Realness and interactivity. In B. Laurel (ed.), *The Art of Human–Computer Interface Design* (pp. 455–459). Reading, MA: Addison-Wesley.

Palmer, M. T. and Simmons, K. B. (1995). Communicating intentions through nonverbal behaviors: conscious and nonconscious encoding of liking. *Human Communication Research*, *22*, 128–160.

Patterson, M. L. (1982). A sequential functional model of nonverbal exchange. *Psychological Review*, *89*, 231–249.

(1994). Strategic functions of nonverbal exchange. In J. A. Daly and J. M. Wiemann (eds), *Strategic Interpersonal Communication* (pp. 273–293). Hillsdale, NJ: Lawrence Erlbaum Associates.

Petersen, A. (2002). *Interpersonale Kommunikation im Medienvergleich [Interpersonal Communication in Media Comparisons]*. Münster, Germany: Waxmann.

Petersen, A. and Bente, G. (2001). Situative und technologische Determinanten des Erlebens Virtueller Realität [Situational and technological determinants of experiencing virtual reality]. *Zeitschrift für Medienpsychologie*, *3*, 138–145.

Petersen, A., Bente, G., and Krämer, N. C. (2002). Virtuelle Stellvertreter: Analyse avatar-vermittelter Kommunikationsprozesse [Virtual representatives: analysis of avatar-mediated communication processes]. In G. Bente, N. C. Krämer, and A. Petersen (eds), *Virtuelle Realitäten* (pp. 227–253). Göttingen: Hogrefe.

Pimental, K. and Teixiera, K. (1993). *Virtual Reality: Through the New Looking Glass*. New York: McGraw-Hill.

Rawlins, C. (1989). The impact of teleconferencing on the leadership of small decision-making groups. *Journal of Organisational Behavior Management*, *10*, 37–54.

Remland, M. (1982). The implicit ad hominem fallacy: nonverbal displays of status in argumentative discourse. *Journal of the American Forensics Association*, *19*, 79–86.

Richards, L., Rollerson, B., and Phillips, J. (1991). Perceptions of submissiveness: implications for victimization. *Journal of Psychology*, *125*, 407–411.

Rickenberg, R. and Reeves, B. (2000). The effects of animated characters on anxiety, task performance, and evaluations of user interfaces. *Letters of CHI 2000*, *April*, 49–56.

Riggio, R. E. and Friedman, H. S. (1986). Impression formation: the role of expressive behavior. *Journal of Personality and Social Psychology*, *50*, 421–427.

Rimé, B. (1983). Nonverbal communication or nonverbal behavior? Towards a cognitive-motor theory of nonverbal behavior. In W. Doise and S. Moscovici (eds), *Current Issues in European Social Psychology* (pp. 85–141). Cambridge University Press.

Rosenfeld, H. M. (1966). Approval-seeking and approval-avoiding functions of verbal and nonverbal responses in the dyad. *Journal of Personality and Social Psychology*, **4**, 597–605.

Ruiter, J. P. de (1998). *Gesture and Speech Production*. Wageningen, The Netherlands: Ponson & Looijen.

Rutter, D. R. and Stephenson, G. M. (1977). The role of visual communication in synchronizing conversation. *European Journal of Social Psychology*, **7**, 29–37.

Rutter, D. R., Stephenson, G. M., Ayling, K., and White, P. A. (1978). The timing of looks in dyadic conversation. *British Journal of Social and Clinical Psychology*, **17**, 17–21.

Sacks, H., Schegloff, E. A., and Jefferson, G. A. (1974). A simplest systematics for the organization of turn-taking in conversation. *Language*, **50**, 696–735.

Sapir, E. (1949 [1928]). The unconscious patterning of behavior in society. In D. G. Mandelbaum (ed.), *Selected Writings of Edward Sapir* (pp. 544–559). Berkeley, CA: University of California Press.

Scheflen, A. E. (1964). The significance of posture in communication systems. *Psychiatry*, **27**, 316–321.

Schlenker, B. R. (1980). *Impression Management: The Self-Concept, Social Identity, and Interpersonal Relations*. Monterey, CA: Brooks/Cole.

Shapiro, M. A. and McDonald, D. G. (1992). I'm not a real doctor, but I play one in virtual reality: implications of virtual reality for judgments about reality. *Journal of Communication*, **42**, 94–114.

Short, J., Williams, E., and Christie, B. (1976). *The Social Psychology of Telecommunications*. London: Wiley.

Sieber, J. E. (1996). Typically unexamined communication processes in research. In B. H. Stanley and J. E. Sieber (eds), *Research Ethics: A Psychological Approach* (pp. 73–104). Lincoln, NE: University of Nebraska Press.

Siegel, S. M., Friedlander, M. L., and Heatherington, L. (1992). Nonverbal relational control in family communication. *Journal of Nonverbal Behavior*, **16**, 117–139.

Slater, M., Howell, J., Steed, A., Pertaub, D.-B., Garau, M., and Springel, S. (2000). Acting in virtual reality. In *Proceedings of the Third ACM Conference on Collaborative Virtual Environments, CVE '2000* (pp. 103–110). www.cs. ucl.ac.uk/staff/m.slater/vr/Projects/Acting/Publications/actingpaper. pdf.

Slater, M., Sadagic, A., Usoh, M., and Schroeder, R. (1998). Small group behaviour in a virtual and real environment: a comparative study. *Paper presented at the BT Workshop on Presence in Shared Virtual Environments*, June. www.cs.ucl.ac.uk/staff/m.slater/BTWorkshop/Inhabit/.

Slater, M. and Steed, A. (2002). Meeting people virtually: experiments in shared virtual environments. In R. Schroeder (ed.), *The Social Life of Avatars: Presence and Interaction in Shared Virtual Environments* (pp. 146–171). London: Springer.

Spears, R. and Lea, M. (1994). Panacea or panopticon? The hidden power in computer-mediated communication. *Communication Research*, **21**, 427–459.

Spears, R., Lea, M., and Lee, S. (1990). De-individuation and group polarisation in computer-mediated communication. *British Journal of Social Psychology,* **29**, 121–134.

Sproull, L. and Kiesler, S. (1986). Reducing social context cues: electronic mail in organizational communication. *Management Science,* **32**, 1492–1512.

Steuer, J. (1992). Defining virtual reality: dimensions determining telepresence. *Journal of Communication,* **42**, 73–93.

Suler, J. (1999). The psychology of avatars and graphical space in multimedia chat communities: a study of the palace. In M. Beiswenger (ed.), *Chat Communication* (pp. 305–344). Stuttgart: Ibidem.

Wallbott, H. G. (1995). Congruence, contagion, and motor mimicry: mutualities in nonverbal exchange. In J. Markova, C. F. Graumann, and K. Foppa (eds), *Mutalities in Dialogue* (pp. 82–98). Cambridge University Press.

Walther, J. B. (1996). Computer-mediated communication: impersonal, inter-personal and hyperpersonal interaction. *Communication Research,* **23**, 3–43.

Watzlawick, P., Beavin, J. H., and Jackson, D. D. (1967). *Pragmatics of Human Communication: A Study of Interactional Patterns, Pathologies, and Paradoxes.* New York: W. W. Norton.

Wortberg, S., Bente, G., and Tietz, B. (2003, March). Genderperzeption und Geschlechtskonstruktion in virtuellen Kommunikationsumgebungen [Gender perception and sex construction in virtual communication environments]. Poster presented at the *45. Tagung experimentell arbeitender Psychologen (TeaP),* Kiel, Germany.

Yngve, V. H. (1970). On getting a word in edgewise. In *Papers from the Sixth Regional Meeting of the Chicago Linguistic Society* (pp. 567–577). Chicago: Chicago Linguistic Society.

Young, D. M. and Beier, E. G. (1977). The role of applicant nonverbal communication in the employment interview. *Journal of Employment Counseling,* **14**, 154–165.

Zeltzer, D. (1992). Autonomity, interaction, and presence. *Presence: Teleoperators and Virtual Environments,* **1**, 127–132.

PART 3

Emotions and visual cues in human–computer interaction

CHAPTER 9

Emotions in human–computer interaction

Veikko Surakka and Toni Vanhala

Overview: Human–computer interaction (HCI) may be significantly improved by incorporating social and emotional processes. Developing appropriate technologies is only one side of the problem. It is also vital to investigate how synthesized emotional information might affect human behavior in the context of information technology. Despite previous suggestions that people treat computers as social actors, we still know relatively little about the possible and supposedly positive effects of utilizing any kind of emotional cues or messages in human–technology interaction. The aim of the present chapter is to provide a theoretical and empirical basis for integrating emotions into the study of HCI. We will first argue and show evidence in favor of the use of virtual emotions in HCI. We will then proceed by studying the possibilities of a computer for analyzing human emotion-related processes and consider some physiological measures used for this purpose in more detail. In this context, we will also briefly describe some new technological prototypes for measuring computer users' behavior. The chapter ends with a discussion summarizing the findings and addressing the advantages of studying emotions in the context of present-day technology.

Introduction

The qualitative improvement and facilitation of human–computer interaction (HCI) has become a central research issue in computer science. Traditionally, attempts to improve HCI have centered on making computers more user-friendly along technical dimensions. In this line of work, perhaps still the most visible milestone for an ordinary user has been the development of a graphical, mouse-driven user interface. This invention dramatically enhanced computer use and raised HCI to a new level. The most important consequences are that the user receives feedback about his or her actions when operating a desktop computer or another kind of information technology, such as handheld devices, televisions, and mobile telephones.

These developments in turn enable the development of various non-traditional input and output channels. For example, computers might be used by touching, speaking, and gazing in their direction. On the other hand, computers themselves might provide rich feedback or output using either the common auditory, visual, or audiovisual channels, or less commonly applied modalities, such as the sense of touch.

Although current computers and user interfaces are reasonably functional (e.g., efficient in computing and relatively easy to use), new problems and lines of research have developed in parallel with the technology itself. Indeed, one of the recently recognized problems relates to the emotional state that working with computers evokes in users. At least two studies have succeeded in bringing attention to the emotional aspects of human–technology relations.

A study by Concord Communications (1999) found that users often admit to help desk managers that they have had violent thoughts and/ or engaged in abusive behavior toward their computers. A study called "Rage Against the Machine," conducted by MORI on behalf of Compaq, found that users swear, consider causing damage, deliberately pull out the plug, and even kick their computers.[1] These examples show that working with computers evokes intense negative emotional reactions. Looking a little deeper, these examples also imply that people actually treat computers as if they were social entities, which they would like to threaten and punish in order to make them operate better in the future.

Curiously, although it is evident on a conscious cognitive level that computers do not share our communicative signals, we seem to forget this when interacting with them. For instance, people really seem to appreciate sharing their feelings with computers as well as virtual expressions of empathy, irrespective of the fact that machines cannot really feel for us (Brave *et al.*, 2005; Klein *et al.*, 2002). Moreover, other social signals, such as simulated emotional touch (i.e., haptics and emotions), simulated proximity, and virtual facial expressions of an embodied agent character may affect our subjective feelings and physiological arousal (Partala *et al.*, 2004; Salminen *et al.*, 2008; Vanhala *et al.*, 2010). Generally speaking, people react to virtual cues of emotion and sociality in much the same manner as they do to those expressed by other humans. According to Nass *et al.* (1994), this is due to our strong tendency for social behavior.

---

[1] www.ipsos-mori.com/researchpublications/researcharchive/poll.aspx?oItemId=1900.

However, we are still left with the fact that computers have limited access to the social signals that we give out, and therefore cannot respond properly to their users. Building *perceptually intelligent* computers is one way to try to construct more socially and emotionally intelligent computers (Pentland, 2000). Concepts such as *perceptually intelligent machines*, *affective computing*, and *emotion and interest sensitive media* refer to a future generation of flexible, trainable, adaptive, and emotionally responsive user interfaces. The ambitious aim of perceptual intelligence is to build machines or interfaces that are as intelligent observers of social and emotional cues as we are. These interfaces utilize, for example, video cameras, microphones, and eye trackers for perceiving users' behaviors and translating them into information that a computer can process.

In addition, various types of physiological indicators (i.e., physiological computing), including correlates of autonomic nervous system activation (e.g., pupil size variation and heart rate), responses of central nervous activation, and electrical activity of facial muscles (Figure 9.1), can be utilized in connecting the user with the computer (Allanson *et al.*, 1999; Anttonen and Surakka, 2005; Barreto *et al.*, 2000; Jacob, 1991; Kübler *et al.*, 1999; Partala *et al.*, 2001, 2005, 2006; Pentland, 2000; Picard, 1997; Surakka *et al.*, 2004; Wolpaw *et al.*, 2002). Although these physiological measures are not readily available for our human communication partners, they can provide rich information for machines that sense them. As physiological activity is a central, underlying factor of all human behavior, it can be argued that computers might potentially have better access to our emotional processes than other people.

Enhancements of the perceptual intelligence of computers need to be matched by corresponding increases in *expressive intelligence*. The ambitious aim in this respect is that computers should be able to express socially and emotionally meaningful information in a human-like manner. Important aspects of communication are sensitivity to the user and appropriate responses to his or her cognitions and emotions. This might be achieved, for example, by the use of friendly visual expressions and even-tempered vocal intonations, while taking into account how users react to them. Work in this field is very much in its infancy. Speech synthesizers, for instance, are slowly beginning to make better use of prosodic features (Ilves and Surakka, 2004). There is also emerging knowledge about the types of virtual cues that are effective in influencing social perceptions of the human perceiver. Recent studies using virtual agents suggest that their gaze direction and other meaningful facial expressions are effective in communicating that they are trustworthy, intelligent social actors (Berry *et al.*, 2005; Schilbach *et al.*,

Figure 9.1 A person interacting with a software agent. This agent records the changes in the level of electrical facial muscle activities, and interprets these activations with the help of signal-processing algorithms. In the prototype, a software agent can be called on for help by raising the eyebrows (a common gesture when one is faced with problems or surprises). This agent can be forced to disappear by lowering the eyebrows (a common gesture used for expressing a negative attitude).

2006). However, these channels have not yet been used to any large extent in actual or real-time human–machine interaction.

Real-time expressive intelligence requires systems that are able to smoothly monitor and interpret users' behaviors via many channels so that the user's reactions to these intelligent expressions can also be taken into account. Computers that utilize video-, bio-, and behavioral signals need efficient signal analysis methods in order to interpret the various sensory signals with which they are faced. Intelligent perception also involves the capability to harness the potential of all available information. In the age of wireless and wearable computing, this means that systems should be able to dynamically integrate new devices (if and when they become available) into their analytical and decision-making processes. Further, they need to drop devices and measurements from their analysis when devices become unavailable (i.e., out of range), and still be able to interpret remaining data properly. These kinds of new developments have been enabled by the recent approaches in software development which emphasize loosely coupled, agent-based architectures (e.g., Vanhala and Surakka, 2005). Thus, complete communicative links can be created between the user and the computer.

An example of a complete communication link between person and machine is a demonstration of the Real Estate Agent (REA) software developed at the Massachusetts Institute of Technology. For example, REA can sense the appearance of a customer or user in front of her with the help of machine vision technology. She (or it) can then make a greeting by speech and nonverbal gestures (i.e., it has both a speech and a gesture database). It is also capable of taking turns during conversation (Cassell *et al.*, 2000). Recently, D'Mello *et al.* (2007) argued that such full communication cycles are needed in intelligent tutoring systems, such as their AutoTutor system. The emotions evoked by AutoTutor were explored with self-reports and observations. Perceptual intelligence was built into the system in the form of several automatic emotion classifiers for conversational cues, and for analyzing postural and facial expression. However, the integration of these separate channels and the intelligent use of this knowledge in an affective loop between the student and AutoTutor is still a work in progress.

We have designed an architecture for building functional prototype software that regulates (i.e., both observes and responds to) users' social and emotional responses (Figure 9.2). The software architecture enables the designer of the system to script the responses of an agent to different predefined scenarios of psychophysiological or psychobehavioral activity. For example, one prototypic system was developed for relaxing the respiration intensity of a person with labored breathing by automatic analysis of his or her heart activity patterns (Vanhala and Surakka, 2005). Depending on the automated higher-level interpretation of low-level electrocardiographic signals extracted from the "user," a virtual agent character would appear and calm the person by instructing a more relaxed breathing pattern in synthesized speech. A second system designed to monitor noninvasively the patterns of mouse and keyboard activity was developed to calm people who become negatively aroused when browsing the web with a mouse and keyboard. Intense levels of arousal while using the computer mouse has also been termed "mouse rage." This "rage" has been shown to exist in day-to-day computer use and can potentially lead to harmful physiological consequences (Marsh and Khor, 2006). When the user becomes negatively aroused, he or she may interpret the lack of feedback from the computer as negative information. This in turn

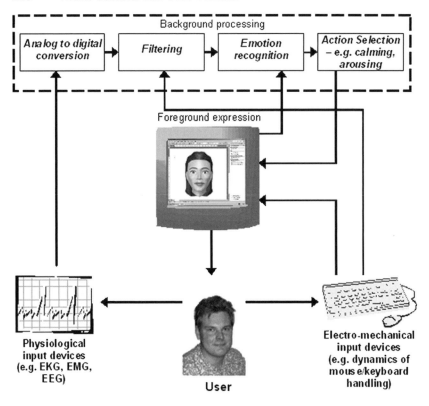

Figure 9.2 A schematic overview of a prototype software developed for detecting users' probable emotion-related responses. For example, significant changes in bioelectrical signals of facial muscles can be recognized with signal-processing algorithms (i.e., psychophysiological computing). In addition, dynamic behavioral changes (i.e., keyboard and mouse manipulation) can be monitored with signals from traditional input devices (i.e., psychobehavioral computing). When predefined algorithmic thresholds are exceeded, for example, an audiovisual agent can be made to appear and communicate in a predefined manner.

may lead to an even greater increase in negative arousal. In this case, our system was designed first to monitor noninvasively the patterns of mouse and keyboard activity, and then, if needed, to invoke a virtual character in order to break the vicious circle.

Although previous examples have shown that contemporary audiovisual agents can be programmed to display socially meaningful signals, this still requires a great deal of effort in preprogramming (i.e., scripting) the behavior of these agents. Even though we are beginning to understand the effectiveness of social and emotional cues in human–computer communication, we are still far from coming up with machines that can independently perform intelligent social emotional communication.

The aim of the present chapter is to provide a basis for a new generation of emotionally intelligent systems. Thus, in the following sections, we will first discuss the advantages of having a technology that is sensitive to emotional and social information. Next, we will present studies that clearly show the potential of emotionally expressive intelligence. Following this, we will present findings on how perceptual and expressive intelligence can be merged to create functional loops of perceptual and expressive intelligence. Finally, we will discuss the findings by adopting a positive perspective for the future.

Emotions and sociality in HCI

A natural approach to the development of social and emotional HCI involves considering which factors are central in human communication and behavior. In addition to the questionnaire and interview findings reported in the introduction, there is other evidence that people use the same kind of social rules in HCI that they use in human–human social communication (Fogg and Nass, 1997; Reeves and Nass, 1996). For example, research on sociality and computers has shown that people automatically interpret a computer agent as extroverted or introverted according to its programmed behavior. It has also been shown that people prefer to interact with agents whose behavior seems to reflect a consistent trait or disposition. For example, they prefer agents that are extroverted and use more courageous language to agents that are extroverted but use more shy language (Nass *et al.*, 2000). Furthermore, there is evidence that people accept and are responsive to flattery and feedback from computers (Aula and Surakka, 2002; Fogg and Nass, 1997). In fact, a research paradigm called "computers are social actors" (CASA) suggests that theories and methods of social psychology are directly applicable to HCI (Nass *et al.*, 1994, 2000; Nass and Moon, 2000; Nass and Steuer, 1993; Reeves and Nass, 1996).

According to Reeves and Nass (1996), our strong tendency to sociality results in people unavoidably reacting to computers' signals as if they had originated from another human being. Although it has not been explicitly stated that the CASA paradigm includes emotions and emotional behavior, it is clear that emotions are one of the most significant factors in social behavior. For example, people like and trust embodied computer agents that display empathic emotions more than agents with self-oriented emotional expressions (Brave *et al.*, 2005). On the other hand, it may also be that inanimate objects, and especially virtual creatures with or without embodiment, automatically evoke our tendency for emotional behavior. This evoked emotional behavior then results in the activation of other social processes. In any case, it is clear that emotional factors are an important component in HCI.

The acknowledged importance of emotions in terms of intra- and interindividual performance and behavior means that the challenge of incorporating emotions into HCI must be faced. For some time, there has been a growing consensus that human emotion systems (physiological, experiential, and expressive) are central factors for rational human behavior (Damasio, 1994; Lang, 1995; Lang *et al.*, 1993; LeDoux, 1994). Affective processes are a necessity for cognitive processing. For example, there is evidence that decision making can be seriously disturbed after brain damage to areas that are important for emotional processing (Damasio, 1994). In a classic paper, Zajonc (1980) suggested that emotional processing can even have primacy over cognition. Because working with computers constantly requires and evokes both affective and cognitive processing, there is no doubt that affective information needs to be considered in the development of interaction with technology. New anthropomorphic interfaces, such as embodied agents, have the potential to enhance the social reactions to computers even further. For example, there is evidence that people react similarly to both virtual and human faces (Schilbach *et al.*, 2005, 2006; Vanhala *et al.*, 2010; Weyers *et al.*, 2006). This may have considerable implications, as, for instance, perception of emotional cues can significantly affect the processing of nonemotional auditory information at a very basic neuronal level (Surakka *et al.*, 1998). Thus, it is becoming increasingly important to take emotions into account in developing alternative new interaction techniques per se and in regulating the quality of human–technology interaction (Aula and Surakka, 2002; Partala and Surakka, 2003, 2004; Salminen *et al.*, 2008; Surakka *et al.*, 2003, 2004).

The argument developed so far implies that fully functional systems need to analyze the aims of the user and the context of use, and be perceptually and expressively intelligent. Clearly, the fulfillment of these aims will require a lot of work. Developing system architectures and programs (as, for example, in Figure 9.2) that are able to process, interpret, and act upon social and emotional information represents a research endeavor in its own right. Although our research team (among others) is ultimately aiming to develop these types of fully functional systems, our recent research efforts have been mainly dealing with the following subtasks.

First, studies that investigate the potential advantages of having expressive intelligence are required. The key question in terms of emotions and human–technology interaction is whether we can evoke reasonable, useful effects with emotional feedback and interventions from technology. Provided that we find useful emotional and social effects, we will then have a well-grounded basis for further developments. Proceeding in this order may initially seem counterintuitive, as perceptual intelligence is actually a precondition for expressive intelligence in fully functional systems. However, if computers were found not to evoke emotional and social responses, further studies would be misguided. In any case, our own studies have shown the clear promise of the potential of emotionally intelligent expression. For this reason, we have proceeded to develop perceptual intelligence. These activities have consisted of both the development of new or alternative hardware-sensing technologies and the analysis of the possibilities of different signal-processing algorithms in interpreting the data flow from various sensing technologies.

Potential of emotionally intelligent expression in HCI

Although people seem to be driven to act socially and emotionally with computers, as yet there is little knowledge regarding what kind of effects (emotional or cognitive) computers expressing this type of information might have on human behavior. The usual and often implicit assumption is that computers that respond to users' stress, frustration, or more specific emotions might significantly improve and facilitate HCI. A related challenge is to identify what measures could be used for detecting these effects automatically in order to build perceptual intelligence into machines. In a sense, these types of investigations can be implemented in a highly similar fashion to investigations in basic emotion research. Thus, we first need to establish, for example, whether pupil size behavior is affected by emotional stimulation. If this proves to be the case, then it is clear that the special nature of HCI needs to be considered at some point by performing pupil size measurements while the user is interacting with a computer.

When we first began to study the potential advantages of emotions in HCI, one of the earlier notions was that tracking the users' gaze direction and pupil size variation could provide an input signal indicating users' interests and emotional states to the computer (e.g., Jacob, 1996). The early results and theories concerning this issue were rather mixed. For example, some studies found pupil constriction to negative emotional stimulation, while others did not find such evidence (e.g., Hess, 1972; Janisse, 1974; Loewenfeld, 1966). Furthermore, gender differences were suggested in some of the early studies (for a review, see Partala and Surakka, 2003). As it was unclear how emotional stimuli would affect the pupil size, it was also unclear whether pupil size variation could be used as an index of users' emotional states. Thus, we conducted studies to address this question, using a set of carefully developed acoustic emotional stimuli called international affective digitized sounds (IADS) by Bradley and Lang (1999, 2000).

In one experiment (Partala *et al.*, 2000; Partala and Surakka, 2003), participants' pupil size was monitored while they were exposed to 30 (10 emotionally negative, 10 neutral, and 10 emotionally positive) stimuli. We found that both negative and positive auditory stimuli evoked significantly greater pupil enlargement than neutral auditory stimuli at the time of presentation. Pupil sizes began to slowly approach the baseline at about 3 s after the stimulus onset, but the statistical differences remained the same even after 2 s from the stimulus offset. We found no evidence of either pupil constrictions or gender differences. The ratings of the stimuli showed that the stimuli elicited the intended emotional responses, and the ratings were in accordance with those of Bradley and Lang (1999). In a further experiment (Experiment 2 in Partala *et al.*, 2000), we found similar results.

The above findings were encouraging in that they showed that auditory emotional stimulation regulates the functioning of the autonomic nervous system as indexed by pupil size variation. The results also showed that subjective experiences could be significantly influenced by auditory stimuli. These findings therefore demonstrate that the measurement of pupil size can be used to reveal possible effects of emotions in the context of HCI.

In a subsequent experiment, we utilized pupil size measurements and ratings of emotional experiences by indexing the users' emotions in the context of HCI. Because pupil size is very sensitive to variations in lighting, we used synthesized speech as a feedback channel during computer interaction. The use of speech synthesis parallels the use of computer agents, but of course without embodiment in this case. In the experiment, we studied the effects of synthesized emotional feedback on cognitive performance and on psychological and physiological reactions during a fully computerized, problem-solving task (Aula and Surakka, 2002). Participants were required to solve series of relatively simple computations (e.g., 3 (?) 3 = 6) in which they had to decide upon the missing (+ or –) operator by pressing a corresponding key. After each series, a Finnish speech synthesizer called Mikropuhe gave *random* negative, neutral, or positive feedback (i.e., feedback that was independent of the participants' performance) with emotional content (e.g., "I am disappointed with your result," "Your result was average," and "Your performance makes me glad," respectively). The feedback messages were controlled so that only the content of the messages varied. Prosodic cues were kept constant across all feedback messages so that there was no variation in intonation, volume, tone, etc. (for more information about the association between vocal cues and emotions, see Scherer *et al.*, 1984). At the end of the experiment, the participants rated their emotional responses to the different feedback messages on two 9-point rating scales assessing emotional valence and arousal (for more information on dimensions of emotions, see, e.g., Lang *et al.*, 1993; Schlosberg, 1954).

In brief, the results from the valence ratings showed that the participants rated different feedback categories as differing significantly in valence (negative as the most unpleasant, positive as the most pleasant). Response times to mathematical tasks were significantly shorter after positive emotional feedback than after negative emotional feedback. Pupil size increased in response to all feedback categories, meaning that autonomic nervous system activity was accentuated as a result of computerized synthetic communication. Interestingly, when tracked over time (5 s from the stimulus offset), the pupil size behavior revealed significant differential pupil responses after the different feedback categories. After positive feedback, there was a greater and faster recovery toward baseline than after neutral feedback.

In sum, the findings suggested that synthetic speech with emotional content regulates emotional responses. Participants experienced feedback messages as emotionally negative, neutral, or positive, and their physiology was consequently affected. The findings also suggest that positive emotional feedback results in improved cognitive performance and faster recovery from physiological arousal than non-emotional feedback. It is noteworthy that the results suggested that positive feedback was effective regardless of the actual performance of the person. This implies that emotional feedback will be effective even with a less than perfect analysis of human performance. This is encouraging for the development of complex emotional technologies. On a more general level, our results clearly showed that synthesized emotional feedback may facilitate the interaction between humans and machines.

Another type of evidence in favor of the use of emotions in human–technology interaction comes from studies using facial EMG and subjective ratings for verifying the evocation of emotional responses in the context of HCI. Unlike earlier findings concerning pupil size, there is an abundance of evidence that facial muscle activity (as measured by EMG) is related to both vocal and facial stimuli that communicate emotions (e.g., Cacioppo and Gardner, 1999; Dimberg, 1990; Hietanen *et al.*, 1998; Larsen *et al.*, 2003; Surakka and Hietanen, 1998). Consequently, there was no particular need to verify the use of facial EMG responses in emotion research, and we were able to proceed more directly in this study. Thus, in another of our experiments (Partala and Surakka, 2004), we assessed facial EMG responses and ratings of emotional experiences in response to synthetic emotions. We also studied the effects of these synthetic emotions in terms of cognitive performance during a computerized problem-solving task.

In this study, participants relocated different color bars with a mouse according to specific instructions. Participants were exposed to preprogrammed mouse delays in this interactive problem-solving task. Following the mouse delays, emotionally worded positive or negative interventions were given via a speech synthesizer (i.e., Mikropuhe), or in the control condition, no intervention was given. For example, one of the positive interventions involved the computer saying: "The functions of the computer were suspended. The problem will happily soon be over." One of the negative interventions was: "The execution of the program was interrupted. This is annoying." As in our previous speech synthesis studies, prosodic cues were kept constant across all interventions, and only the contents of the interventions varied. Facial EMG responses were recorded from above corrugator supercilii (activated when frowning) and zygomaticus major (activated when smiling) muscle sites (e.g., Fridlund and Cacioppo, 1986). We also measured, among other things, participants' task performance after the different interventions. Finally, participants were asked to rate the different intervention categories on 9-point scales on the dimensions of valence and arousal.

The results showed that subjects rated the interventions as intended, meaning that positive interventions were rated significantly more positively than negative ones. Analysis of problem-solving performance showed better performance following positive than negative interventions. EMG activity was analyzed during and after the different interventions. These results showed that smiling activity was significantly higher during the positive interventions than during the other interventions. It was also significantly higher after the positive than the control condition. Interestingly, frowning activity generally decreased from the baseline during both positive and negative interventions. EMG activity was still below baseline 3 s after the interventions. Frowning activity was significantly lower after the positive interventions than in the control condition. To summarize, the results showed that synthetic speech with emotional content regulated both emotional and cognitive processes. Thus, the results again emphasized the utility of emotions in general and positive emotions in particular (Partala and Surakka, 2004).

It should not be interpreted from the above findings that only positive feedback or intervention is of value in HCI. On the contrary, the results speak in favor of the use of emotions in general because, for example, frowning activity relaxed in response to both negative and positive interventions. Furthermore, negative emotional cues may serve important functions in HCI as well. In a very recent study (Vanhala *et al.*, 2010), we explored how embodied emotionally expressive agents would affect ratings of emotion and attention-related dimensions and physiological responses. Participants were shown a set of female and male embodied agents displaying a negative, a neutral, or a positive facial expression. In addition to the facial cues, the apparent proximity level of the agent was varied by displaying the agent in three different sizes.

The results showed that negative virtual facial cues were effective in capturing attention. Participants rated frowning agents as significantly less pleasant, less relaxing, and more arousing, dominating, conspicuous, and distracting than neutral and smiling agents. The physiological measures provided preliminary evidence suggesting that negative expressions required less mental effort to process. For example, mental effort has been linked with sympathetic activation of the autonomous nervous system (e.g., Chen and Vertegaal, 2004) Sympathetic activity was decreased during negative expressions of the male agent according to our low-frequency heart-rate variability analysis. Thus, the reactions to negative, threatening facial cues seem to be special in terms of the subjective experiences and physiological reactions that they evoke. Regardless of the fact that they are emotionally negative, their utility lies in the fact that they can more efficiently catch one's attention, and that can be very useful for many purposes.

Somewhat similar findings that demonstrate an *anger pop-out* or *threat superiority* effect in responses to human faces have been reported by other researchers (e.g., Fox and Damjanovic, 2006; Hansen and Hansen, 1988). Our study also replicated the earlier results showing that simulated proximity to a computer agent significantly affects the level of the feeling of being in control, so that the bigger the agent, the lower is the experience of being in control (Partala *et al.*, 2004). In both of these studies, agents that appeared to be closer were rated as more dominating than agents that seemed to be further away. Overall, findings from our studies with embodied virtual characters parallel the implications of CASA; that is, similar social and emotional cues (e.g., proximity and facial expressions) seem to be active both in HCI and in human–human interaction. Taking advantage and conscious control of these cues has the potential to significantly facilitate HCI by effecting relatively fast and automatic processes; for example, the rapid allocation of attention to emotional cues in virtual faces.

Developments in emotional perceptual intelligence

Methods for perceptual intelligence require quite complex efforts in different research areas. First, we need engineers to develop new hardware prototypes for unobtrusive measurement technology. Then, the prototypes need to be tested; for example, in the respect that they are able to reliably measure emotion-related responses. Typically, these developments require several iterations before they become functional. Signal-processing methods need to be developed in a similar iterative fashion in order to give computers capacity for lower- and higher-level interpretations from the measured signals. Finally, everything should be coupled together. In the next section, we aim to describe investigations that have dealt with both hardware and software developments in the context of emotions and HCI.

With respect to other emotion-related autonomic nervous system activation correlates, we have recently begun to study different heart-activity measures. Similar to pupil size measurements, recent technological advances have made these measures relatively noninvasive, wireless, and convenient. For example, in one of the earlier studies investigating the relation between emotions and heart rate, heart-rate responses were measured with a regular-looking office chair (Anttonen and Surakka, 2005). This chair contains embedded sensors that are able to detect the heart rate of the person sitting on it. While validating the concept of a nonintrusive measurement chair, we discovered that the chair was able to detect significant changes in heart rate during auditory, visual, and audiovisual stimuli with emotional content. The mean heart rate decelerated in response to emotional stimulation in line with previous findings (e.g., Levenson and Ekman, 2002; Rainville *et al.*, 2006). Further results revealed that heart rate decelerated the most in response to negative stimuli as compared with responses to positive and neutral stimuli.

As both facial activity and heart rate changes have been found to be associated with emotional responding, we performed a further study investigating what kind of heart rate responses could be evoked by computer-guided voluntary facial muscle activations (Vanhala and Surakka, 2007b). Participants were required to activate their facial muscles according to different guidelines as visualized by the computer. Paralleling the methods of biofeedback, participants received real-time visual feedback about the intensity level of their corrugator supercilii and zygomaticus major muscle activations as measured by EMG. Heart activity was registered with a prototype of a wireless electrocardiogram (ECG) measurement patch (Vehkaoja and Lekkala, 2004). We found that activations of both muscles resulted in a deceleration of the mean heart rate, which was extracted from the wireless ECG. This effect was strongest for the moderate intensity level of activations, which were also rated as the most pleasant and easy to perform. The results were encouraging, as they demonstrated how computers can effectively help in regulating emotional and physiological processes.

In a subsequent study, we investigated whether the heart-rate effects could be automatically detected and classified (Vanhala and Surakka, 2007a). The results showed that heart-rate responses to voluntary facial activations could be detected in real time with less than half a second of heart-rate data. In summary, these studies utilizing heart activity have suggested that physiological responses to emotional stimulation can be identified from unobtrusively acquired heart-rate data and that computers can really help in regulating these responses.

Because the facial musculature system is richly developed and well represented in the brain's motor cortex, human facial activity is one promising channel for taking measures to distinguish emotional reactions (e.g., Ekman, 1994; Rinn, 1991). In fact, computing systems built for classifying emotional states into negative, neutral, and positive from continuous facial EMG recordings have shown some promise (Partala *et al.*, 2005, 2006). The setup was as follows. Participants were shown emotionally arousing pictures and videos, and their task was to rate their emotional experiences on a dimensional scale following each stimulation. At the same time, the computer, using various computational regression models, estimated the participants' ratings on the basis of their facial EMG activity. Next, the subjective ratings and the computer's estimations were compared with one another. The comparison showed that the best models were able to estimate the participants' positive and negative ratings of pictorial and video stimuli with average accuracies of over 70 and 80 percent, respectively. Thus, facial EMG is yet another promising method upon which to build perceptual intelligence.

Following these promising results, the development of new wireless electrode measurement technologies has begun (see www.cs.uta.fi/~wtpc/). One of these is an elastic, comfortable-to-wear, facial EMG headband that contains embroidered silver thread electrodes that are "attached" simply by wearing the band. The band includes signal amplifying and radio technology to send the amplified signals wirelessly to machines with computing power. First studies with this prototype have been successful (Nöjd *et al.*, 2005; Vehkaoja *et al.*, 2005). It is firmly believed that these kinds of advances in technology will bring physiological measurement devices into a wider use in the future.

As a whole, the above research and development has shown that there are several measurements and technologies that can be integrated into computer systems in order to create perceptually intelligent machines. Importantly, many of the measures are becoming increasingly noninvasive, ubiquitous, and convenient. In many cases, the process of carefully attaching sensors according to clinical and experimental standards could be eliminated for the end user of the system. The user would instead merely wear a common accessory (e.g., headband or hat) or be seated on a regular chair that contains unobtrusive sensors.

Discussion

We began our analysis from descriptive findings about surprisingly strong emotional reactions while working with computers. Our further analysis from more controlled experimental studies showed that computers are able to evoke and regulate human emotions while people are working with them. These reactions were more modest than those reported in the public media. However, the findings were clear. It may be that our strong tendency to interpret information socially is the central cause for emotional reactions in HCI, as argued earlier (Brave *et al.*, 2005; Reeves and Nass, 1996). On the other hand, it might also be that inanimate objects and especially virtual creatures with or without embodiment automatically evoke our tendency for emotional behavior as a first priority. Following emotions, other social processes like politeness, for example, are activated. In either case, emotions are very much operational and effective in HCI.

Emotions evoked by technology were also found to be otherwise beneficial, as clear proof was found of their effects on participants' emotions and cognitive performance. Positive emotional feedback was found to enhance human mathematical computations. This was the case regardless of the fact that the feedback was randomized, meaning that it had nothing to do with actual performance (Aula and Surakka, 2002). Thus, it may be that positive emotional feedback in particular will be effective even with less than perfect timing and analysis of human performance. Research on emotional interventions (Partala and Surakka, 2004) again showed that emotional messages given by a computer operated in a similar fashion to that in the above study.

The studies reviewed above concerning expressive emotional intelligence showed that even relatively mild, emotion-related social cues can have significant experiential, behavioral, and physiological effects. The use of positive emotional cues seemed to have especially beneficial effects. However, negative cues also showed promise as a method for evoking reactions; for example, in order to draw attention to critical information (Vanhala *et al.*, 2010). The use of negatively toned emotional cues may, in fact, require much more fine-grained analysis of the timing for delivering such cues and more fine-grained analysis of the user performance. Of course, in both cases (i.e., positive or negative emotional cues), more research is needed on the requirements for user performance analysis; for example, with respect to optimal timing for launching emotional interaction between humans and computers. We have shown that it is possible to unobtrusively monitor heart rate and, moreover, to automatically classify changes in the heart rate (Anttonen and Surakka, 2005; Vanhala and Surakka, 2007a). Thus, in this light, automatic analysis of the levels of various physiological processes (e.g., heart rate) is one possibility for detecting the appropriate moments for intervening in users' behaviors. It is possible that people will become annoyed over wrongly timed interventions and feedback, although we have not observed anything to suggest this in our own studies. It is even possible that people will become annoyed over more properly timed communication. There really is much work to do in investigating the synchrony of communication between humans and technology. At this point, we would still like to highlight our finding that people are affected by artificial emotions on many levels (affective, cognitive, social). Perhaps it is well worth risking people's annoyance about computer-generated communication if, on the whole, the benefits clearly outweigh the possibly quite infrequent annoyances.

Moreover, in real life, people tend to be forgiving and tolerant of all kinds of interactions with asynchronies. In this vein, it can be argued that because we tend to treat technology in a human-like manner, we will also be tolerant and forgiving in HCI.

Findings showing promise and potential for expressive intelligence were argued to act as a precondition for further developments in the area of perceptual intelligence. As there is evidence of this potential, there are grounds for developing perceptual intelligence as well. At the moment, there is ongoing work that has already shown that it is possible to develop less obtrusive hardware technologies than, for example, traditional electrode measurement technology. Further technological breakthroughs of this kind are required in the future if we wish to achieve wider acceptance of emotional computing. Our ongoing work has also proved that at least up to a point, software (i.e., signal-processing methods) is capable of continuously analyzing higher-level user processes such as emotional experiences. Of course, there is still a lot to do even regarding these types of inferring algorithms. Moreover, the inclusion of hardware and software technology in the context of use is very much in its early stages.

Studying the effects of emotions and social information in the context of information technology (e.g., HCI, CMC, videoconferencing) clearly reveals the constrained nature of communicative cues available in this context. Due to the limitations of technology, it is unavoidable that, for example, only a face and voice (virtual or real) can be made perceptible. If synthetic characters are used, there is still much to do before they can perfectly mimic human performance, although they do enable the use of a wider range of social cues, such as virtual proximity and facial expressions. At first glance, these shortcomings can be seen as critical barriers to trying to study the possibilities of using this kind of information. However, in some ways, much of the past and current research on human–human emotion has also dealt with virtual or artificial stimuli. For example, studies have widely utilized only facial stimuli (i.e., without voice and body), digitized auditory stimuli (without face and body), etc., yet significant scientific advances concerning human emotions have been made with these stimuli of limited ecological validity. Thus, upon closer inspection, one might argue that studying the effects of emotions in the context of HCI represents the continuation of a relatively well-established research tradition. Furthermore, one could also argue that virtual agents like speech synthesizers, virtual faces, and artificial persons really do offer useful tools for controlled experimentation on the effects of communicative signals on human performance (e.g., Massaro and Egan, 1996). If this is the case, it is reasonable to assume that findings from HCI can be applied directly to human–human interaction.

It is clear that working with computers requires both cognitive and emotional resources even in the absence of dramatic reactions such as swearing at and kicking computers. Perhaps working with computers imposes a continuous cognitive-emotional load, leading to accentuated physiological and psychological arousal. If this arousal is negatively valenced, in the long run there may be serious side effects on our mental and physical health. For example, sympathetic arousal similar to what we have found in response to synthesized emotional cues is known to result, in the long term, in elevated risk of cardiovascular diseases (Malliani *et al.*, 1991). One self-evident argument for the necessity of emotionally intelligent technology is that, as we have now seen, computers evoke social and emotional responses in any case. Thus, the question that arises is whether we neglect this or whether we are willing to use this phenomenon in our own favor.

This chapter has presented encouraging findings in favor of using emotional information in HCI. The studies have suggested that emotions can be systematically evoked and regulated by technology in the context of information technology. This kind of emotional HCI can facilitate cognitive performance, regulate attentive processing, and reduce negative physiological arousal. Technology is, and will continue to be, pervasive in everyday life to such an extent that we cannot afford to neglect its effects on emotions. Emotions themselves are equally pervasive factors for all human performance in any context, including HCI.

Acknowledgments

This research has been supported by the Academy of Finland (project numbers 1202183, 177857, 1115997), and the Graduate School in User-Centered Information Technology, Tampere, Finland. Parts of this chapter were published by Surakka (2004) in *Psykologia*, a journal of the Finnish Psychological Association.

References

Allanson, J., Rodden, T., and Mariani, J. (1999). A toolkit exploring electro-physiological human–computer interaction. In M. A. Sasse and C. Johnson (eds), *Human–Computer Interaction – Interact '99* (pp. 231–237). Amsterdam: IOS Press.

Anttonen, J. and Surakka, V. (2005). Emotions and heart rate while sitting on a chair. In *Proceedings of the SIGCHI Conference on Human Factors in Computing Systems, CHI 2005*, (pp. 491–499). Portland, OR: ACM Press.

Aula, A. and Surakka, V. (2002). Auditory emotional feedback facilitates human–computer interaction. In X. Faulkner, J. Finlay, and F. Détienne (eds), *People and Computers XVI: Memorable Yet Invisible, Proceedings of the British HCI* (pp. 337–349). London: Springer.

Barreto, A., Scargle, S., and Adjouadi, M. (2000). A practical EMG-based human–computer interface for users with motor disabilities. *Journal of Rehabilitation Research and Development*, *37*, 53–64.

Berry, D. C., Butler, L. T., and de Rosis, F. (2005). Evaluating a realistic agent in an advice-giving task. *International Journal of Human–Computer Studies*, *63*, 304–327.

Bradley, M. M. and Lang, P. J. (1999). *International Affective Digitized Sounds (IADS): Stimuli, Instruction Manual and Affective Ratings*. Technical Report B-2. Gainesville, FL: University of Florida: Center for Research in Psychophysiology.

(2000). Affective reactions to acoustic stimuli. *Psychophysiology*, *37*, 204–215.

Brave, S., Nass, C., and Hutchinson, K. (2005). Computers that care: investigating the effects of orientation of emotion exhibited by an embodied computer agent. *International Journal of Human–Computer Studies*, *62*, 161–178.

Cacioppo, J. T. and Gardner, W. L. (1999). Emotion. *Annual Review of Psychology* *50*, 191–214.

Cassell, J., Bickmore, T., Campbell, L., Vilhjálmsson, H., and Yan, H. (2000). Human conversation as a system framework: designing embodied conversational agents. In J. Cassell, J. Sullivan, S. Prevost, and E. Churchill (eds), *Embodied Conversational Agents* (pp. 29–63). Cambridge, MA: MIT Press.

Chen, D. and Vertegaal, R. (2004). Using mental load for managing interruptions in physiologically attentive user interfaces. In E. Dykstra-Erickson and M. Tscheligi (eds), *Extended Abstracts of the 2004 Conference on Human Factors and Computing Systems* (pp. 1513–1516). Vienna: ACM Press.

Concord Communications (1999). Concord network rage survey. www.concord.com/library/network_rage/.

Damasio, A. (1994). *Descartes' Error: Emotion, Reason and the Human Brain*. New York: Grosset.

Dimberg, U. (1990). Facial electromyography and emotional reactions. *Psychophysiology*, *27*, 481–494.

Ekman, P. (1994). Strong evidence for universals in facial expressions: a reply to Russell's mistaken critique. *Psychological Bulletin*, *115*, 268–287.

Fogg, B. J. and Nass, C. (1997). Silicon sycophants: the effects of computers that flatter. *International Journal of Human–Computer Studies*, *46*, 551–561.

Fox, E. and Damjanovic, L. (2006). The eyes are sufficient to produce a threat superiority effect. *Emotion*, *6*, 534–539.

Fridlund, A. J. and Cacioppo, J. T. (1986). Guidelines for human electromyographic research. *Psychophysiology*, *23*, 567–589.

Hansen, C. H. and Hansen, R. D. (1988). Finding the face in the crowd: an anger superiority effect. *Journal of Personality and Social Psychology*, *54*, 917–924.

Hess, E. H. (1972). Pupillometrics. In N. S. Greenfield and R. A. Sternbach (eds), *Handbook of Psychophysiology* (pp. 491–531). New York: Holt, Rinehart & Winston.

Hietanen, J. K., Surakka, V., and Linnankoski, I. (1998). Facial electromyographic responses to vocal affect expressions. *Psychophysiology*, *35*, 530–536.

Ilves, M. and Surakka, V. (2004). Subjective and physiological responses to emotional content of synthesized speech. In N. Magnenat-Thalmann, C. Joslin, and H. Kim (eds), *Proceedings of the 17th International Conference on Computer Animation and Social Agents, CASA 2004* (pp. 19–26). Geneva: Computer Graphics Society (CGS).

Jacob, R. J. K. (1991). The use of eye movements in human computer interaction techniques: what you look at is what you get. *ACM Transactions on Information Systems*, *9*, 152–169.

(1996). The future of input devices. *ACM Computing Surveys*, *28*(A) (Annex), December.

Janisse, M. P. (1974). Pupil size, affect and exposure frequency. *Social Behavior and Personality*, *2*, 125–146.

Klein, J., Moon, Y., and Picard, R. W. (2002). This computer responds to user frustration: theory, design, and results. *Interacting with Computers*, *14*, 119–140.

Kübler, A., Kotchoubey, B., Hinterberger, T., Ghanayim, N., Perelmouter, J., Schauer, M., Fritsch, C., Taub, E., and Birbaumer, N. (1999). The thought translation device: a neurophysiological approach to communication in total paralysis. *Experimental Brain Research*, *124*, 223–232.

Lang, P. J. (1995). The emotion probe: studies of motivation and attention. *American Psychologist*, *50*, 372–385.

Lang, P. J., Bradley, M. M., and Cuthbert, B. N. (1995). *International Affective Picture System (IAPS): Photographic Slides*. Gainesville, FL: University of Florida, Center for the Study of Emotion and Attention.

Lang, P. J., Greenwald, M. K., Bradley, M. M., and Hamm, A. O. (1993). Looking at pictures: affective, facial, visceral, and behavioral reactions. *Psychophysiology*, *30*, 261–273.

Larsen, J. T., Norris, C. J., and Cacioppo, J. T. (2003). Effects of positive and negative affect on electromyographic activity over zygomaticus major and corrugator supercilii. *Psychophysiology*, *40*, 776–785.

LeDoux, J. E. (1994). Emotion, memory and the brain. *Scientific American*, *270* (6), 32–39.

(1998). *The Emotional Brain*. New York: Simon & Schuster.

Levenson, R. W. and Ekman, P. (2002). Difficulty does not account for emotion-specific heart rate changes in the directed facial action task. *Psychophysiology*, *39*, 397–405.

Loewenfeld, I. E. (1966). Pupil size. *Survey of Ophthalmology*, *11*, 291–294.

Malliani, A., Pagani, M., Lombardi, F., and Cerutti, S. (1991). Cardiovascular neural regulation explored in the frequency domain. *Circulation*, *84*, 482–492.

Marsh, P. and Khor, Z. (2006). Life online: mouse rage! Social Issues Research Centre. www.sirc.org/publik/mouse_rage.pdf.

Massaro, D. W. and Egan, P. B. (1996). Perceiving affect from the voice and the face. *Psychonomic Bulletin and Review*, *3*, 215–221.

D'Mello, S., Graesser, A., and Picard, R. W. (2007). Toward an affect-sensitive AutoTutor. *IEEE Intelligent Systems*, *22*(4), 53–61.

Nass, C., Isbister, K., and Eun, J. L. (2000). Truth is beauty: researching embodied conversational agents. In J. Cassell, J. Sullivan, S. Prevost, and

E. Churchill (eds), *Embodied Conversational Agents* (pp. 374–402). Cambridge, MA: MIT Press.

Nass, C. and Moon, Y. (2000). Machines and mindlessness: social responses to computers. *Journal of Social Issues*, **56**, 81–103.

Nass, C. and Steuer, J. (1993). Voices, boxes, and sources of messages: computers and social actors. *Human Communication Research*, **19**, 504–527.

Nass, C., Steuer, J., and Tauber, E. R. (1994). Computers are social actors. *Proceedings of CHI '94*, (pp. 72–78). Boston: ACM.

Nöjd, N., Puurtinen, M., Niemenlehto, P., Vehkaoja, A., Verho, J., Vanhala, T., Hyttinen, J., Juhola, M., Lekkala, J., and Surakka, V. (2005). Wireless wearable EMG and EOG measurement system for psychophysiological applications. In R. Lundström, B. Andersson, and H. Grip (eds), *Proceedings of the Nordic Baltic Conference on Biomedical Engineering and Medical Physics* (pp. 144–145). Umeå: Swedish Society for Medical Engineering and Medical Physics.

Partala, T., Jokiniemi, M., and Surakka, V. (2000). Pupillary responses to emotionally provocative stimuli. In A. T. Duchowski (ed.), *Proceedings of ETRA 2000, Eye Tracking Research and Applications* (123–129). Palm Beach Gardens, FL: ACM Press.

Partala, T., Aula, A., and Surakka, V. (2001). Combined voluntary gaze direction and facial muscle activity as a new pointing technique. In M. Hirose (ed.), *Proceedings of INTERACT 2001* (pp. 100–107). Tokyo: IOS Press.

Partala, T. and Surakka, V. (2003). Pupil size variation as an indication of affective processing. *International Journal of Human Computer Studies*, **591**–2, 185–198.

(2004). The effects of affective interventions in human–computer interaction. *Interacting with Computers*, **16**, 295–309.

Partala, T. Surakka, V., and Lahti, J. (2004). Affective effects of agent proximity in conversational systems. In *NordiCHI: Proceedings of the Third Nordic Conference on Human–Computer Interaction* (pp. 353–356). New York: ACM Press.

Partala, T., Surakka, V., and Vanhala, T. (2005). Person-independent estimation of emotional experiences from facial expressions. In J. Riedl, A. Jameson, D. Billsus, and T. Lau (eds), *Proceedings of the 10th International Conference on Intelligent User Interfaces* (pp. 246–248). New York: ACM Press.

(2006). Real-time estimation of emotional experiences from facial expressions. *Interacting with Computers*, **18**, 208–226.

Pentland, A. (2000). Perceptual intelligence. *Communications of the ACM*, **43**, 35–44.

Picard, R. (1997). *Affective Computing*. Cambridge, MA: MIT Press.

Rainville, P., Bechara, A., Naqvi, N., and Damasio, A. R. (2006). Basic emotions are associated with distinct patterns of cardiorespiratory activity. *International Journal of Psychophysiology*, **61**, 5–18.

Reeves, B. and Nass, C. (1996). *The Media Equation: How People Treat Computers, Television, and New Media Like Real People and Places*. Cambridge University Press.

Rinn, W. E. (1991). The neuropsychology of facial expression. In R. S. Feldman and B. Rimé (eds), *Fundamentals of Nonverbal Behavior* (pp. 3–30). Cambridge University Press.

Salminen, K., Surakka, V., Lylykangas, J., Raisamo, J., Saarinen, R., Rantala, J., Raisamo, R., and Evreinov, G. (2008). Emotional and behavioral responses to haptic stimulation. In *Proceedings of SIGCHI Conference on Human Factors in Computing Systems* (pp. 1555–1652). New York: ACM Press.

Scherer, K. R., Ladd, D. R., and Silverman, K. E. A. (1984). Vocal cues to speaker affect: testing two models. *Journal of the Acoustical Society of America*, **76**, 1346–1356.

Schilbach, L., Helmert, J. R., Mojzisch, A., Pannasch, S., Velichkovsky, B. M., and Vogeley, K. (2005). Neural correlates, visual attention and facial expression during social interaction with virtual others. In *Proceedings of ICCS-2005 Symposium, Toward Social Mechanisms of Android Science*, Stresa, Italy (74–86).

Schilbach, L., Wohlschlaeger, A. M., Kraemer, N. C., Newen, A., Shah, N. J., Fink, G. R., and Vogeley, K. (2006). Being with virtual others: neural correlates of social interaction. *Neuropsychologia*, **44**, 718–730.

Schlosberg, H. (1954). Three dimensions of emotion. *Psychological Review*, **61**, 81–88.

Surakka, V. (2004). Tunteet ja sosiaalisuus ihminen-tietokone vuorovaikutuksessa [Emotions and sociality in human–computer interaction]. *Psykologia*, **39**, 19–28.

Surakka, V. and Hietanen, J. K. (1998). Facial and emotional reactions to Duchenne and non-Duchenne smiles. *International Journal of Psychophysiology*, **29**(1), 23–33.

Surakka, V., Illi, M., and Isokoski, P. (2003). Voluntary eye movements in human–computer interaction. In J. Hyönä, R. Radach, and H. Deubel (eds), *The Mind's Eyes: Cognitive and Applied Aspects of Oculomotor Research* (pp. 473–491). Oxford: Elsevier Science.

(2004). Gazing and frowning as a new human–computer interaction technique. *ACM Transactions on Applied Perception*, **1**, 40–56.

Surakka, V., Tenhunen-Eskelinen, M., Hietanen, J. K., and Sams, M. (1998). Modulation of human auditory information processing by visual emotional stimuli. *Cognitive Brain Research*, **7**, 159–163.

Vanhala, T. and Surakka, V. (2005). An agent framework for the development of psycho-physiologically interactive systems. In *Proceedings of HCI International 2005*. CD-ROM. Mahwah, NJ: Lawrence Erlbaum.

(2007a). Recognizing the effects of voluntary facial activations using heart rate patterns. In *Proceedings of the 11th WSEAS International Conference on Computers*, 628–632.

(2007b). Facial activation control effect (FACE). In A. Paiva, R. Prada, and R. W. Picard (eds), *Proceedings of ACII 2007, Lecture Notes in Computer Science*, vol. 4738 (pp. 278–289). Lisbon: Springer.

Vanhala, T., Surakka, V., Siirtola, H., Räihä, K.-J., Morel, B., and Ach, L. (2010). Virtual proximity and facial expressions of computer agents regulate human emotions and attention. *Computer Animation and Virtual Worlds*, **21**, 215–224.

Vehkaoja, A. and Lekkala, J. (2004). Wearable wireless biopotential measurement device. In *Proceedings of the IEEE EMBS 2004* (pp. 2177–2179). San Francisco, CA: IEEE Press.

(2006). Wireless measurement band for EEG mismatch negativity registration in mobile activities. *IMEKO XVIII World Congress and IV Brazilian Congress of Metrology*.

Vehkaoja, A., Verho, J., Puurtinen, M., Nöjd, N., Lekkala, J., and Hyttinen, J. (2005). Wireless Head Cap for EOG and Facial EMG Measurements. *27th Annual International Conference of the IEEE Engineering in Medicine and Biology Society*, *6*, 5865–5868.

Weyers, P., Mühlberger, A., Hefele, C., and Pauli, P. (2006). Electromyographic responses to static and dynamic avatar emotional facial expressions. *Psychophysiology*, *43*, 450–453.

Wolpaw, R. J., Birbaumer, N., Mcfarland, D. J., Pfurtscheller, G., and Vaughan, T. M. (2002). Brain–computer interfaces for communication and control. *Clinical Neurophysiology*, *113*, 767–791.

Zajonc, R. B. (1980). Feelings and thinking: preferences need no inferences. *American Psychologist*, *35*(2), 151–175.

CHAPTER 10

Embodiment and expressive communication on the internet

Elisabeth Oberzaucher, Karl Grammer, and Susanne Schmehl

Overview: Human brains are basically social, and use communication mechanisms that have evolved during our evolutionary past. Thus, we suggest that even in communication with and by machines, humans will tend to react socially and use communication mechanisms that are primarily social and embodied. One of these mechanisms is communicative feedback, which refers to unobtrusive (usually short) vocal or bodily expressions, whereby a recipient of information can inform a contributor of information about whether he or she is able and willing to communicate, perceive the information, and understand the information. We will show how feedback can be modeled in virtual agents on facial expressions of a virtual agent or verbot and thus contribute to human–human communication over the internet. We will present a simple model based on a pleasure, arousal, and dominance space, which allows a complex stimulus generation program to be driven with only a few parameters.

Humans are social – but what about human–machine communication?

Internet communication consists of two major domains: communication with a machine and human–human communication through a machine. Both processes involve different but comparable elements in order to be efficient, as we will outline here.

In its early years, the internet was used by a rather small group of scientists for communication via email and bulletin boards. As compared to phone calls and direct face-to-face communication, it seemed to be missing a social component, thus leading to the introduction of emoticons such as the well-known smiley, which constituted a first attempt to fill this gap. Fahlmann (2007), who introduced the smileys, proposed them in order to identify sarcastic remarks – so that everybody would get the joke. Emoticons have since developed into a highly sophisticated emotional language with many expressions.

The introduction of the *http* protocol made the internet an informational one-way street, with the exceptions of bulletin boards and email. This changed dramatically with the introduction of chat rooms, which still rely on emoticons. As a next step, visual chat rooms with video connections were introduced, but direct audio- and video-chats are not quite comparable to the relatively anonymous original chat room, and are faced with the bandwidth problem.

Visual chat rooms added animations and representations of virtual people to the chat. These additions consist of virtual 2D or 3D figures (avatars), a graphic representation of the user. One of the first anthropomorphic 3D representations was introduced by the Japanese artist Ken-ichi Kutsugi. "Terai Yuki" (Figure 10.1) was a virtual idol, with a family history, who made music and other videos. She was able to walk around on a user's screen, to exchange emails, etc. In the following years, this "verbot" concept was taken over by Microsoft, resulting in the MS Agent software for controlling and creating agents on the screen (Microsoft, 2003). These representations were able to greet users, provide guided tours through the operating system, or look up information on the web. Unfortunately, the first implementation was the strange paperclip Figure in Microsoft Word, whose non-acceptance by the public might have been due to the lack of identification and emotionality. Other verbots, such as "Julia" (who can retrieve information from the internet) from Lycos, Inc., try to overcome this problem – yet the acceptance of such verbots seems to be low. In our view, the mere existence of desktop agents and verbots reveals a general human tendency, which has also led to the development of emoticons – that is, communication is primarily social and the user feels lonely in front of a machine with abstract representations of communication.

In their book *The Media Equation*, Reeves and Nass (1996) report that people interact with computers as they would with real people. This may also indicate that people themselves prefer to be treated by computers in an emotional way. But what form should an interaction between man and machine take in order to meet the social and emotional demands of humans, and to be comparable to real-life situations? One method is the implementation of emotional feedback from the computer via nonverbal behavior, since people react most strongly to nonverbal communication, even if it is abstract (Reeves and Nass, 1996).

Indeed, humans seem to have a general perceptual strategy that leads to phenomena of animism and anthropomorphism. Animism is the attribution of life to the nonliving, whereas anthropomorphism is the interpretation of nonhuman beings and things in human terms (Guthrie, 1993). Such a hyperactive agent detection device is assumed

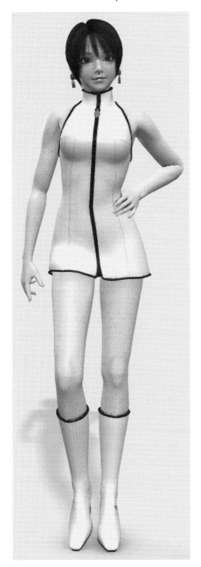

Figure 10.1 The first virtual idol, "Terai Yuki," is not only a singer and movie star but also a virtual agent on Japanese computer screens.

to have evolved because the adaptive advantage of detecting every agent is much higher than the costs of being mistaken (Bulbulia, 2004). As a result, we tend to treat our object environment socially (Guthrie, 1993). Our brain tries to interpret even its nonsocial environment by social rules (Cosmides and Tooby, 1992), because of the adaptive advantage of gathering information from faces, such as personal identity, possible kin relationships, personality, emotional states, and action tendencies.

One argument against the use of virtual agents for communication and computer interfaces is that they are artificial, and human–human communication is a poor model for human–computer interaction (Shneiderman, 1989). Xiao (2001) stated that machines should build trust in their users by showing traces and explanations. One of the basic hurdles is that 3D agents, being artificial, might hinder the creation of trust. However, Moser *et al.* (2006) showed that realistic artificial faces activate the same brain regions for emotional processing as human faces. Thus, avatars can introduce a social element in computer environments.

The flow of human communication is controlled by a variety of evolved mechanisms such as turn-taking, feedback, and emotional expression, which are embodied – this means that they are not encoded in language itself, but are instead signaled via motion of the human body and paralinguistic features of speech. These mechanisms enable humans to communicate fluently and convey not only factual but also social information, and this is necessary for the structuring of their own behaviour.

Our brains are not prepared to deal with abstract information only. This is why modern media technologies like *Second Life*, *World of Warcraft*, or avatar-controlled browsing are being given new, embodied, and personalized interfaces, thus responding to the social needs of humans. The social preoccupation of the human brain might also explain the success of Web 2.0, which is a social networking tool for creating online communities and sharing social information.

The same is true of the existence of chatterbots and virtual agents, which try to exploit users. Recently, CNET issued a warning regarding "flirting robots," which apparently try to induce trust in a user in order to obtain confidential and private information (Fried, 2007). Cyber-Lover invites its victims to disclose personal information and does so by sending friendly social signals. But how can such a system create trust? The responses of chat room users are apparently used to tailor its interaction accordingly by a series of simple, social, user-centered dialogues.

Human communication is not only the transfer of information – it is also social and embodied. In recent years, embodiment has found enormous theoretical attention in language, speech, and communication research in general. "Classic" communication models that emphasize symbolic information transfer neglect the decisive influence of nonsymbolic signals, which play a crucial role especially in face-to-face communication.

Evolutionary constraints on communication

Based on an evolutionary approach, we propose a dynamic, multilevel communication model, which operates simultaneously on a signal continuum from indexes (e.g., pitch, body motion, gesticulation) and icons (gestures, facial expressions) to a symbolic level (spoken words) (Allwood *et al.*, 2008; Grammer and Kopp *et al.*, 2008; Oberzaucher, 2006). This approach also assumes that on the index level, human communication is primarily analogous and not signal-oriented. As contradistinguished from symbolic communication (e.g., intentional use of speech and signs with conventional semantics), it consists of nonverbal indicators of nonconscious and nonverbalizable mental concepts. Both interaction partners continuously adjust to the flow of communication through an appraisal/evaluation process that is not necessarily conscious (Figure 10.2).

Why is the index level so important for communication? The primary function of communication is to share information. Usually, two or more communicators take turns in contributing new information. The selection pressures during human evolution not only ensured that communicative processes can take place, but they also imposed constraints, which are still present. The evolutionary constraints on communication are as follows:

- the control of communication success
- mutual manipulation attempts
- the possibility of deception.

Thus, we propose that there are evolved functions in communication that cope with these constraints. Communication success can be monitored by a feedback system. Mutual manipulation can be achieved by displaying signals, which promote the action tendencies of the signaler. Deception is an important element in generating and maintaining one's adaptive communicational advantage over potential competitors. As Dawkins and Krebs (1978) propose, presenting one's intentions in a communication may be a costly mistake, since the intentions of one organism may be exactly the opposite of the intentions of another organism. An adaptation to the social aspect of the environment of evolutionary adaptedness (EEA) (Cosmides and Tooby, 1992) is important, as a great deal of an organism's well-being, prospects for survival, and reproduction prospects depend on its successful communication with other members of the group.

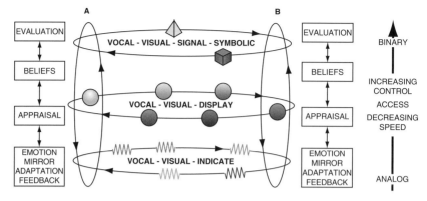

Figure 10.2 The Bielefeld model of communication depicts several levels and layers of communication, which reach from the exchange of symbolic information displays down to an indexed level, which is supposed to control the interaction flow via control processes like evaluation and appraisal.

Our ancestors therefore had to develop a means of concealing their intentions or psychophysical features that could affect the achievement of their goals negatively. Since communication is a tool to satisfy individual needs, it is also employed to manipulate others (Dawkins and Krebs, 1978). In this communicative arms race, interaction partners aim to find out others´ goals in order to maximize their own benefits. The sender tries to keep his or her own goals secret; thus, deception and manipulation of intelligence has evolved. On the receiver side, the need to know others' goals led to the evolution of antideception intelligence. Both systems are subject to permanent optimization; neither the sender nor the receiver will ever be completely adapted.

But of course, we have to trust our communication partner to a certain extent – otherwise communication would be pointless. Nevertheless, we do not trust blindly, but constantly try to validate the information perceived. In this context, nonverbal behavior – both accompanying speech and feedback – is of central importance.

Confidence and trust – feedback in communication with virtual agents

The term "feedback" stems from the cybernetic theory of Wiener (1948) and describes "processes by which a control unit gets information about the effects and consequences of its actions." Feedback can be verbal, like short utterances ("yes"), but it is obviously more than just a verbal phenomenon. Listeners employ nonverbal means, such as posture, facial expression, gaze, gesture, or prosody, to give feedback, often in combination with acoustic back channels. For example, prosodic and temporal features carry information about the successful integration of the information into the listener's existing body of knowledge (Ehlich, 1986); head nods and jerks frequently accompany and can even change the meaning of verbal feedback (Houck and Gass, 1997).

Yngve (1970) introduced the term "back channel" to emphasize the permanent bidirectionality of human communication. Allwood *et al.* (1992) assume that feedback is a central functional subsystem of human communication. It consists of methods that unobtrusively provide information about the most basic communicative elements in face-to-face dialogue without interrupting or breaking dialogue rules. Feedback consists of unobtrusive (usually short) expressions whereby a recipient of information signals to the contributor about his or her ability and willingness to communicate (have contact), to perceive, and to understand the information (Allwood *et al.*, 1992). A feedback utterance at the right time can communicate to the speaker that he or she should, for example, repeat the previous utterance and speak more clearly, or use words that are easier to understand. Feedback can communicate whether the recipient is accepting the main evocative intention of the contribution; i.e., whether a statement is believed, a question can be answered, or a request be complied with. Furthermore, feedback can indicate the emotions and attitudes triggered by the information in the recipient. Clearly, the essential role of feedback in natural communication makes it a crucial issue in the development of artificial conversational agents.

Every expression, considered as a behavioral feedback unit, has two functional sides. On the one hand, it can evoke reactions from the interlocutor, and on the other hand, it can respond to evocative aspects of a previous contribution. Each feedback behavior may thereby serve the four basic responsive feedback functions (Allwood *et al.*, 1992): contact (C), perception (P), understanding (U), and acceptance/agreement (A). In addition, further emotional or attitudinal information (E) may be expressed concurrently; e.g., by an enthusiastic prosody and a friendly smile, or by affect bursts like a sigh, a yawn, or a "wow!" (Scherer, 1994).

Thus, feedback is manipulative on the one hand and responsive on the other, as predicted by evolutionary theories. But where does trust come into the game? Most nonverbal communication is difficult to control consciously. Faked facial expressions, for instance, are easy to recognize. The reason for this seems to lie in the fact that they are difficult to produce in the ongoing flow of behavior and their conscious production imposes a cognitive load on the producer. We seem to trust nonverbal signals more than the verbal channel – and missing feedback signs on an indexed level of communication might be perceived as signs of lacking commitment and thus of possible deception. This is why embodiment is of such crucial importance for creating trust in human–machine communication.

Feedback in conversational agents

Almost every existing conversational agent system involves, implicitly or explicitly, aspects of communicative feedback by presenting emotional feedback, usually given through continuously adapted expressions, often combined with prosodic cues. Such feedback can either express the agent's own emotional state, and its changes over the course of dialogue (Becker *et al.*, 2004), or it can be used to intentionally convey affective states like commiseration. In the GRETA character (de Rosis *et al.*, 2003; Poggi *et al.*, 2005), thematic and rhematic parts of a communicative act are assigned to an affective state, yielding facial expressions that are drawn from large lexicons of codified behavior. Thórisson (1996) employs pause duration models to generate agent feedback; i.e., verbal back-channel utterances or nods are given after a silent pause of a certain duration (110 ms) in the speaker's utterance. The agent "Gandalf" simulates turn-taking behavior by looking away from the listener while speaking, and returning his gaze when finishing the turn. The Rea system (Cassell *et al.*, 1999) also uses a pause duration model and employs different modalities for feedback (nods, short feedback utterances). When the dialogue partner has finished a turn, she nods; if she did not understand the utterance, she raises her eyebrows and asks a repair question (e.g., "Could you repeat that?"). Beun and van Eijk (2004) propose a model to generate elementary feedback sequences at the knowledge level of dialogue participants. Based on an explicit model of the mental states of the dialogue partners, they create dialogue rules to enable a computer system to generate corrective feedback sequences when a user and a computer system have different conceptualizations of a particular discourse domain.

We are building a computational model of feedback behavior based on our theoretical and empirical studies, which can be simulated and tested in the embodied agent "Max" (Allwood *et al.*, 2008; Kopp *et al.*, 2008). Max is a virtual human under development by the artificial intelligence (AI) group at Bielefeld University. The system we use is already applied as a conversational information kiosk in the Heinz-Nixdorf-MuseumsForum (HNF), where Max engages visitors in face-to-face small talk and provides information about the museum, the exhibition, and other topics. Users can enter language input to the system using a keyboard, and Max responds with synthetic German speech and nonverbal behaviors such as gestures, facial expressions, gaze, and locomotion (Kopp *et al.*, 2005).

Max is equipped with an emotion system that runs a dynamic simulation to model the agent's emotional state (Becker *et al.*, 2004). The current emotional state is distributed within the architecture, and continuously modulates subtle aspects of the agent's behavior such as pitch, speech rate, variation width of the voice, or the rate of breathing and eye blinking. Likewise, the current emotion is mapped onto Max's facial expression and deliberative processes. Max therefore becomes "cognitively aware" of his emotional state and can include it in further deliberations. The emotion system, in turn, receives input from both the perception and the deliberative component. For example, seeing a person or achieving a goal triggers a positive stimulus, while detecting obscene or politically incorrect wordings in the user input leads to negative impulses on Max's emotional system.

In the following, we will outline how emotional feedback can be realized, identify the necessary mechanisms, and describe how control architectures could map appraisal/evaluation to the actual production of behavior.

Bodily expression as a feedback device: the mapping problem

AI tries to model adaptive behavior in autonomous agents (Staller and Petta, 1998), which are situated in highly complex dynamic environments. Although the implementation of emotion processes in such systems is highly sophisticated (usually based on the functional appraisal theory of emotion), none of the current projects offer a convincing solution for the action expression problem (i.e., mapping behavioral output on emotions). For example, Petta *et al.* (1999) describe the construction of such a system, but they do not provide a rationale as to how the emotional state and the expressive behaviour (precaptured motions and surface color changes) of their agent are linked. In their outline of the emotional architecture, Staller and Petta (1998) linked 24 emotion categories to 14 action-response categories with over a thousand individual actions. It is unclear, however, how the categories and actions were connected, and why. Existing attempts to incorporate emotional signals in embodied systems are library solutions; i.e., they map emotions on expressive behaviors manually. It is obvious that such systems are not flexible and tend to be perceived as monotonous. In social interactions, signals tend to be more complex.

If people want to interact socially with machines, what is conveyed by these agents has to be comparable to the information we usually process in emotional communication.

One can assume that facial expressions (like the smiling emoticon) are the emotional core information a user may use as feedback. However, the implementation of such a system is far from trivial, because it requires fundamental theoretical and methodological considerations. Here, we present an approach which we call *reverse engineering*, in accordance with the technical term that describes the process of taking apart an object to see how it works in order to duplicate or enhance it.

Basically, any expression simulation system consists of two parts. One part is the control architecture and the other part is the expressive output. The control architecture determines which facial expression has to be shown under what circumstances. It must include variables, which generate facial expressions under defined circumstances. Thus, a linkage between emotion theories and facial expressions is necessary. The second part seems to be more trivial – faces are equipped with muscles, which deform the surface of a face, thus generating form patterns of facial expressions. The construction of an expressive system can rely either on top-down constructed expressive templates (whole expressions) or a bottom-up approach, where single muscles are animated (see below).

One untackled problem in the construction of avatars is the fact that neutral faces per se already hold emotional information (Lee *et al.*, 2008); i.e., the basic construction of a face and a body put emotional information in an avatar. Gender-specific expectations regarding dominance and affiliative markers change the perception of a face (Hess *et al.*, 2004). Even the attractiveness of the avatar can change its perception. Rules in actual facial measurements and perception of a face and the attribution of personality traits have been widely discussed (for a review, see Grammer *et al.*, 2003).

We tested the quality of an emotional expressive system by segmenting it into its parts (according to the reverse-engineering concept). On this basis, we reconstructed a new system by means of simulation and tested its performance in interactions with real people.

Our approach relies on a series of methods: first, the observation of human communicative behavior in dyadic interactions and the analysis of verbal and nonverbal behavior; second, self-reports for the description of internal states; and third, the simulation of either randomized expressions or prototypes gained from real-life data and their perception. This combination allows a model to be built of how nonverbal behavior is linked to internal states and how they are perceived.

This is an ambitious project – and we are a long way from completing it. Here, we present our first results.

However, before we turn to the details of our empirical research, we need to discuss some of the very basics of emotion and facial expression theories.

Control architecture: emotion theories, feedback, and facial expression

Facial expressions are defined as expressive movements of facial muscles and the resulting positioning of the facial features. Research on facial expressions deals with the type of information conveyed. The scientific interest mainly lies in the link between emotions and facial expressions. Are emotions the reason for facial expression and/or inevitably connected to them, thus signaling an emotional state? Are facial expressions a mere communication mechanism, which is independent of emotions? Is the link between facial expressions and emotions merely coincidental rather than causal? The presumed association between emotions and corresponding facial expressions inevitably leads to the question: What are emotions?

This question has given scientists significant numbers of headaches in the past. A paper by Kleinginna and Kleinginna (1981) took stock of various definitions proposed by more than 100 authors. The paper, together with the lively history of about 100 years of psychological study into emotional processes, has led some current researchers to conclude that there is only limited agreement as to what emotions actually are.

Generally speaking, emotions are composed of neurophysiological and behavioral components as well as subjective experiences. The drawback of this definition is that it fails to distinguish emotions from intentions, motives, desires, and other psychological concepts. Various attempts to define emotions have not yet led to a satisfactory result: The precision necessary for a scientific concept seems out of reach. The approach by Paul Ekman (1984) was probably the most successful attempt: Emotions last from 500 ms to 4 s, and are elicited by universal triggers. These triggers can be defined for different emotions, such as loss for sadness, unexpected events for surprise, etc. Consequently, an emotion is always clearly connected to a trigger.

The James–Lange theory (1890) states that emotions are the result of somatic changes. When a stimulus is perceived, the brain triggers somatic changes, which are experienced as emotions by the individual. "We do not cry because we are sad, but we are sad because we cry."

On this basis, Tomkins (1962), Ekman (1971), and Izard (1971) proposed the theory of a facial expression program, suggesting a connection between internal physiological processes and emotions. When we experience an emotion, a cascade of electrical impulses (arising from the emotion centers of the brain) triggers a special facial expression, and certain physiological changes, such as changes in blood pressure or heart rate. Ekman defines the so-called *basic emotions* as those emotions that are hardwired and linked to a specific facial expression. All facial expressions can be regarded as the result of mixtures of basic emotions. This approach is supported by neurophysiology; e.g., Panksepp (1992) identifies brain circuits that correspond to the base emotions. On the perceptual level, a basic emotion can be correctly assigned to a certain facial expression independently of the context. Emotions are regarded as physiological adaptations to external situations, facilitating the predictability of actions and reactions. Facial expressions are the external signals of these emotions, and we assume that it has been evolutionarily advantageous to signal one's internal state to the environment.

However, facial expressions are not necessarily always directly linked to a person's emotional state, as there are culturally determined "display rules," which are transmitted by social learning. These rules determine in which situations facial expressions are appropriate and when they must be altered, suppressed, or masked by other facial expressions (Ekman and Friesen, 1969).

According to the behavioral ecology view theory (Fridlund, 1991, 1994), facial expressions are social tools that mimic signal intentions and social motives, but are not necessarily linked to emotions. One social motive can be associated with more than one emotion. Comprehension of the meaning of expressions has developed in co-evolution with the signals. Hence, expressions must be reliable signals for future actions and selection must work against unintended displays of internal states if these displays might be disadvantageous to the sender. The sender should only signal his internal state if this promises an advantage; e.g., cry if he wants to be comforted *and* if there is a good chance of getting solace from somebody. Facial expressions can thus be regarded as manipulation tools in social interactions, and they have a meaning only in a certain context. According to this theory, facial expressions have evolved for only one reason: to activate particular reactions and behaviors in a face-to-face interaction. This view is consistent with the theories on communication which we presented at the beginning of this chapter – expressive behavior is evocative and thus manipulative, but in addition it controls the structuring of interactions.

Russell (1995) also rejects the categorical model of basic emotions, stating that basic emotions can hardly ever be observed in real-life situations, but rather occur as "melodramatic poses" in conversations, underlining the spoken words. He further suggests that the context is most important for understanding and interpreting facial expressions. Russell claims that the face does not convey more information about emotions than the rest of the body (e.g., body posture, words, intonation), but rather signals the person's global feelings. He had found earlier (1991) that when rating faces, participants were able to assess only the level of arousal and valence, but could not attribute specific emotions. Only when the context was known could specific emotions be recognized.

According to Russell, facial expressions contain information that is understood automatically, quickly, and universally: Quasi-physical information, such as muscular contractions, skin color, tears, sweat, etc., communicate the dimensions of pleasure and arousal. This primary information is associated with the context of the situation. An emotion is attributed to the expression-context unit. Shame, fear, and guilt, for example, can adopt similar values of pleasure and arousal although their context is completely different.

Theories on the dimensional nature of emotions first emerged as early as the 1920s. Wundt (1924) describes three main dimensions for the classification of feelings: delight–aversion, arousal–calmness, tension–relief. Woodworth (1938) tried to systematically describe emotions and facial expressions. He found that certain emotions were often associated with certain facial expressions and that categories of emotions could be collocated along a continuum. Osgood (1966) claimed that emotional attributions to expressions can be described by dimensions. Mehrabian and Russell's (1974) model on emotions is also a dimensional one. They describe three dimensions, namely arousal (calm–aroused), dominance (dominant–submissive), and valence (pleasant–unpleasant). The authors state that three dimensions are necessary and sufficient to describe all possible emotional states.

In Russell's circumplex model (Russell, 1980), emotional states can be collocated in a 2D space, circularly around the zero point representing the "neutral state," and along the axes representing arousal–sleep and displeasure–pleasure (Figure 10.3). Russell (1978) claims that two axes are sufficient, as further dimensions can only be components of some, but not of all, emotions. In his model, the distance between two emotions in the pleasure-arousal (PA) space reflects their similarity. Specific values of pleasure and arousal can be assigned to all emotions and facial expressions. This model is implemented in the simulation "MAX."

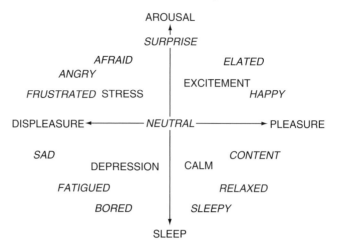

Figure 10.3 The circumplex model of emotions – the dimensions range from displeasure to pleasure (or valence) and from sleep to arousal. Basic emotions are distributed at specific points within the PA space.

Constructing control architecture: appraisal

Appraisal theories of emotion hypothesize that emotions are the result of an analysis in which an individual evaluates the personal significance of a stimulus occurring in the environment (Lazarus, 1991). Ekman (1980) describes this process as an automatic appraisal mechanism, which is a cognitive subsystem, able to operate independently of other cognitive systems and dedicated to determining whether or not a stimulus will elicit a basic emotion – joy, fear, surprise, anxiety, disgust, anger, or contempt (Figure 10.4). The appraisal of a situation generates a certain emotional state that evokes specific actions, which are appropriate in this situation. Emotions are internal states that are expressed by certain components of facial expressions. Activation of these components can intensify and modify communication, but although they may suit other purposes, all facial expressions result from emotions in the first place (Ekman 1980).

The "componential approach to emotions" (Frijda, 1986; Lang, 1995; Lazarus, 1991; Scherer, 1984) extends this assumption to the degree that emotions are structures consisting of certain, correlated components. Affect, appraisal, action disposition, and physiological reaction are described as main components in this model. Facial expressions thus mirror action readiness – in other words, the willingness to

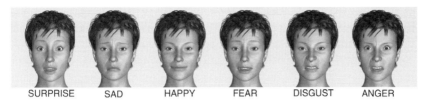

SURPRISE   SAD   HAPPY   FEAR   DISGUST   ANGER

Figure 10.4 The six basic emotions from the categorical expression program rendered in our system.

interact – and can help an interacting person to adjust behavior to the sender's current state.

According to Scherer (1999, 2001), emotions are a response to the evaluation of an external or internal stimulus event on a cognitively nonaccessible level. This emotion model proposes different elements: cognitive appraisal, physiological arousal, motor system activation, subjective feeling, and the motivational system. In other words, facial expressions are an intrinsic part of a feedback system, which evokes and controls actions in an interaction.

During cognitive appraisal, an individual constantly evaluates the situation according to its relevance (novelty check, intrinsic pleasantness, goal relevance check), implications (causal attribution check, outcome probability check, discrepancy from expectation check, goal/need conduciveness check, urgency check), coping potential (control check, power check, adjustment check), and normative significance (internal and external standard check). In Scherer's terms, the resulting patterns of appraisal are associated with specific emotions, like joy, fear, sadness, or anger. As different subsystems of appraisal might bring different evaluative results, the resulting emotion can be a mixture of the basic emotion dimensions.

In Griffiths' (1990) view, such low-level appraisal systems are indeed automatic and operating independently of the cognitive system, and lead to conscious verbally reportable appraisals. High-level appraisal is verbally reportable and integrated with the organism's beliefs. Both levels are finally integrated to create the emotion response. Frijda (1986) points out that emotional appraisal results in action tendencies – where the emotion presents the possibilities for action of an environment.

All of the approaches cited above have difficulty in mapping actual behavior onto emotional states. The discrete approach suffers from the fact that basic emotions are not represented by only one distinct facial expression. Instead, basic emotions form expression families, and it is unclear upon which specific pattern the result of an appraisal should be mapped. The componential approach is rather vague regarding the mapping problem. The situation is further complicated by the introduction of high-level appraisal, for which it is even less clear how it should be integrated and finally mapped onto expression output.

We therefore decided to base our approach on Mehrabian and Russell's (1974; Russell, 1980) circumplex model. It is possible to map the outcome of any appraisal system directly onto this space as continuous vectors in terms of pleasantness, arousal, and dominance. In addition, this model allows the mapping of both low-level behavioral data, like muscle movements, intonation, etc., and iconic and symbolic behaviors onto the PA space. However, in order to realize this, a corpus of real interactions has to be analyzed, mapped, and tested in terms of its reliability and validity.

The reverse-engineering method reveals that all existing theories use at least some overlapping building blocks. At first, every theory needs some appraisal process in order to elicit an emotion. The result of this appraisal process is then fed into a base module, which calculates the respective variables for the emotion elicitation process. At this point, any control architecture needs some expert system to decide which emotion should occur. Whether or not a facial expression occurs is again decided by an expert system. Basically, all three main theoretical approaches, the expression program, the componential approach, and the circumplex model, can be modeled this way. This was done successfully for the componential approach by Wehrle and Scherer (2001). The basic problem for all theoretical approaches is the fact that two expert systems are needed: one for translating appraisal into emotions and the other for generating the expression output. In Figure 10.5, we created a flowchart delineating this procedure for the expression program in the circumplex model.

Figure 10.6 combines the circumplex model with the "stimulus evaluation check" of Scherer (2001). An appraisal process triggers two dimensions: arousal and valence. These values can be mapped directly on the facial muscles in an expert system. In our further analysis, we will present the data for pleasure and arousal two-dimensionally – a 3D model which incorporates dominance should be easy to accomplish.

To map appraisal onto the PAD circumplex model, we administered two questionnaires to 123 male and female students (mean age 24.3): the Geneva Appraisal Questionnaire (GAQ) (Scherer, 1997) and an 18-item PAD list (Russell et al., 1978).

The principal component analysis of the PAD explains 65 percent of the variance with the factors pleasure, arousal, and dominance.

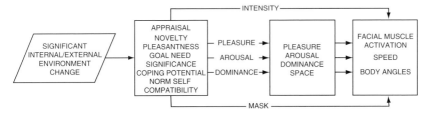

Figure 10.5 This flowchart delineates the architecture for a program that reacts to a significant stimulus change in the environment. This stimulus is mapped by an appraisal process to pleasure, arousal, and dominance. These three variables are then mapped continuously on facial expressions, their contraction speed, and body angles, which cause posture shifts. The expression can also be masked and varied in intensity. For the mapping of expressions on the PDA space, either real-life data and self-reports or third-party ratings can be used. Other behaviors, like blink rate, gesticulation, or breathing, can be incorporated.

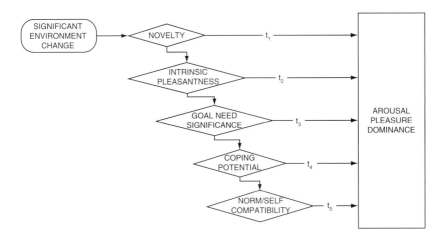

Figure 10.6 This flowchart shows the appraisal process modeled, based on the model proposed by Scherer (1999), but the appraisal is mapped on pleasure, arousal, and dominance instead of the categorized emotions.

The GAQ scores were calculated for seven basic items according to the manual. We then regressed the GAQ items on pleasure, arousal, and dominance. This resulted in the translation of the evaluation of an emotional event into the dimensions of the PAD space.

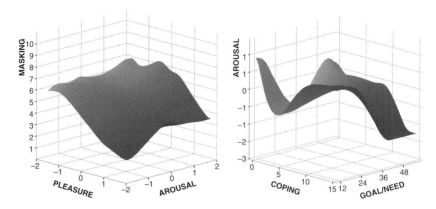

Figure 10.7 This figure shows the mapping of the tendency to mask an expression on pleasure and arousal (left) and the mapping of arousal on the ability to cope with a situation and the goal/need check (right).

The only remaining hurdle is to determine which events correspond to what extent to the respective appraisal outcomes. If this can be achieved, the rest of the simulation becomes self-evident in the PAD space. Novelty is positively related to arousal and pleasantness, goal-need increases pleasantness and dominance, coping relates negatively to pleasure and positively to dominance, and norm compatibility is pleasurable. In addition, we calculated an intensity factor, which is negatively related to pleasure and the tendency to mask the emotion. These two variables are paramount for the simulation, as they control whether an expression occurs and with what intensity.

These results make it clear that an appraisal process can deliver the respective scores for all processes by using regression of pleasure, arousal, and dominance on the five appraisal domains. As an outcome, we then have three values of pleasure, arousal, and dominance, which can be fed into the next step, which is expression mapping on pleasure, arousal, and dominance (Figure 10.7). The advantage of this approach is that it relies on real-life data – so no manual mapping and scripting are necessary, because we have a continuous process.

Constructing facial expressions and body postures

Research on facial expressions relies on two types of approaches: interpretative methods and objective descriptive methods. Interpretative methods concentrate on the assessment of the perceivers, who are confronted with stimuli showing different expressions under standardized conditions and are asked to evaluate them. This requires an interpretation from the observer and leads to insights into the perception of the observer rather than into the quality of facial expressions. Descriptive methods characterize the objective change in expressions, refraining completely from interpretations. They can provide an insight as to what kind of expressive behavior is possible under which circumstances, but give no clue about the meaning of facial expressions.

Most studies on the meaning of facial expressions followed a typical top-down approach: A certain facial expression was presented and an emotion term had to be attributed. Mostly, only a limited number of emotions were provided as possible answers. This method (which was already used by Charles Darwin in the nineteenth century) assumes that concordance in the attributions to a certain facial expression allows the conclusion that the attributed emotion is the reason for this facial expression.

Single facial movements (i.e., changes caused by a single muscle), which comprise a facial expression, have often been identified, but the meaning of these single components has rarely been the subject of scientific research. Snodgrass (1992) was one of the first researchers to apply a bottom-up approach: Single muscle components were rated according to their degree of pleasure and arousal. In a second step, they were attributed to emotion terms. In both settings, subjects showed a high agreement in their ratings. Additionally, the attributed emotion was associated with the values in the pleasure and arousal dimensions. These findings support the assumption of Russell (1980), who stated that the information conveyed by a facial expression is present even in the single components.

The great advantage of the bottom-up approach is the means to investigate any type of expressive behavior, and not merely a limited set of emotions. Note that by using dimensions rather than emotions in the ratings, the bottom-up approach can be applied to both stimulus and evaluation.

Past research on emotional expressions used photographs. These photographs usually show the basic emotions at a very high intensity. The shortcomings of this method are obvious: There is no way to exclude personal information, and it is not possible to vary the intensity of the expressions systematically. Therefore, expressions of low intensity have not been investigated so far. This is even more regrettable since we experience in our everyday lives that we are capable of understanding subtle facial expressions just as well as ones of high intensity.

Therefore, we use computer models, which allow us to manipulate their appearance and expressions systematically. The first face models on the computer were developed in the 1970s. Parke (1972) developed a parametric 3D model, and Gillenson (1974) created the first interactive 2D model. Platt and Badler (1981) designed the first model based on muscular actions, using FACS (facial action coding system) (Ekman and Friesen, 1978) as a basis for the control of facial expressions.

FACS is the most widely used and versatile method for measuring facial behavior. Paul Ekman and Wallace Friesen (1978) developed FACS by determining how the contraction of each facial muscle (singly and in combination with other muscles) changes the appearance of the face. They examined videotapes of facial behavior to identify the specific changes that occur with muscular contractions and to determine how they differ. Their goal was to create a reliable means for skilled human scorers to categorize facial behavior.

FACS measurement units are action units (AUs), not muscles, for two reasons. First, some muscles were combined into a single AU because the changes in appearance which they produced could not be distinguished. Second, the appearance changes produced by one muscle were sometimes separated into 2 or more AUs to represent relatively independent actions of different parts of the muscle.

The great advantage of FACS is that all possible facial changes and movements, respectively, can be recorded and cataloged. It is strictly descriptive and has no need to refer to emotions. The main drawback is that only outwardly visible changes are covered; changes with no effect on external appearance, as is the case for changes in muscular tonus, cannot be recorded. Visible changes other than deformations are not included either: There are no variables covering changes in face color (blushing and blanching), perspiration, and tears. FACS also has shortcomings in terms of real-time application, since movements with a duration shorter than 200 ms can only be perceived in slow motion.

Spencer-Smith *et al.* (2001) developed a 3D model that allows the creation of stimuli with 16 different AUs and defined intensities based on FACS. The limited number of embedded AUs is one of its major shortcomings, taking into account that FACS consists of 46 AUs for facial expressions and 12 AUs for head and eye movements. Moreover, the basic character of this model has rather few polygons, with the result that the simulated facial expressions are rather crude approximations, lacking in detail.

Implementing FACS on a 3D computer face

We used the computer program Poser 6 (Curious Labs, Santa Cruz, CA, USA) as a test bed for our approach. Such a software environment has the advantage that the lighting conditions, camera angle, and focus length are exactly the same for all pictures. The avatars

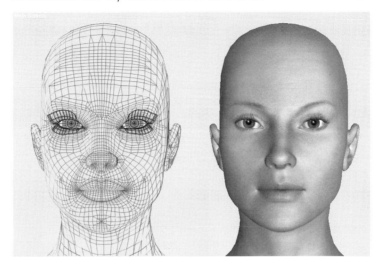

Figure 10.8 On the left is the wire frame mesh we used for the 3D avatar and on the right the rendered photo-realistic textured version.

are 3D mesh models, consisting of single polygons, which can be textured arbitrarily according to the desired appearance of the resulting figure (Figure 10.8). By adding hair models and photo-realistic, high-resolution textures, highly realistic models can be created. We used the model Victoria V.2 from DAZ (Digital Art Zone, Draper, UT, USA) with a polygon count of 10,434 for the head. The high number of polygons and their different shapes allow the anatomically correct simulation of muscular movements. This enables highly realistic expressions to be created, because subtle changes can also be incorporated. Based on FACS, we modeled the facial AUs onto the virtual character's face. The highly sophisticated description and illustration of AUs allows a 3D modeler to model all AUs systematically and precisely.

Using our reverse-engineering approach, we modeled all AUs as a system of morph targets at their maximum contraction directly on the head mesh in the modeling program CINEMA 4D (MAXON Computer, Inc., Newbury Park, CA, USA). The quality of the morph targets is the most crucial element in this model, since this is the key to natural stimuli. The meshes were translated by scientists and constantly rechecked by trained FACS coders. The intensity of the applied mesh deformation can vary between 0 and 1, corresponding to not applied or full expression. A total of 25 AUs were implemented in this way and finally tested for interactions with codes from the FACS

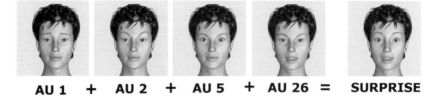

AU 1 + AU 2 + AU 5 + AU 26 = SURPRISE

Figure 10.9 This picture shows how single-modeled facial AUs from the FACS can add up to a complex expressive facial pattern (AU_1, inner brow raise; AU_2, outer brow raise; AU_5, upper lid raise; AU_26, jaw drop).

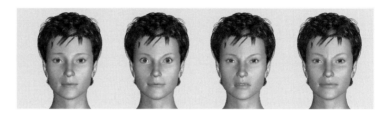

Figure 10.10 Faces with randomly activated AUs, which were used in the study. Picture 1 (from left): AU_1, 0.47; AU_9, 0.19; AU_14, 0.56; AU_24, 0.58. Picture 2: AU_5, 0.57; AU_17, 0.33; AU_20, 0.62; AU_23, 0.63. Picture 3: AU_4, 0.3; AU_7, 0.6; AU_10, 0.34; AU_15, 0.19. Picture 4: AU_2, 0.28; AU_4, 0.29; AU_6, 0.66; AU_12, 0.58; AU_15, 0.41.

handbook. This was necessary in order to avoid folding and distortion of the wire frame mesh.

By activating the single morphs of AUs in almost any intensity and combination, virtually any type of facial expression can be reconstructed (Figure 10.9). Additionally, if a random element is added to the activation, two emotional expressions will never be the same. Thus, the major problem of facial animation – sterility through repetition – is eliminated.

Methods of stimulus generation and presentation

With these developments, Grammer and Oberzaucher (2006) were able to use a radical bottom-up approach. We developed a Python program called Face Randomizer, which allowed the intensities of the activations of single morph targets to be altered randomly. This means that no expression occurred twice, and each participant rated different expressions of the same person (Figure 10.10).

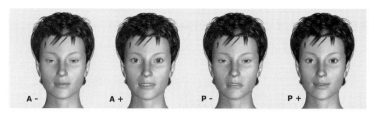

Figure 10.11 Visualization of the regression analysis of muscle activation on pleasure (P+), displeasure (P–), arousal (A+), and nonarousal (A–). In this case, either 50 percent or all AUs were randomly activated. Thus, this regression is part of the occurrence of muscle activation in the facial context – i.e., the activation of other muscles.

In total, 403 male and female students (mean age 22.4) were recruited as participants on a voluntary basis. Each rating situation took approximately 25 min; on average, each participant rated eleven different faces. Overall, n = 4,453 randomly generated expressive faces were rated in this study.

2D regression analysis of pleasure and arousal on AU activation

In order to ascertain whether there are distinct PA spaces, a LOESS regression was applied to pleasure and arousal for each AU activation (Grammer and Oberzaucher, 2006). The single AU regression spaces were all calculated and the regression area was resampled with a grid from –3.5 to 3.5 for both pleasure and arousal, with a step width of 0.125. The resulting data set is shown in Figure 10.11 for AU_1, AU_5, and AU_12. The data suggest that the PA space is not a linear space for all AUs. In the case of AU_1 (inner brow raise), we see that this AU is activated when pleasure is high and arousal is low, but there is a second peak with medium pleasure and high arousal. This is different for AU_5 (upper lid raise), which is activated by high arousal and high pleasure. AU_12 (lip corner puller), which is responsible for smiling, is active under high arousal and high pleasure (Figure 10.12).

With this information, the complete PA space can be reconstructed. The activation values of all AUs at a distinct point in the PA space can be recomposed into the expression communicating to the respective emotion (Figure 10.13). The PA spaces of all AUs now can be used to drive a simulation on the basis of only two variables – arousal and pleasure – and create the corresponding facial expression automatically.

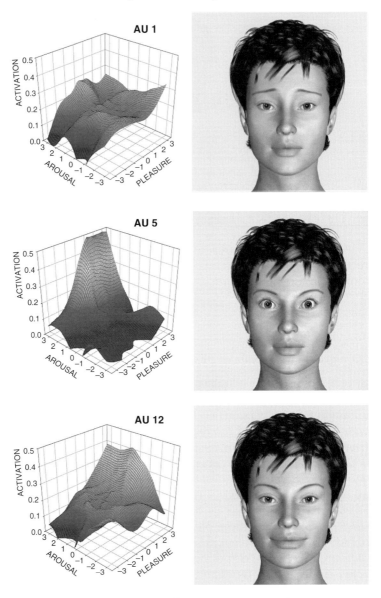

Figure 10.12 The activation of single AUs in a pleasure and arousal space. Note that these distributions differ between AUs.

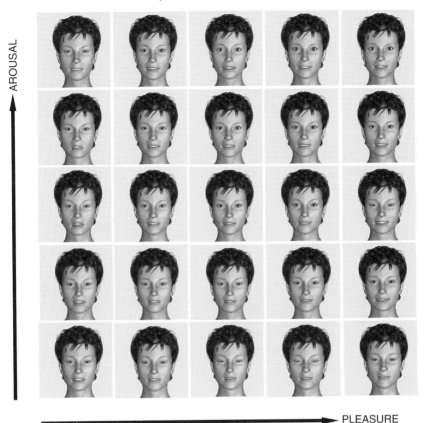

AROUSAL

PLEASURE

Figure 10.13 The completely reconstructed pleasure and arousal space.

Reconstruction of basic emotions in the PA space

In a last step, we tried to establish whether the two models, the expression program and the circumplex model, could actually be unified, at least empirically. In order to accomplish this, we calculated the PA spaces for categorical emotions from the AUs which constitute them. This is a single adding-up of all values of activation at any point of the space.

The categorical emotions are not distributed uniformly in the PA space. Surprise (AU_1 + AU_2 + AU_5 + AU_26) occurs most often when pleasure is neutral and arousal is high. Sadness (AU_1 + AU_4 + AU_15) coincides with low pleasure and slightly raised arousal, but the plane also indicates that sadness could occur in situations of low arousal and high pleasure. Happiness (AU_6 + AU_12) occurs when pleasure is high and arousal slightly above neutral. Fear (AU_1 + AU_2 + AU_4 + AU_20 + AU_26) shows relations to low pleasure and high arousal, as does disgust (AU_9 + AU_10). The difference between fear and disgust is that fear does not occur at medium arousal and low pleasure, but disgust does. The last of the six basic emotions is anger (AU_4 + AU_5 + AU_7 + AU_10 + AU_23 + AU_26). It occurs under high arousal and low pleasure conditions but also under high arousal and high pleasure conditions and even under low arousal and high pleasure conditions. With these results, we are now able to map the categorical model onto the circumplex model. We propose that the first is a subspace of the latter model (Figure 10.14).

Modeling emotional postures

It is taken for granted that the nonverbal information we acquire from a person's body posture and position affects our perception of others. However, to date, complete human body postures have never been described on an empirical level. This study is the first approach to tackle the unexplored topic of human postures and their communicative value as concerns emotional states. Ekman and Friesen (1969) see the communicative relevance of postures mainly in expressing the intensity of an emotion, whose quality is conveyed mainly by facial expressions. Later, Coulson (2004) showed that postures taken by actors instructed to display the basic emotions can express them to a certain extent.

In the present study (Grammer *et al.*, 2004), we combined two approaches: traditional behavior observation and modern morphometric analysis. Photographs of 100 passersby were taken when they came to a halt in response to being asked to participate in a survey. The participants filled out a questionnaire about their current affective state (PANAS; Watson *et al.*, 1988) and their attitude to the interviewer. The body postures of the participants were transferred to a 3D virtual environment (Poser), and 55 body angles were measured. A principal component analysis of the items of the affect questionnaire revealed five main factors: aversion, openness, irritation, happiness, and self-confidence. These factors were regressed onto the body angles. The respective postures were reconstructed in 3D avatars. This method enables extrapolation of the interaction of affective state and body angles. We used this possibility to construct both the positive and the negative end of the regression (i.e., an extrapolation that leads to postures that did not exist in our original data set). Fifty subjects then

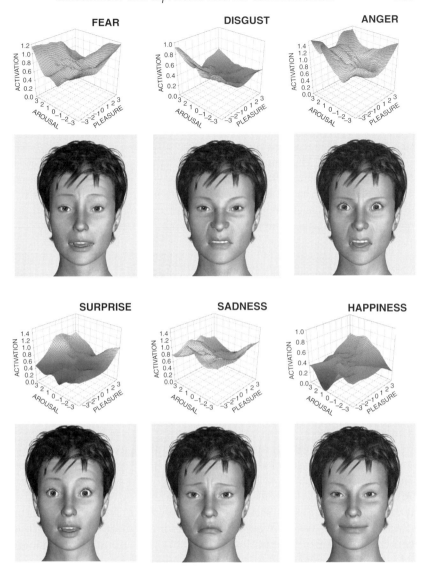

Figure 10.14 The reconstruction of categorical emotion expressions in the pleasure and arousal space. In comparison to the predictions from Figure 10.1, we find an almost complete match – but there are also exceptions; i.e., the same categorical emotion can occur under different pleasure and arousal combinations.

rated the reconstructed postures on 5-point Likert scales for the principal components from the self-reports.

The ratings of the reconstructed postures were of high interrater reliability (Cronbach's alpha 0.69–0.89, and intraclass correlation 0.77–0.91). We found the ratings to be valid and accurate with respect to the five factors. Paired t-tests of the positive and negative posture dimensions of the factors showed that for all affect components, the negative posture was rated significantly as the opposite of the corresponding positive posture (Figure 10.15).

After verifying the self-reports and comparing them to third-party ratings, we calculated the regressions from a PA rating to the body angles; thus, each body angle has a representation of its size in a PA space. This allows pleasure, arousal, and dominance to be changed continuously to attain the respective change in body posture.

Modeling muscle contraction speed and dynamics

In 1997, Grammer, Filova, and Fieder introduced a new paradigm into the analysis of behavioral information processing. This approach emphasizes the human ability to "assess elementary dimensions of behaviour like speed, acceleration and amount of movement or motion quality" (Grammer *et al.*, 1997). The novelty of this concept was the assumption that behavioral dynamics and qualities convey meaning, not only static expressive configurations. The quality of a movement lies in its dynamics, and precisely this quality might be integral to the signal as well as its interpretation (Grammer *et al.*, 2002). The quality of a movement is one of the many behavior elements which had been neglected in the traditional classification of static expressions.

Besides the possibilities for researching static expressions, reverse engineering opens a new horizon for the timing aspect of behavior. In this context, facial expressions can be understood as the apex, which is framed by an onset- and an offset-movement. The relation of the duration of these three periods (onset–apex–offset) might be one source of dynamic information. Above that, the timing of the single AUs within the onset and offset period could modulate the meaning of an expression; i.e., whether they are activated simultaneously or sequentially.

Static facial expressions have been a subject of emotion research for the last few decades. The meanings attributed to facial expressions are not always unambiguous: The perception of smile meanings varies greatly and can range from aggressive intentions and mockery to pleasant feelings and seduction (Ekman, 1984). Extensive research has been devoted to the genuineness of smiles. Similarly, brow-raising,

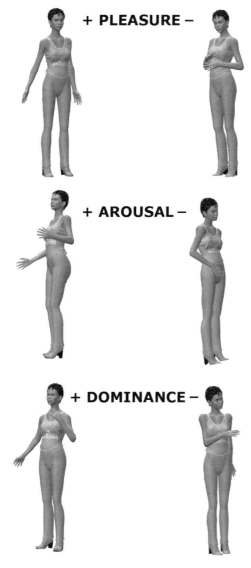

Figure 10.15 Reconstruction of postures from a regression analysis of real observed postures (body angles) on the PA space.

which consists of the contraction and relaxation of the M. frontalis, M. pars medialis, and M. lateralis, is used to signal many emotional states. Eibl-Eibesfeldt and Hass (1967) identified two basic brow movements: first, a very quick raising of the brow, often observed during social greetings, which they christened "eye-greeting" (Grammer *et al.*, 1988); and second, a temporally persistent raising of the brows which is thought to express angry surprise and displeasure.

Currently, scientists are beginning to tackle the distinction of a variety of multifaceted facial expressions by these innovative methods. Krumhuber and Kappas (2005) conducted three experiments in order to illustrate the role of dynamics in the perception of the genuineness of a smile by using Poser 4. Consistent with Grammer *et al.* (1997), all three of Krumhuber and Kappas' experiments confirmed that certain durations of onset, apex, and offset in Duchenne smiles conveyed authenticity to the facial expression. The dynamics, therefore, may indicate, or at least influence, the expression's underlying meaning.

The present study reinvestigated the role of dynamic components in the perception of expressive genuineness. In addition, it analyzed whether dynamic changes in smiles and brow raises have an impact on the ascription of meaning to facial expressive movements. These two facial expressions were chosen since in-depth, up-to-date litera-ture could only be found on the dynamic qualities of these two facial expressions. The dynamics of smiles and brow-raising have little in common: While smile onsets last, on average, 700 ms and are accompanied by other facial movements (Schmidt and Cohen, 2002), brows shoot up in 80 ms, after a pause of all other facial movements (Grammer *et al.*, 1988). Smiles last for at least 3–4 s, while brow-raising usually lasts for only about 0.8 s. However, as stated above, both expressions have been found to have temporally consistent movement patterns. Onset is defined as the time span during which a face moves from a neutral state to a full-blown expression, apex is the duration of the peak expression of the trait, and offset refers to the duration in which the face returns from a full-blown expression to a neutral state.

We conducted two experiments to establish the influence of muscu-lar dynamics on the reading of facial expressions. The first experiment focused on brow-raising, which is thought to accompany many differ-ent emotions. The second investigated Duchenne smiles, which are called genuinely "felt" smiles in emotion research. We used embodied agents, created in Poser 5 in combination with Ekman and Friesen's AUs (1978), to manipulate the dynamics of these two expressions. Each expression was divided into three periods – onset, apex, and offset – whose duration (short, medium, and long) was combined randomly. This resulted in 54 videos (27 male and 27 female stimuli) for both smiling and brow-raising. These videos were shown to 521 participants (302 women, 209 men), who ascribed meaning to each expression (Figure 10.16).

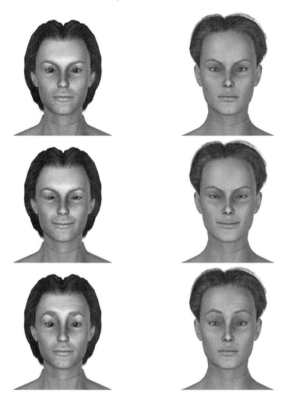

Figure 10.16 Male and female stimuli used in the analysis of muscle contraction speed and meaning of smiles and brow-raising.

A short onset of brow raises is associated with high arousal, a long apex conveys coyness, and the offset does not affect the meaning of this expression. In smiles, long onsets convey pleasure, genuineness, and less arousal and coyness. A short apex is attributed as negative, aggressive, unhappy, and false. A short offset makes a smile appear more aggressive.

The results suggest that the dynamics of facial expressions do influence the attribution of an underlying emotion. Furthermore, the findings identify dynamics as significant in the act of decoding and ascription, perhaps even more so than static configuration. In a next step, we again mapped the speed data in the PAD space – thus, we have speed information for pleasure arousal and dominance for at least two muscles – the smile (M. zygomaticus major) and the brow raise (M. pars medialis, M. pars lateralis) (Figure 10.17).

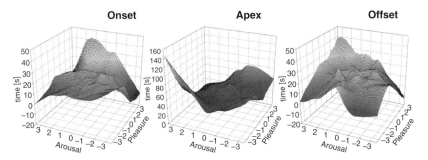

Figure 10.17 Results of the speed analysis and the distribution of onset, apex, and offset duration in relation to pleasure and arousal. High pleasure and high arousal have a fast onset, short apex, and long offset.

Head movements

In the next study, we investigated the communicative function of head movements. We filmed interactions between two people and analyzed their behavior, using Anvil (Kipp, 2001). We focused on head movements as feedback signals and translated them into head movements of an avatar in Poser 7. Then, 62 participants (32 women, 30 men) assessed the stimuli regarding the three dimensions "pleasure," "arousal," and "dominance." Each participant evaluated 10 videos. Altogether, we had 41 videos, which included single and repeated nods and jerks. A head movement is defined as a nod when the head goes down and then up, and as a jerk when the head moves up first and then down.

The results show that jerks are perceived as more dominant than nods. Moreover, jerks are associated with higher values of pleasure. Arousal is linked to the speed of the head movements – the faster a movement is, the more aroused it appears to be. Additionally, high arousal is related to fewer minima (i.e., greatest movement of the head toward the chest) than dominance. Dominance is also expressed in reduced emphasis of movements. High pleasure is connected with a larger number of maxima (i.e., the greatest backward movements) (Figure 10.18).

Our findings show that head movements are suitable signals for the dimensions pleasure, arousal, and dominance.

Krämer (2001) explored the effect of head activity and head tilts on the perception of a virtual agent. An agent that shows head activity is perceived as friendlier, more attentive, but also more intrusive and masculine than a static agent. Head tilts to the right (seen from

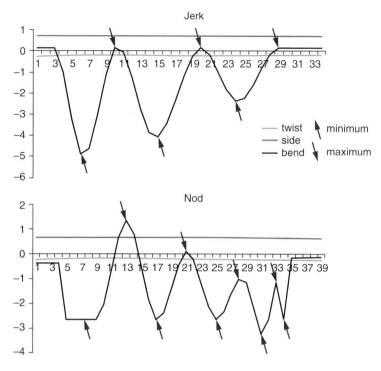

Figure 10.18 These graphs show the dynamics of head movements typical of a jerk and a nod. The main movements are in bending the head. The minimum characterizes the greatest movement toward the chest, while the maximum is the greatest backward movement of the head. The speed of the movement is described by the length of the curve.

the avatar's perspective) are perceived as more repellent, unconcerned, competent, and authentic than upright heads. Tilts to the left yield more positive evaluations than tilts to the right. It seems that movements to the right can mean something different from tilts to the left. The reason for this remains unclear, as tilts can be perceived as referring to some surroundings, such as an asymmetric screen.

Putting it all together: timing issues

In the last few years, several systems have tried to predict the right time for feedback. Ward and Tsukahara (2000), noticing that feedback is often interlaced into pauses between two words or phrases of the speaker, describe a pause-duration model that also incorporates prosodic cues based on the best fit to a speech corpus. It can be stated in a rule-based fashion: After a relatively low pitch for at least 110 ms, following at least 700 ms of speech, and given that you have had no output back-channel feedback within the preceding 800 ms, wait another 700 ms and then produce back-channel feedback. Takeuchi *et al.* (2004) augment this approach with incrementally obtained information about word classes. Fujie *et al.* (2004), in addition to analyzing prosody information to extract proper feedback timing, employ a network of finite state transducers, including one that maps recognized words onto content for possible feedback before the end of the utterance.

Usually, feedback is implemented at the end of an utterance, but Allwood *et al.* (2008) show that this is not necessarily the case – in the analysis of dyadic interactions, they find that more than 70 percent of feedback occurs during and parallel to speech. Thus, the appraisal has to be continuous, as suggested by Kopp *et al.* (2008) and implemented in MAX.

We have accumulated empirical data on different elements of emotional expressions and feedback. Now, we can test and verify the whole system. For this purpose we can use events from our appraisal study. One description for an event is: "I was sitting in my chair working on my PC, when my girlfriend stepped behind me and told me she is pregnant."

We took the original values from the questionnaire and used the combined scores to calculate the respective PAD scores from our regressions for a visualization of what should have happened in the face and posture of the subject. We calculated this sequentially; i.e., for each of the five appraisal steps, we calculated the activation of the AUs. We simulated the sequence of expressions with each appraisal step lasting for five frames. This number is chosen here only for demonstration; we are currently investigating the actual time course of an appraisal process. The result is a complex, time-structured facial expression somewhere between pleasure and surprise. Novelty check increases arousal, the news is perceived as pleasant, and the goal/need check then causes even more arousal, whereas pleasure drops. The appraisal of coping then lowers pleasure and arousal, whereas with the norm-compatibility check, pleasure rises again. What we see here is that the simulation can produce highly complex sequences of facial expression. The posture is only depicted for the novelty check (Figure 10.19). The final movie can be downloaded from our website.

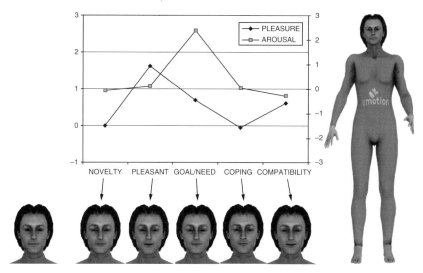

Figure 10.19 This depicts the reconstruction of a reported emotional event. The graph shows the time changes for the different stimulus evaluation checks and the pleasure and arousal values created by them. In the lower pictures (neutral face on the left), we see the corresponding muscle activations, and on the right we see the posture taken after the novelty check.

Expression simulation in communication over the internet

In this explorative work, we have demonstrated that it seems to be possible to create a control architecture for expression simulation on the basis of only two controlling variables – pleasure and arousal – which can generate highly complex and variable facial and bodily expressions. This architecture can easily be implemented under a variety of conditions. This approach provides a simple solution for the action expression problem in virtual agents and embodied systems.

The system can generate virtually endless combinations of AU activations, and thus the expressive behavior of such an agent will never become monotonous. Our research also shows that a radical bottom-up approach in nonverbal behavior research is feasible and generates convincing results. For the construction of avatars and embodied systems, in our view this is the only approach that is able to solve the action expression problem.

Besides the finding that the control architecture is feasible, we have also demonstrated that even apparently contradicting emotion theories can be implemented under the same control architecture. For instance, it should be possible to weigh AUs according to emotional arousal. This means that these AUs would be shown preferably according to the given emotional conditions. With this architecture, it would be possible to let an avatar show emotions that apparently contradict the context – i.e., crying under highly happy circumstances.

Literally all emotion theories can be mapped onto facial expressions with this procedure, as long as a semantic differential for this theory can be constructed. For instance, it would be plausible to have subjects rate random faces in the six basic emotions and then calculate the regression values for each AU and basic emotions. This demonstrates that our approach is versatile and can be used to test the validity of emotion theories. However, there is a general caveat. In the case of random faces, there is no information about the internal state of the sender. This information would be necessary to create a complete, accurate, and valid model.

Many aspects of expression simulation have not yet been touched upon by this first approach, as, for example, the occurrence of facial asymmetries in expression. With our methods, this would be easy to implement by simply splitting the morph targets that compose the AUs. Control architectures for asymmetries can then be built in the same way as for the symmetric expressions. Other semantic differentials can also be used. For example, differentials covering the honesty of the expression would only add one variable to our system. Currently, we are extending the model on the same basis for blink rates, gaze directions, saccadic eye movements, breathing, gesticulation, and prosodics. The final database will be available under open-source licensing conditions from our website.

Another problem that is touched upon only rarely in facial expression research is the assessment of dynamics. However, once again, we suggest that this can be done in the same way as for the symmetric facial expressions. We suggest that it is possible to put all other types of nonverbal behavior – from head and eye movements and gestures, to postures and emotional patterns in speech – in a comparable system.

The reverse engineering approach generally consists of a collection of either simulated or real-life data. In the case of real-life observation data, self-descriptions can be collected in parallel. In a second step, the resulting stimuli are rated by observers and then a regression analysis of the data is made. The prerequisite is that the behavior data are extremely low-level, like muscle movements or body angles. Based on these regressions, new stimuli can be created, which can then be rated again and compared to self-description.

However, the present approach has consequences not only for control architecture research but also for the field of nonverbal behavior research itself. If such an approach is widely adopted, it could help in overcoming the stagnation of research in nonverbal behavior. This tool creates the opportunity to address open questions in facial expression research by the new methodological possibilities. By the ability to manipulate facial expressions with high-resolution and sufficient realism, the nature and meaning of facial expressions can be investigated in more detail. For example, it is possible to look at the meaning of single AUs more thoroughly – what is the threshold intensity above which they can convey a meaning? By introducing asymmetry, these phenomena can also be studied. Interaction effects of AUs can also be addressed; i.e., which combination of AUs is necessary and/or sufficient to create a convincingly prototypical emotion expression, and what variations in facial expression are attributed to the same basic emotion? How are facial expressions appraised that are composed of parts of the AUs defining a basic emotion? This latter question would discriminate between compulsory and facultative elements of the expressions of basic emotions as they are described by Ekman and Friesen (1978). Using reverse engineering, research is no longer limited to expressions of basic emotions of rather high intensity. By applying this technique, every combination and intensity of AUs can be investigated. This enables the analysis of mixed emotions; i.e., overlaps or combinations of basic emotions.

Another open question refers to the existence of conversational signals, which control interactions (Fridlund, 1994). When facial signals occur to emphasize certain parts of speech, the control architecture will become slightly more difficult. We suggest that an approach that takes into account the behavioral ecology view simply adds a new layer to our control architecture, as is the case for the emotion program theory.

However, these are not actually all of the possible dimensions: When a motivational layer is added, even the necessities created by the componential approach to emotions (Frijda, 1986) can be covered. All in all, the present study is only the first step, both for research based on reverse engineering and implementing emotional behavior in avatars. Our results hint at the qualities of this approach for both fields. In research on nonverbal behavior, the ability to modulate behavioral output (in combination with a metric measurement) creates the opportunity to analyze the qualitative meaning of behavior elements. In behavior simulation, this method allows complex behavior patterns to be implemented with a comparably simple architecture combined with high plasticity and variability in the output. Thus, both computer engineering and research on the theory of emotions will benefit from this approach.

Indeed, in accordance with Grammer *et al.*'s (1997) hypothesis, research conducted by Johansson (1973, 1976) and Grammer *et al.* (1988) has shown that dynamic and qualitative properties enable successful differentiation between behavior and its intention. Very recent research has shown that dynamic and qualitative changes in facial expression can be perceived. With the discovery of the so-called mirror neurons (MNs), Gallese and Goldmann (1998) suggested that human "mind-reading" abilities, in the case of this study the ascription of meaning to expressive stimuli, rely on the capacity to adopt simulation. This capacity might have evolved from an action-execution-observation matching system whose neural substrate is the MNs, only recently discovered in the macaque monkey's premotor cortex. MNs are thought to underlie the process of mind reading, or at least serve as precursors to such a process. Based on these findings, Rizzolatti *et al.* (2001) derived the "direct-matching hypothesis." This proposes that humans understand actions by mapping an observed action onto their own area of motor representation. Thus, an action, in the case of this study a facial expression, can be "read" when its observation causes the motor system of the observer to "resonate." According to this approach, the observer's "motor knowledge" is used to devise the observed action. In other words, we "understand" an action because the motor representation of that action is activated in our brain.

This is why communication over the internet has to become embodied.

References

Allwood, J., Nivre, J., and Ahlsén, E. (1992). On the semantics and pragmatics of linguistic feedback. *Journal of Semantics, 9*(1), 1–26.

Allwood, J., Kopp, S., Grammer, K., Ahlsén, E., Oberzaucher, E., and Koppensteiner, M. (2008). The analysis of embodied communicative feedback in multimodal corpora – a prerequisite for behavior simulation. *Journal of Language Resources and Evaluation* (Special Issue on Multimodal Corpora), *41*(3–4), 255–272.

Becker, C., Kopp, S., and Wachsmuth, I. (2004). Simulating the emotion dynamics of a multimodal conversational agent. In E. André (ed.), *Proceedings of Affective Dialogue Systems Conference (ADS '04)*, LNAI 3068 (pp. 154–165). Berlin: Springer.

Beun, R. J. and Van Eijk, R. M. (2004). A cooperative dialogue game for resolving ontological discrepancies. In F. Dignum, F. (ed.), *Advances in Agent Communication* (pp. 349–363). Berlin: Springer.

Bulbulia, J. (2004). Religious costs as adaptations that signal altruistic intention. *Evolution and Cognition, 10*(1), 19–42.

Cassell, J. (2004). Towards a model of technology and literacy development: story listening systems. *Journal of Applied Developmental Psychology*, **25**(1), 75–105.

Cassell, J. and Thórisson, K. R. (1999). The power of a nod and a glance: envelope vs. emotional feedback in animated conversational agents. *Applied Artificial Intelligence*, **13**, 519–538.

Cassell, J., Bickmore, T., Billinghurst, M., Campbell, L., Chang, K., Vilhjálmsson, H., and Yan, H. (1999). Embodiment in conversational interfaces: Rea. In *CHI '99 Conference Proceedings* (pp. 520–527). New York: ACM Press.

Cassell, J., Vilhjálmsson, H., and Bickmore, T. (2001). BEAT: the Behavior Expression Animation Toolkit. In *Proceedings of SIGGRAPH '01* (pp. 477–486). New York: ACM Press.

Cleveland, W. S. (1979). Robust locally weighted regression and smoothing scatterplots. *Journal of the American Statistical Association*, **74**, 829–836.

Cleveland, W. S. and Devlin, S. J. (1988). Locally weighted regression: an approach to regression analysis by local fitting. *Journal of the American Statistical Association*, **83**, 596–610.

Cosmides, L. and Tooby, J. (1992). Cognitive adaptations for social exchange. In J. Barkow, L. Cosmides, and J. Tooby (eds), *The Adapted Mind: Evolutionary Psychology and the Generation of Culture* (pp. 163–228). New York: Oxford University Press.

Cosmides, L., Tooby, J., and Barkow, J. H. (1992). *Evolutionary Psychology and Conceptual Integration*. Oxford University Press.

Coulson, M. (2004). Attributing emotion to static body postures: recognition accuracy, confusions, and viewpoint dependence. *Journal of Nonverbal Behavior*, **28**, 117–139.

Darwin, C. (1872). *The Expression of the Emotions in Man and Animals*. New York: D. Appleton and Company.

Dawkins, R. and Krebs, J. R. (1978). Animal signals: information or manipulation? In J. R. Krebs and N. B. Davies (eds), *Behavioural Ecology: An Evolutionary Approach* (pp. 282–309). Sunderland, MA: Sinauer.

De Rosis, F., Pelachaud, C., Poggi, I., Carofiglio, V., and De Carolis, B. (2003). From Greta's mind to her face: modeling the dynamics of affective states in a conversational embodied agent. *International Journal of Human–Computer Studies*, **59**, 81–118.

Ehlich, K. (1986). *Interjektionen*. Tübingen: Niemeyer.

Eibl-Eibesfeldt, I. and Hass, H. (1967). Neue Wege der Humanethologie [*New Ways in Human Ethology*], *Homo*, **18**, 13–23.

Ekman, P. (1969). The repertoire of nonverbal behavior – categories, origins, usage and coding. *Semiotica*, **1**, 49–98.

  (1971). Universals and cultural differences in facial expressions of emotion. *Nebraska Symposium on Motivation*, **19**, 207–283.

  (1980). Biological and cultural contributions to body and facial movement in the expression of emotions. In A. O. Rorty (ed.), *Explaining Emotions* (pp. 73–101). Berkeley, CA: University of California Press.

  (1984). Expression and the nature of emotion. In K. Scherer and P. Ekman (eds), *Approaches to Emotion* (pp. 319–343). Hillsdale, NJ: Lawrence Erlbaum.

  (1994). Strong evidence for universals in facial expressions: a reply to Russell's mistaken critique. *Psychological Bulletin*, **115**, 268–287.

276   *Elisabeth Oberzaucher, Karl Grammer, and Susanne Schmehl*

Ekman, P. and Friesen, W. V. (1978). *Investigator's Guide: Facial Action Coding System*. Palo Alto, CA: Consulting Psychologists Press.

Fahlmann, S. E. (2007). Smiley lore :-). www.cs.cmu.edu/~sef/sefSmiley.htm.

Fridlund, A. J. (1991). Sociality and solitary smiling: potentiation by an implicit audience. *Journal of Personality and Social Psychology, 60,* 229–240.

(1994). *Human facial expression: An Evolutionary View.* San Diego, CA: Academic Press.

Fried, I. (2007). Warning sounded over 'flirting robots.' www.news.com/beyond-binary/8301-13860_3-9831133-56.html.

Frijda, N. H. (1986). *The Emotions.* Cambridge University Press.

Fujie, S., Fukushima, K., and Kobayashi, T. (2004). A conversation robot with back-channel feedback function based on linguistic and nonlinguistic information. In *Proceedings of the International Conference on Autonomous Robots and Agents* (pp. 379–384).

Gallese, V. and Goldmann, A. (1998). Mirror neurons and the simulation theory of mind-reading. *Trends in Cognitive Science, 2,* 493–501.

Gillenson, M. L. (1974). *The Interactive Generation of Facial Images on a CRT Using a Heuristic Strategy.* Ohio State University, Computer Graphics Research Group.

Grammer, K., Schiefenhovel, W., Schleidt, M., Lorenz, B., and Eibl-Eibesfeldt, I. (1988). Patterns on the face: the eyebrow flash in crosscultural comparison. *Ethology, 77,* 279–299.

Grammer, K. and Fieder, M. (1997). A neural network approach for the classification of body movements (Abstract). In A. Schmitt, K. Atzwanger, K. Grammer, and K. Schäfer (eds), *New Aspects of Human Ethology* (pp. 202–203). New York: Plenum Press.

Grammer, K., Filova, V., and Fieder, M. (1997). The communication paradox and possible solutions: towards a radical empiricism. In A. Schmitt, K. Atzwanger, K. Grammer, and K. Schäfer (eds), *New Aspects of Human Ethology* (pp. 91–120). New York: Plenum Press.

Grammer, K., Fink, B., and Renninger, L. (2002). Dynamic systems and inferential information processing in human communication. *Neuro Endocrinological Letters* (Special Issue), *23*(4), 15–22.

Grammer, K., Fink, B., Møller, A. P., and Thornhill, R. (2003). Darwinian aesthetics: sexual selection and the biology of beauty. *Biological Reviews, 78*(3), 385–340.

Grammer, K., Fink, B., Oberzaucher, E., Atzmueller, M., Blantar, I., and Mitteroecker, P. (2004). The representation of self-reported affect in body posture and body posture simulation. *Collegium Anthropologicum, 28*(2), 159–173.

Grammer, K. and Oberzaucher, E. (2006). The reconstruction of facial expressions in embodied systems: new approaches to an old problem. *ZIF Mitteilungen, 2,* 14–31.

Griffiths, P. E. (1990). Modularity and the psychoevolutionary theory of emotion. *Biology & Philosophy, 5,* 175–196.

Guthrie, S. (1993). *Faces in the Clouds: A New Theory of Religion.* Oxford University Press.

Hess, U., Adams, R. S., and Kleck, R. E. (2004). Facial appearance, gender, and emotion expression. *Emotion, 4,* 378–388.

Houck, N. and Gass, S. M. (1997). Cross-cultural back channels in English refusals: a source of trouble. In A. Jaworski (ed.), *Silence – Interdisciplinary Perspectives* (pp. 285–308). Berlin: Mouton de Gruyter.

Izard, C. E. (1971). *The Face of Emotion*. New York: Appleton-Century-Crofts.

(1977). *Human Emotions*. New York: Plenum.

(1991). *The Psychology of Emotions*. New York: Plenum.

James, W. (1950 [1890]). *The Principles of Psychology*. New York: Dover.

Johansson, G. (1973). Visual perception of biological motion and a model of its analysis. *Perception & Psychophysics*, *14*, 201–211.

(1976). Spatio-temporal differentiation and integration in visual motion perception. *Psychological Research*, *38*, 379–398.

Kipp, M. (2001). **Anvil** – a generic annotation tool for multimodal dialogue. In *Proceedings of Eurospeech 2001*, Aalborg (pp. 1367–1370).

Kleinginna, P. R. and Kleinginna, A. M. (1981). A categorized list of emotion definitions with suggestions for a consensual definition. *Motivation and Emotion*, *5*, 345–379.

Kopp, S., Gesellsetter, L., Krämer, N.C., and Wachsmuth, I. (2005). A conversational agent as a museum guide. Design and evaluation of a real-world application. In T. Panayiotopoulos *et al.* (eds), *Intelligent Virtual Agents 2005* (pp. 329–343). Hamburg: Springer.

Kopp, S., Allwood, J., Ahlsén, E., Grammer, K., and Stocksmeier, T. (2008). Modeling embodied feedback with virtual humans. In I. Wachsmuth and G. Knoblich (eds), *Modeling Communication with Robots and Virtual Humans* (pp. 18–37). Berlin: Springer.

Krämer, N. C. (2001). *Bewegende Bewegung. Sozio-emotionale Wirkungen nonverbalen Verhaltens und deren experimentelle Untersuchung mittels Computeranimation.* [*Moving Movements. Socio-emotional Effects of Nonverbal Behavior and Their Experimental Analysis by Means of Computer Animation*] Lengerich: Pabst Science Publishers.

Krebs, J. R. and Dawkins, R. (1984). Animal signals: mind reading and manipulation. In J. R. Krebs and N. B. Davies (eds), *Behavioural Ecology: An Evolutionary Approach* (pp. 380–402). Oxford: Blackwell Scientific.

Krumhuber, E. and Kappas, A. (2005). Moving smiles: the role of dynamic components for the perception of the genuineness of smiles. *Journal of Nonverbal Behavior*, *29*, 3–24.

Lang, P. J. (1995). The emotion probe. *American Psychologist*, *50*, 372–385.

Lazarus, R. S. (1991). *Emotion and Adaption*. New York: Oxford University Press.

Lee, E., Kang, J. I., Park, I. H., Kim, J.-J., and An, S. K. (2008). Is a neutral face really evaluated as being emotionally neutral? *Psychiatry Research*, *157*, 77–85.

Mehrabian, A. and Russell, J. A. (1974). *An Approach to Environmental Psychology*. Cambridge, MA: MIT Press.

Microsoft (2003). Microsoft Agent product information. (www.microsoft.com/msagent/prodinfo/).

Moser, E., Derntl, B., Robinson, S., Fink, B., Gur, R. C., and Grammer, K. (2006). Amygdala activation at 3T in response to human and avatar facial expressions of emotions. *Journal of Neuroscience Methods*, *161*(1), 126–133.

Ortony, A. and Turner, T. J. (1990). What's basic about basic emotions? *Psychological Review*, *97*, 315–331.

Osgood, C. E. (1966). Dimensionality of the semantic space for communication via facial expressions. *Scandinavian Journal of Psychology*, *7*, 1–30.

Panksepp, J. (1992). A critical role for "affective neuroscience" in resolving what is basic about basic emotions. *Psychological Review, 99*(3), 554–560.

Parke, F. I. (1972). Computer-generated animation of faces. *Proceedings of ACM National Conference* (vol. I, pp. 451–457).

Petta, P., Staller, A., Trappl, R., Mantler, S., Szalavari, Z., Psik, T., and Gervautz, M. (1999). Towards engaging full-body interaction. In H.-J. Bullinger and P. H. Vossen (eds), *Adjunct Conference Proceedings, HCI International '99, 8th International Conference on Human–Computer Interaction* (pp. 280–281). Stuttgart: Fraunhofer IRB Verlag.

Platt, S. M. and Badler, N. (1981). Animating facial expression. *Computer Graphics, 15*(3), 245–252.

Poggi, I., Pelachaud, C., de Rosis, F., Carofiglio, V., and De Carolis, B. (2005). GRETA. A believable embodied conversational agent. In O. Stock and M. Zancarano (eds), *Multimodal Intelligent Information Presentation.* (pp. 3–25). Dordrecht: Kluwer.

Reeves, B. and Nass, C. (1996). *The Media Equation. How People Treat Computers, Television, and New Media like Real People and Places.* New York: Cambridge University Press.

Russell, J. A. (1978). Evidence of convergent validity on the dimensions of affect. *Journal of Personality and Social Psychology, 36*, 1152–1168.

(1980). A circumplex model of affect. *Journal of Personality and Social Psychology, 39*, 1161–1178.

(1991). In defense of a prototype approach to emotion concepts. *Journal of Personality and Social Psychology, 60*, 425–438.

(1995). Facial expression of emotion: what lies beyond minimal universality? *Psychological Bulletin, 118*, 379–391.

Russell, J. A. and Mehrabian, A. (1977). Evidence for a three-factor theory of emotions. *Journal of Research in Personality, 11*, 273–294.

Scherer, K. R. (1984). On the nature and function of emotion: a component process approach. In K. R. Scherer and P. Ekman (eds), *Approaches to Emotion* (pp. 293–317). Hillsdale, NJ: Erlbaum.

(1994). Affect bursts. In S. van Goozen, N. E. van de Poll, and J. A. Sergeant (eds), *Emotions: Essays on Emotion Theory* (pp. 161–193). Hillsdale, NJ: Lawrence Erlbaum.

(1997). Profiles of emotion-antecedent appraisal: testing theoretical predictions across cultures. *Cognition and Emotion, 11*, 113–150.

(1999). Appraisal theory. In T. Dalgleish and M. J. Power (eds), *Handbook of Emotion and Cognition* (pp. 637–663). New York: Wiley.

(2001). Appraisal considered as a process of multi-level sequential checking. In R. Scherer, A. Schorr, and T. Johnstone (eds), *Appraisal Processes in Emotion: Theory, Methods, Research* (pp. 92–120). New York: Oxford University Press.

Schmidt, K. L. and Cohen, J. F. (2002). Human facial expressions as adaptations: evolutionary questions in facial expression research. *Yearbook of Physical Anthropology, 44*, 3–24.

Shneiderman, B. (1989). Social and individual impact. *Educational Media International, 26*(2), 101–106.

Smith, C. A. and Scott, H. S. (1997). Spontaneous facial behavior during intense emotional episodes: artistic truth and optical truth. In J. A. Russell and J. M. Fernández-Dols (eds), *The Psychology of Facial Expression* (pp. 229–254). Cambridge University Press.

Snodgrass, J. (1992). Judgment of Feeling States from Facial Behavior: A Bottom-up Approach. Unpublished doctoral dissertation, University of British Columbia.

Spencer-Smith, J., Wild, H., Innes-Ker, A. H., Townsend, J. T., Duffy, C., Edwards, C., Ervin, K., Merritt, N., and Paik, J. W. (2001). Making faces: creating three-dimensional parameterized models of facial expression. *Behavior Research Methods, Instruments and Computers*, *33*, 115–123.

Staller, A. and Petta, P. (1998). Towards a tractable appraisal-based architecture for situated cognizers. In D. Canamero, C. Numaoka, and P. Petta (eds), *Grounding Emotions in Adaptive Systems, Workshop Notes, 5th International Conference of the Society for Adaptive Behavior* (pp. 56–61). Zurich: Society for Adaptive Behavior.

Takeuchi, M., Kitaoka, N., and Nakagawa, S. (2004). Timing detection for realtime dialog systems using prosodic and linguistic information. In *Proceedings of the International Conference on Speech Prosody* (pp. 529–532).

Thórisson, K. R. (1996). Communicative Humanoids – A Computational Model of Psychological Dialogue Skills. PhD thesis, School of Architecture and Planning, Massachusetts Institute of Technology.

Tomkins, S. S. (1962). *Affect Imagery Consciousness: Vol. I. The Positive Affects*. New York: Springer.

Ward, N. and Tsukahara, W. (2000). Prosodic features which cue back-channel responses in English and Japanese. *Journal of Pragmatics*, *32*(8), 1177–1207.

Watson, D., Clark, L. A., and Tellegen, A. (1988). Development and validation of brief measures of positive and negative affect: the PANAS scales. *Journal of Personality and Social Psychology*, *54*(6), 1063–1070.

Wehrle, T. and Scherer, K. R. (2001). Towards computational modeling of appraisal theories. In K. R. Scherer, A. Schorr, and T. Johnstone (eds), *Appraisal Processes in Emotion: Theory, Methods, Research* (pp. 350–365). New York: Oxford University Press.

Wiener, N. (1984). *Cybernetics and Control and Communication in the Animal and the Machine*. Cambridge, MA: MIT Press.

Woodworth, R. S. (1938). *Experimental Psychology*. New York: Holt.

Wundt, W. (1924 [1912]). *An Introduction to Psychology* (R. Pinter, Trans.). London: Allen and Unwin.

Xiao, J. (2001). *Understanding the Use and Utility of Anthropomorphic Interface Agents*. Student Poster at the CHI 2001 in Seattle, WA, USA.

Yngve, V. H. (1970). On getting a word in edgewise. In *Papers from the Sixth Regional Meeting of the Chicago Linguistics Society* (pp. 567–578). Chicago: Chicago Linguistics Society.

Index

Studies in Emotion and Social Interaction